STILL DYING FOR A LIVING

Law and Society Series
W. Wesley Pue, General Editor

The Law and Society Series explores law as a socially embedded phenomenon. It is premised on the understanding that the conventional division of law from society creates false dichotomies in thinking, scholarship, educational practice, and social life. Books in the series treat law and society as mutually constitutive and highlight scholarship emerging from the interdisciplinary engagement of law with fields such as politics, social theory, history, political economy, and gender studies.

A list of titles in the series appears at the end of the book.

Steven Bittle

STILL DYING FOR A LIVING

Corporate Criminal Liability after the
Westray Mine Disaster

UBCPress · Vancouver · Toronto

© UBC Press 2012

All rights reserved. No part of this publication may be reproduced, stored in a retrieval system, or transmitted, in any form or by any means, without prior written permission of the publisher, or, in Canada, in the case of photocopying or other reprographic copying, a licence from Access Copyright, www.accesscopyright.ca.

21 20 19 18 17 16 15 14 13 12   5 4 3 2 1

Printed in Canada on FSC-certified ancient-forest-free paper
(100% post-consumer recycled) that is processed chlorine- and acid-free.

Library and Archives Canada Cataloguing in Publication

Still dying for a living : corporate criminal liability after the Westray Mine disaster /
Steven Bittle.

(Law & society)
Includes bibliographical references and index.
Issued also in electronic format.
ISBN 978-0-7748-2359-3 (bound); ISBN 978-0-7748-2360-9 (pbk.)

    1. Criminal liability of juristic persons – Canada. 2. Corporations – Corrupt practices – Canada. 3. Corporation law – Canada – Criminal provisions. 4. Canada. Act to Amend the Criminal Code (Criminal Liability of Organizations). I. Title. II. Series: Law and society series (Vancouver, B.C.)

| HV6771.C3B57 2012 | 345.71'0268 | C2012-903969-1 |

Canadä

UBC Press gratefully acknowledges the financial support for our publishing program of the Government of Canada (through the Canada Book Fund), the Canada Council for the Arts, and the British Columbia Arts Council.

This book has been published with the help of a grant from the Canadian Federation for the Humanities and Social Sciences, through the Aid to Scholarly Publications Program, using funds provided by the Social Sciences and Humanities Research Council of Canada.

UBC Press
The University of British Columbia
2029 West Mall
Vancouver, BC V6T 1Z2
www.ubcpress.ca

On 9 May 1992, twenty-six miners were killed
in an underground explosion at the
Westray coal mine in Pictou County, Nova Scotia.
This book is dedicated to their memory and the hope that
someday workers can finally stop dying for a living.

Contents

Foreword: The Struggle for Corporate Accountability / ix
STEVE TOMBS

Preface / xv

Acknowledgments / xvii

Abbreviations / xx

1 Introduction: What Is Crime? / 1

2 Criminal Liability and the Corporate Form / 14

3 Theorizing Corporate Harm and Wrongdoing / 38

4 Constituting the Corporate Criminal through Law / 71

5 Visions of Economic Grandeur: The Influence of Corporate Capitalism / 115

6 Obscuring Corporate Crime and the Corporate Criminal / 148

7 Disciplining Capital: More of the Same or Hope for the Future? / 183

Appendices

A Members of the Standing Committee on Justice and
   Human Rights / 194

B Details Regarding Data Sources / 195

C Witnesses Appearing before the Standing Committee on
   Justice and Human Rights / 198

D Interview Participants / 201

E Interview Schedule / 203

Notes / 207

References / 218

Index / 231

Foreword: The Struggle for Corporate Accountability

In September 2008, in contrast to any other social catastrophe – global warming, widespread hunger, poverty, the routine deaths of millions of children, AIDS, and tuberculosis and malaria epidemics, about which "there always seemed to be time to reflect, to postpone decisions" (Žižek 2009, 80) – one issue presented itself as "an unconditional imperative which must be met with immediate action," namely that the "banks," for which read finance capital in particular and the global neo-liberal order in general, had to be saved (80). In the United States, this unconditional imperative spawned the "Paulson Plan." Sketchier than many undergraduate essays, this three-page document was a gun pointed by three men at everybody else with the message "give us $700 billion or else" (Harvey 2009). This "financial coup" – repeated in the United Kingdom to the tune of £850 billion – marked the beginning of a new "age of austerity," characterized by sovereign debt, where the most vulnerable within and across societies were now targeted as the price worth paying for capitalist recovery (ibid). As Karl Marx (1976, cited in Dienst 2011, 29) had once remarked, "the only part of the so-called national wealth that actually enters into the collective possession of a modern nation is – their national debt."

Thus, within the "age of austerity" – which reflected the price of "recovery" (recovery to what, one might ask) – the social wage across the Western world has been under attack. Government debt, re-cast as state over-spending rather than as the socialization of the effects of reckless, capitalist profit taking, has meant that unemployment insurance, the deferred wages that are pensions, public services, and the often still minimal protections offered by regulation are luxuries that can now be barely afforded. Moreover, if the nature and level of regulation of finance capital had been a key factor in generating the crisis, one would not have noticed this from the state responses to it. The "free market" did not look quite so "free" when governments were forced to rescue banks and other financial institutions. The fact that it was only governments that *could* respond to the crisis – under the guise of creating "the conditions for a new expansion" – is not in itself at all remarkable (Gamble 2009, 97). What is remarkable, however, is that, in so doing, the idea of the necessity and desirability of regulatory retreat has persisted across mainstream political spectrums. In the United Kingdom, for example, all three major political parties that fought the general election in 2010 were committed to reducing regulation – regulation in general was inherently burdensome and only to be an option of last resort, a minimalist necessary evil, which, in any case, entailed costs for both the state and for business, costs that had to be restricted in the new "age of austerity." Thus, regulatory costs had to be minimized, on the one hand, as part of the overall attempt to tackle the new fiscal crisis of the state and, on the other hand, to reduce the costs for the private sector, which was seen as the only vehicle for economic recovery. Absent from this political discourse was any sustained, critical consideration of the forms of state regulation that had fuelled the unsustainable levels of profit maximization on the part of financial services operating in the shadow-economy of derivatives and securities – a toxic process that had created the very crisis to which more of the same poison was to prove to be the necessary cure.

At the same time, it is worth emphasizing that in the United Kingdom, certainly, there has been no attempt to re-regulate the financial services sector, save for a belated proposal for a flimsy fence between retail and investment banking – not to be erected until 2019 (well beyond the life of the government) – no inclination to alter radically those parts of it that are now effectively under state ownership; no thoroughgoing inquiry into the potential illegalities involved in the near collapse of this sector; no significant prosecutions developed by the Serious Fraud Office or the Financial Services Authority; and certainly no ideological or material undermining of political faith in "light touch" regulation across all other areas that "affect" business life, even in the light of our current collective experience of its manifest failures. Specifically, we do not know, nor are we ever likely to know, to what extent criminal activity was implicated in the events leading up to the crisis. And with a few notable exceptions, criminologists on either side of the Atlantic have barely bothered to give the crisis a second glance (Burdis and Tombs 2012; McGurrin and Friedrichs 2010).

Of course, while different states are characterized by their own specificities, the lack of effective legislative response to the crisis is hardly confined to the United Kingdom. In the United States, for example, brief periods of optimism for advocates of regulation, engendered first by the wake-up calls that developed following the demise of Enron, WorldCom, and Tyco, followed by the introduction of the *Public Company Accounting Reform and Investor Protection Act of 2002 (Sarbanes-Oxley Act)*, and then encouraged, later in the decade, with the election of Barack Obama as the US president, were both short lived and ultimately of little import in responding to corporate crime and harm.[1] The *Sarbanes-Oxley Act* proved to be relatively ineffectual, at best seeking to address the symptomatic issues of corporate governance rather than the underlying structural issues of neo-liberal capitalism that systematically produce crime and harm (Soederberg 2008). Meanwhile, the approach of the Obama administration to corporate wrongdoing, not least in the wake of the economic crisis, is most pithily encapsulated in the classic Who line: "Meet the New Boss. Same as the Old Boss."[2] Thus, the crisis has prompted little or no credible legislative response: "None of the key guilty parties have been sent to prison; rather, Wall Street almost immediately called for returning to 'business as usual,' has aggressively contested relatively modest new regulatory initiatives, and has altogether done well for itself while much of the balance of the economy and the American people continue to suffer" (Friedrichs 2011). Meanwhile, in Canada, if the first decade of the twenty-first century "witnessed renewed interest in the regulation of corporate crimes," the two key pieces of legislation that the Canadian state was forced to enact – Bills C-45, which was ostensibly designed to address safety crimes (and the subject of this book), and C-13, aimed at tackling market fraud – were almost immediately to "fall into a state of virtual disuse" (Bittle and Snider 2011, 373 and 374).

The ideological foundations upon which our economy is based have hardly been undermined, then. Rather, if somewhat paradoxically, these factors may in fact have been strengthened by the economic crisis – private capital has been trumpeted as the only feasible response to economic crisis. Of course, the pro-capitalist cheerleaders in government have not had, and will not have, it all their own way. Governmental efforts to re-cast a new, post-welfare capitalist settlement have met little popular resentment and resistance. State responses have followed similar patterns – a combination of ideological mystification backed by the often heavy hand of power, which has been flexed brutally on the streets of London, New York, Athens, Toronto, and numerous other cities and towns across the world.

Foreword

If regulation remains a dirty word across much of the Western world, it is not homogenous, neither by state nor by sphere of regulation. In the United Kingdom, the one form of regulation that has been consistently and most vehemently singled out for "reform" is that which, formally, provides occupational health and safety protection. A slew of deregulatory reforms have been passed in the first eighteen months of the new Coalition government, while the United Kingdom's record on workplace health and safety deteriorates on almost any indicator one might choose. In the world's fifth largest economy, you are more likely to die or be hospitalized as a result of working in the United Kingdom than to be a victim of the kind of violent crime that attracts the interest of politicians, the police, the media, and, of course, academics. And the United Kingdom is not an exception. Work is a major killer across the globe. The International Labour Organization attributes some 2.3 million deaths per annum to work, meaning that there are more than 6,000 work-related deaths every day. For every fatality, there are another 500-2,000 injuries, depending on the type of job. Many millions more suffer long-term, debilitating, chronic illnesses through working for a living. This situation is routine, systematic corporate violence – albeit such deaths, injuries, and illnesses are rarely discussed in such terms. It is a violence comprehensible "not in the pathology of evil individuals but in the culture and structure of large-scale bureaucratic organisations within a particular political economy" (Hills 1987, 190).

This violence, and the systematic poverty of state efforts to respond adequately to it, not least through the legal system, is the subject of *Still Dying for a Living*. Steven Bittle's text is remarkable for both being a forensic dissection of a specific piece of law – Bill C-45, *An Act to Amend the Criminal Code (Criminal Liability of Organizations)* (Westray bill) – within the context of a specific social issue – corporate manslaughter – while at the same time offering a broader analysis of the ways in which power is exercised in contemporary capitalist economies.[3] Drawing upon Foucauldian and Marxist literatures, *Still Dying for a Living* documents how material and ideological power have combined to produce a bill that will continue to isolate corporate violence from "real" crimes of violence. However, it is more than a study of law's failure to challenge systematic, routine corporate violence. It also contributes to our understandings of the class-based nature and operation of a criminal justice system; of the significance of the state in understanding the contours of contemporary life; of the ways in which dominant legal, economic, and cultural discourses are created, sustained, and utilized; and, thus, of our sense of how moral *un*-panics (Davis 2000) are constructed – as opposed, of course, to the fears over knives, illegal drugs, pedophiles, gangs, even dangerous dogs, which pervade the broadcast and print media, the sites of formal political debate, and, regrettably, texts and courses in criminology across the West.

Still Dying for a Living is a painstakingly researched and powerfully argued key to understanding our anti-regulatory times and a significant empirical, theoretical, and epistemological contribution to a literature that is still relatively marginal to criminology and socio-legal studies. Very much focused upon the politics of regulation in Canada, its analysis and conclusions span national borders and legal cultures. Moreover, and mercifully, it stands as a rare corrective to the overwhelming majority of the academic literature on regulation, a small industry that is a torrent of self-referential banality from which considerations of power, capital, class, and even crime are notable for their absences. Therein, regulation is viewed largely as a technical issue, a search for mechanisms to empower anthropomorphized, essentially responsible firms to comply with the law in a world of stakeholders and conversations, where those who might suggest resort to criminal law are simplistic, anachronistic embarrassments – a world where power is never concentrated but dispersed, where sources of influence are polycentric, and where the state is certainly decentred and relatively and increasingly impotent, just one among a range of actors, not least those that inhabit the private sector itself. So regulation might be responsive, better, smart, twin-tracked, and risk-based, but it is always so "realistic" that it is never about controlling pathological, calculating, profit-maximizing entities as one element of a broader struggle for social justice. Typically, then, in one of the rare treatments of the economic crisis from a criminological perspective, the editors of a special issue of *Criminology and Public Policy* were able to conclude thus:

> There is currently a remarkably optimistic consensus in some academic quarters about how to reduce the harm caused by privileged predators. The heart of it lies in the presumed promise of pluralistic, cooperative approaches, and responsive regulation. These assumptions highlight the need for enhanced prevention, more diverse and more effective internal oversight and self-monitoring, and more efficient and effective external oversight. They have gained use throughout a variety of regulatory realms, many since their earliest, albeit embryonic, formulation nearly three decades ago ... They make sense theoretically, and we endorse them. We do so not because they have a record of demonstrable success but principally because sole or excessive reliance on state oversight and threat of criminal prosecution is difficult, costly,

Foreword

and uncertain. Still, we are mindful, as others should be, that the onset of the Great Recession occurred during and despite the tight embrace of self-regulation, pluralistic oversight, and notions of self-regulating markets by policy makers and many academicians. (Grabosky and Shover 2010, 641-42)

Bittle's book should be compulsory reading for all those who persist in their "assumptions" regarding the "presumed promise of pluralistic, cooperative approaches, and responsive regulation" – albeit with the knowledge that the policy approaches they suggest have no "record of demonstrable success." Neither I nor Steven Bittle share these assumptions, this optimism, and this "remarkably optimistic consensus." For as Bittle documents, by contrast, regulation often only ever erupts onto any political agenda following large-scale loss of life and limb or other forms of serious economic, physical, or social harms. The regulatory "settlement" that is then reached is the outcome of an always incomplete struggle, the product of asymmetric power. And, thus, if the Westray bill – hoisted onto the statute books following twenty-six eminently preventable deaths – in its diluted form and its timid application, is hardly a challenge to the power of corporate capital and the daily carnage upon which its profits are based, it is also, as he documents here, not a mere irrelevance. As with its UK equivalent, the *Corporate Manslaughter and Corporate Homicide Act,* the very existence of the Westray bill offers "a new and symbolically important way to speak of corporate wrongdoing" (see Chapter 7 in this text).[4] If it offers little in terms of corporate accountability, it is one material and discursive tool in the struggle for such accountability. It allows us to name, and to seek to process legally, one subset of corporate violence. It pierces the din of business-as-usual in order to scream that men and women are not just dying for a living – they are also being killed for a profit.

Steve Tombs
Professor of Sociology
School of Humanities and Social Science
John Moores University
Liverpool, UK

Preface

Each year, hundreds of Canadians are killed on the job or die from work-related illnesses, while thousands more suffer debilitating injuries, including amputations, broken bones, and burns. Despite the frequency and seriousness of these incidences, they face little public, political, and academic scrutiny and are rarely treated as crimes worthy of criminal justice intervention. Defined away as unfortunate "accidents" – the regrettable but largely unavoidable risks that go along with the pursuit of profit – injury and death in the workplace is an invisible crime (Glasbeek 2002; Tombs and Whyte 2007). Crime is about the perils of guns, gangs, and drugs, or so we are told, not the harms that we experience while trying to earn a living.

Given the low priority accorded to workplace injury and death, it was thus significant when, in March 2004, the Canadian government introduced *Criminal Code* legislation aimed at strengthening corporate criminal liability.[1] Bill C-45, *An Act to Amend the Criminal Code (Criminal Liability of Organizations)* (Westray bill), introduced a legal duty for "all persons directing work to take reasonable steps to ensure the safety of workers and the public," attributed criminal liability to an "organization" if a senior officer knew, or ought to have known, about the offence, and introduced sentencing provisions specifically for the organizational setting.[2] Colloquially referred to as the Westray bill, the law's enactment followed the deaths of twenty-six workers at the Westray mine in Pictou County, Nova Scotia, in 1992, a disaster caused by dangerous and illegal working conditions.

The federal government declared the Westray bill an important step toward ensuring the accountability of organizations for the actions taken by their representatives. Pundits predicted that it would "revolutionize" corporate criminal liability (Archibald, Jull, and Roach 2004, 368), ending the lenient treatment of corporations through the introduction of "stricter penalties" and improved "enforcement tools" (Mann 2004, 29). However, peeling back the veneer of this so-called crackdown on corporate crime reveals a much different picture. To start, the law's introduction was anything but expeditious, subject to a long and drawn-out process in Canada's Parliament that raised questions about the need for reform. What is more, since the law took effect in 2004 there have been only a handful of charges and few convictions – not exactly a revolution in corporate accountability.

Still Dying for a Living critically examines the introduction of Canada's corporate criminal liability legislation, exploring the factors leading to the law's enactment and why, despite promises to the contrary, it is rarely enforced. The goal is to provide readers with a comprehensive and contemporary understanding of the constitution of corporate crime by interrogating the assumptions, agendas, and relations of power that informed the Westray bill's development and enforcement – the factors that produce legal categorizations of corporate harm and wrongdoing. Of particular interest are the official discourses that animated the nature and scope of the Westray bill and the ways in which these discourses correspond to the broader social-political-economic context.

Drawing theoretical inspiration from Foucauldian and neo-Marxist literatures, and weaving together the results of in-depth interviews and a detailed examination of parliamentary transcripts, *Still Dying for a Living* argues that dominant legal, economic, and cultural discourses converged around the Westray bill to downplay the seriousness of workplace injury and death and effectively isolate "these crimes from 'crime, law and order' agendas" (Tombs and Whyte 2007, 69). In addition to helping (re)enforce and (re)produce the dominance of corporate capitalism, this production of corporate crime and corporate criminal liability throws serious doubt on the state's ability to hold corporations accountable for their harmful, anti-social acts. There is little reason to believe the Westray bill will produce a crackdown on the most powerful economic actors or seriously challenge companies to reduce workplace injuries and death in industries where fixing these conditions is complex and expensive. Although it will hold some corporations and corporate actors accountable – thus far, the smallest and weakest – the primary causes of injury and death on the job continue unabated (for example, the tension between profit maximization and the costs of safety and the relative worth of workers/employees versus owners and investors).

Acknowledgments

That this book reached its final form is a credit to the many people who provided encouragement, feedback, and assistance along the way. With the usual disclaimer that any errors or omissions are mine only, I would like to thank the following individuals and organizations for their many and important contributions to this book. I first want to thank everyone who took the time out of their busy schedules to participate in an interview for this study. Their insights were instrumental in helping me to understand the factors that contributed to the development and (lack of) enforcement of Bill C-45, *An Act to Amend the Criminal Code (Criminal Liability of Organizations)*. I would also like to thank several people who provided encouragement, guidance, and assistance while I was completing my research. For such efforts, I acknowledge Rob Beamish, Colin Campbell, Michelle Ellis, Ken Hatt, Anne Henderson, Vince Sacco, and Wendy Schuler. Thank you to Paul Paton for his constructive feedback on my research plan and to Sergio Sismondo for his insightful comments and suggestions on an earlier draft of the text. Fiona Kay offered extensive and constructive suggestions on all aspects of my work – thank you, Fiona, for all of your time and consideration.

I owe an enormous debt of gratitude to Steve Tombs for providing invaluable feedback and suggestions on an earlier version of the text and for graciously taking the time out of his busy schedule to write the foreword. The influence of Steve's work on my own thinking about the regulation of corporate crime is evident in the pages that follow. Frank Pearce provided incredible support and encouragement along the way, offering unique and thoughtful insights that helped stimulate my interest in issues of corporate crime control and political economy. I benefited in immeasurable ways from the many conversations that I had with Frank about the nature and scope of my research.

I struggle to find the words to express my gratitude to Laureen Snider. Laureen provided incisive comments on all stages of my work, never wavering in her commitment to seeing me complete this book. Intellectually engaging and inspiring, she constantly challenged me to think critically about issues of corporate crime. Laureen is a kind and caring person who is always giving of her time and endlessly encouraging in her support of my research and writing. I am very fortunate to have Laureen as a mentor, friend, and colleague.

Many friends and colleagues offered generous words of advice and encouragement along the way as well as the occasional and much-needed distraction from writing. I am extremely grateful for all of the love and support that I received, and continue to receive, from my family. My mother is a constant source of unconditional love and support. Thanks, Mom, for always being there. My father, who passed away at far too young an age, is a constant source of inspiration – I miss him always.

Thank you to everyone at UBC Press who helped bring this book to its completion: Stacy Belden, Laraine Coates, Ann Macklem, Peter Milroy, Valerie Nair, and Melissa Pitts. Special thanks are due to Randy Schmidt, senior editor at UBC Press, for his sage advice and guidance throughout the course of this project. I would also like to acknowledge the two anonymous reviewers whose extremely thoughtful comments and suggestions motivated me to rethink and revise various sections of the book. The Faculty of Social Science Research Committee at the University of Ottawa provided much appreciated supporting funds for this project through its publications program.

Revised sections of my research findings (Chapters 4-6) were used in the following articles, for which I thank the publishers for their permissions to use in this book: (with L. Snider) "From Manslaughter to Preventable Accident: Shaping Corporate Criminal Liability," *Law and Policy* (October 2006) 28(4): 470-96; (with L. Snider) "'Moral Panics' Deflected: The Failed Legislative Response to Canada's Safety Crimes and Markets Fraud Legislation," *Crime, Law and Social Change* (2011) 56: 373-87. Some of the study's results also inform a chapter on state-corporate crime that appears in the following publication: "Corporate Crime and the Neo-Liberal State," in K. Gorkoff and R. Jochelson, eds., *Thinking about Justice: A Book of Readings* (Halifax, NS: Fernwood, 2012).

Finally, and certainly not least, mere thanks are not enough to express the gratitude that I owe my partner, Ruth Code. Ruth's kindness, caring, and support helped me stick with it in moments of doubt, and she was an unbeliev-able source of hope and strength when life presented us with a few bumps along the road. Quite simply, I would not have completed this book without her love and encouragement.

Abbreviations

CBA	Canadian Bar Association
PC	Progressive Conservative
ILO	International Labour Organization
LRCC	Law Reform Commission of Canada
MP	Member of Parliament
NDP	New Democratic Party
NGO	non-governmental organization
QFL	Quebec Federation of Labour
SHARE	Shareholder Association for Research and Education

STILL DYING FOR A LIVING

1

Introduction: What Is Crime?

I abhor what happened to the twenty-six men and their families, the hell all of us
have gone through because of this, and the possibility that maybe, just maybe,
nothing will ever be done about it. It worries me to think about how many other
businesses might be protected by dirty politicians, making safety rules and
regulations only words written on paper. I can only hope that a government
with backbone will make company officials like Westray's straighten up and run
responsible and safe businesses or close their doors.

– Shaun Comish (1993, 52)

In contemporary Western society, it is difficult to escape the constant bombardment of political, media, and popular culture chatter about the perils of crime and disorder. Politicians frequently decry the need for greater crime control to deter those who purportedly make it unsafe for us to carry out our daily routines (Garland 2001). Media commonly report sensationalistic crimes – the street-level violent offences committed by strangers – giving meaning to the familiar media adage: "If it bleeds, let it lead" (Ericson, Baranek, and Chan 1991). Similar ominous messages emerge through popular culture – particularly movies and television – underscoring the prevailing assumption that menacing and dangerous individuals await us around every street corner (Menzies, Chunn, and Boyd 2001, 11). Fear of crime sells in contemporary capitalist society and there appears to be a limitless supply of consumers willing to purchase its key messages and concomitant law-and-order strategies (Taylor 1999).

Consistent with the cultural obsession over crime control, the Canadian government introduced stringent anti-violence legislation in the fall of 2003 aimed at some of Canada's worst offenders – those with a well-documented track record of reckless behaviour and responsibility for multiple and egregious acts of violence. The legislation had all-party support, signalling a consensus for the need to better protect Canadians from violent crime (Archibald, Jull, and Roach 2004, 367). The government characterized its legislative initiative as a significant step toward ensuring that offenders are held criminally responsible for their harmful behaviour (Department of Justice Canada 2003). Legal observers suggested that it represented a fundamental change, perhaps even a revolution, in assigning criminal liability (Archibald, Jull, and Roach 2004, 368). News items cautioned would-be criminals that they were in for a wake-up call once the new law took effect (Mann 2004, 29). It thus appeared that if violent crime was the problem, then harsh new penalties were the solution.

However, peeling back the veneer of the federal government's so-called crackdown on violent crime reveals a much different story. To start, it took more than ten years to introduce a new law in response to a violent and mass killing in which twenty-six Canadians died. What is more, despite widespread political support, many politicians – particularly those with an affinity for law-and-order policies – cautioned against going too far in trying to hold offenders criminally responsible for their actions (Bittle and Snider 2006). Also curious was the fact that both the media and general public expressed little interest in the new law, hardly the status quo for issues of violent crime. Moreover, since its enactment, only a handful of charges have been laid – a particularly worrisome trend given that research reveals an increase in the forms of violence that the law purports to address (Sharpe and Hardt 2006). In fact, it would appear that the most significant development associated with the new legislation is the emergence of a crime *(un)control* industry, one in which lawyers and consultants offer for-fee courses that potential offenders can take to learn about the new law and the steps they must follow to avoid criminal responsibility (for example, see Gonzalez 2005; Guthrie 2004).

Contextualizing Corporate Harm

The preceding scenario appears highly improbable given the predominance of contemporary law-and-order politics (Menzies, Chunn, and Boyd 2001). Politicians would fear for their political lives for perceived inaction against comparable increases in street crime, youth offending, gang activity, or official homicide rates, all of which frequently serve as barometers to the efficacy of the criminal justice system (Garland 2001; Taylor 1999). However, in this instance, the reality is much different. Despite legislative condemnation and continued violence, there has been little public outcry and few media inquiries, and a majority of politicians have appeared content to leave the issue off the political radar. So what accounts for this seemingly improbable chain of events? The short answer is that it is not a story about traditional street crime but, instead, about legislation relating to culpable injury and death in the workplace. It is a story about the government of Canada's enactment of corporate criminal liability legislation.

Although political rhetoric generates fear of violent street crime, the truth is that most people are much more likely to be victimized on the job than on the street (Snider 1993; Tombs and Whyte 2007). In 2001, the International Labour Organization (ILO) estimated that there were 268 million workplace accidents worldwide that caused an employee to miss three or more workdays. During the same year, 351,000 people suffered fatal workplace injuries, a number that skyrockets to 2.2 million when including work-related deaths due to illnesses such as cancers and respiratory and circulatory diseases (International Labour Organization 2005, 1; Tombs and Whyte 2007, 37).

In Canada, there were 928 workplace fatalities in 2004 (Association of Workers' Compensation Boards of Canada 2006) and 1,097 in 2005 (Sharpe and Hardt 2006).[1] In comparison, there were 622 reported homicides in Canada in 2004 (Dauvergne 2005, 1) and 658 in 2005 (Statistics Canada 2006). Furthermore, while police investigate and lay criminal charges in a majority of homicides, the same cannot be said for workplace fatalities, despite research suggesting that at least two-thirds of these incidences include some form of criminal culpability (Tombs 2004, 164-65, 174-75).[2] In cases where individuals or a company do face criminal charges for workplace fatalities, convictions are few and far between, and, even if found guilty, punishments pale in comparison to those meted out for street-level crimes (Glasbeek 2002).

The history of occupational health and safety law and its enforcement reveals striking inconsistencies and, at times, apathy when it comes to developing effective strategies for holding corporations and executives to legal account for injury and death in the workplace (Pearce and Snider 1995; Pearce and Tombs 1998). The record illustrates a general reluctance to equate harm and wrongdoing by corporations with serious crimes – that is, they are deemed *mala prohibita* (wrong because prohibited) as opposed to *malum in se* (inherently wrong or evil) (Snider 2000, 184). This apathy, however, does not suggest a total disregard for workers' safety. Today's worker enjoys a much safer working environment than his or her counterpart did in previous generations (Snider

1987, 54). At the same time, reforms are typically slow, hard fought, and rarely result in dramatic improvements to workplace health and safety (Snider 1987; 1993). In this respect, the Canadian government's introduction of corporate criminal liability legislation is an important, symbolic event. This book undertakes to critically examine the development of this law.

Canada's Corporate Criminal Liability Legislation

On 7 November 2003, following a period of protracted political discussion and debate, the Canadian government introduced Bill C-45, *An Act to Amend the Criminal Code (Criminal Liability of Organizations)* (Westray bill). Bill C-45 attributes criminal liability to organizations for acts or omissions by their representatives, introduces a legal duty for "all persons directing work to take reasonable steps to ensure the safety of workers and the public," and outlines factors for courts to consider when sentencing corporations, including probation orders specifically crafted for organizational settings.[3] This legal development marked the first time that the Canadian government had introduced *Criminal Code* provisions relating to corporate criminal liability.[4]

As is often the case, it was a much-publicized disaster that piqued the government's interest in corporate crime law reform (Braithwaite 2005, 61; Snider 1993, 89-113). On 9 May 1992, an underground explosion at the Westray mine in Plymouth, Nova Scotia, killed twenty-six miners. The blast, apparently caused when sparks from a continuous mining machine ignited methane gas, was so intense that "it blew the top off the mine entrance, more than a mile above the blast centre" (McMullan 2001, 135), shaking houses and breaking windows in nearby communities (McMullan 2005, 24). Rescue workers searched frantically for survivors, but the explosion's devastating impact meant that death was probably immediate and certainly inevitable (24). Workers were crushed by falling debris, burned from the intense heat of the methane gas explosion, or succumbed to carbon monoxide poisoning. Although rescuers eventually recovered fifteen bodies, officials deemed the conditions of the mine to be too dangerous to recover the remaining eleven victims, whose bodies remain entombed underground to this day (Glasbeek 2002, 61).

Although the mine owners, Curragh Resources, eventually were charged criminally, no one was ever convicted. A combination of prosecutorial mishaps and difficulties determining legal responsibility conspired to ensure that nobody was held to criminal account (McMullan 2001, 136; 2005, 30).[5] Despite these problems, within five days of the explosion the Nova Scotia government announced a public inquiry to investigate how and why the miners died.[6] Five years later, the inquiry's report, *The Westray Story: A Predictable Path to Disaster* (Richard 1997), characterized the tragedy as "foreseeable and preventable," unearthing evidence that, prior to the explosion, management received more than fifty warnings about workplace health and safety violations, all of which they ignored (Glasbeek 2002, 62). Tragically, the final warning came just ten days before the explosion, when a Department of Labour inspector issued mine management with a written order to clean up the site to prevent a coal dust explosion or face prosecution. Unfortunately, the order's fourteen-day waiting period did not have a chance to expire before inspectors could take further action (McMullan 2005, 26).[7]

The inquiry's report contained seventy-four recommendations aimed at preventing similar incidents and improving workplace health and safety. The Nova Scotia government officially accepted them all, including recommending that the federal government change the Canadian *Criminal Code* to make corporate officials "properly accountable for workplace safety" (Richard 1997, 600-1). This recommendation provided the impetus for what eventually became Bill C-45, colloquially referred to as the Westray bill. The process of translating the inquiry's recommendations into *Criminal Code* legislation was anything but expeditious. In 1993, a year after the disaster, a parliamentary sub-committee of the Standing Committee on Justice and Human Rights (Justice Committee) recommended legal changes modelled on a 1987 Law Reform Commission of Canada report, which suggested that corporations (including directors, officers, or employees) be accountable for negligent or reckless behaviour resulting in injury or death to workers or consumers. In November 1993, a federal government white paper proposed that corporations be made liable for any "collective failure" to exercise reasonable care by any corporate "representatives" (Minister of Justice Canada 1993). Six years later, in 1999, the leader of Canada's democratic socialist party, the New Democratic Party (NDP), sponsored a private members' bill, which died on the order paper following Parliament's dissolution.[8] On 9 February 2000, the Justice Committee tabled its fifteenth report, requesting that the government consider a program of corporate criminal liability law reform.[9] A year and a half later, upset by the federal government's continued inaction, the NDP tabled another private members' bill, Bill C-284, *An Act to Amend the Criminal Code (Offences by Corporations, Directors and Officers)*.[10] This legislation was the forerunner to the Westray bill.

Bill C-284 was withdrawn at second reading and sent to the Justice Committee for study and review (Goetz 2003, 7). Two months later, hearings began. Thirty-four witnesses appeared before the Justice Committee, which like all House of Commons committees includes members of parliament from all political parties. Witnesses either requested an audience or the committee invited them to testify because of their expertise or personal connection with the issues at hand (for example, family members of Westray victims, union representatives, and legal experts). After the hearings, the Justice Committee was to draw up a consensus-based report; however, members could not agree on the appropriate model of corporate criminal liability to recommend. This impasse allowed the government's law writers (the legislative drafters at the federal Department of Justice) to "draw [their] own conclusions" from the hearings (Department of Justice Canada 2002b). As its starting point, the government agreed with the Justice Committee's position that reforms were needed to reflect the "reality of corporate decision-making and delegation of operational responsibility in complex organizations" (ibid). Following an examination of the committee's evidence, and considering the strengths and limitations of various reform proposals, the government introduced the Westray bill.

The Focus of *Still Dying for a Living*

As the preceding discussion begins to reveal, protracted political discussion and debate, tensions, controversies, false starts, and restarts characterized the introduction of Canada's corporate criminal liability legislation. The circuitous route leading to the law's enactment raises important questions regarding its development. Using the Westray bill as its empirical focus, *Still Dying for a Living* critically interrogates the evolution of corporate criminal liability in Canada – the production of corporate crime. In addition to accounting for the broader context within which growing concerns over corporate malfeasance emerged, it explores the specific factors that gave rise to, and shaped, the Westray bill. It accounts for the transformations that occurred in the nature and scope of corporate criminal liability, beginning with the recommendation by the Westray inquiry's report to introduce specific *Criminal Code* provisions, through the parliamentary process that brought the legislation to fruition, including the tabling of different iterations of the bill, and ending with the Justice Committee hearings that helped establish the law's parameters.

The goal is to understand and explain the constitution of corporate criminal liability, the factors that contribute to legal categorizations of corporate harm and wrongdoing. Of particular interest are the discourses that shaped the conceptualizations of corporate crime and corporate criminal liability and, in turn, how these discourses correspond to the broader social-political-economic context. Language matters – it does not determine but, rather, shapes our thinking and actions (Ericson and Haggerty 1997). In many Western democratic nations, it is increasingly commonplace to debate the merits of corporate crime-related legislation, something largely absent from the neo-liberal political lexicon of the 1980s and early 1990s (McMullan 1992, 116; Pearce and Tombs 1998, 289). Canada's corporate criminal liability legislation therefore represents a new way to speak of corporate harm and wrongdoing.

At the same time, however, language does not emerge in a vacuum. In many complex and contradictory ways, discourses about corporate crime shape, and are shaped by, the broader context (Tombs and Whyte 2007, 69). For this reason, *Still Dying for a Living* examines how various discourses have coalesced within particular "law-state-economy" relations to establish the parameters for criminalizing corporate malfeasance and effectively (re)produce the dominant social formation (Dupont and Pearce 2001, 150). In this respect, it endeavours to develop a political economy of corporate criminal liability law reform that accounts for the links between various discursive formations and dominant notions of corporate capitalism, the primary vehicle for structuring the workplace within the capitalist mode of production (Pearce and Tombs 1998).

A series of questions frame the analysis and help illuminate the factors that inform the development of Canada's corporate criminal liability legislation:

- What contributed to the formulation and introduction of corporate criminal liability legislation?
- What social-political-economic factors dominated and characterized the law reform process?
- How was corporate criminal liability conceptualized and constructed through the reform process?
- Who were the "authorized knowers," the individuals asked to testify before the Justice Committee that examined the issue of corporate criminal liability?
- What knowledge claims helped constitute corporate crime and corporate criminal liability?
- What are the implications of the reform process and resulting legislation for corporate crime control?
- How has the law been enforced? How has it been implemented alongside provincial occupational health and safety regulations?

- What is the likelihood that corporations and corporate actors will be held to account for their criminal acts? Will it "revolutionize" corporate criminal liability, as some observers have suggested (for example, Archibald, Jull, and Roach 2004)?
- What are the implications for how we "think" about corporate harm and wrongdoing?

Theoretical Lens

Informing these lines of inquiry is a theoretical framework that combines Michel Foucault's ([1972] 2001) notion of discursive formations with neo-Marxism (Althusser 1969, [1971] 2001; Althusser and Balibar 1968; Resnick and Wolff 1985, 1987, 2006). As we shall see, this theoretical integration provides a rich analytical lens to examine the relationships between discourse and social structures, particularly regarding discourse and the class relations that are integral to the capitalist mode of production. It brings together Foucault's interest in the "how" of "economic exploitation and political domination" with Marxist concerns with the "why" of "capital accumulation and state power" (Jessop 2007, 40; see also Hunt 2004). Undertaking this endeavour entails moving beyond conceptions of the social as invariably and inevitably determined by the economic to consider how social and political relations correspond to the mode of production – the extent to which class relations are "implicated in the phenomenon under inquiry" (Hunt 2004, 601-2).

Foucault's ([1972] 2001) insights help to explore the legal, economic, and cultural discourses that constitute the dominant knowledge claims in relation to corporate crime and corporate criminal liability. Whose knowledge claims had legs when it came to defining the nature and scope of corporate crime and corporate criminal liability (Snider 2000)? Neo-Marxist contributions are useful for exploring the ways in which these discourses are inculcated in the capitalist mode of production. What are the various discourses that run through these relations that help to characterize corporate crime and corporate criminal liability? How do these characterizations support or challenge dominant notions of corporate capitalism? How do they reflect class struggles to define and control the means of production?

The goal is to illuminate the productive nature of corporate criminal liability law reform – how particular legal, economic, and cultural discourses shape, but do not determine, corporate criminal liability in Canada. Although these discourses have their own genesis – they are developed through varying and relatively unrelated historical contexts and, therefore, do not influence each other in any predetermined ways – they nevertheless have coalesced within particular discursive and social conditions to produce specific characterizations of corporate crime and corporate criminal liability. Of interest is how these discursive formations are constitutive of class struggles over the role of the corporate form in extracting surplus labour and accumulating capital. To underscore the productive nature of capitalist social relations, and to extend beyond essentialist or teleological characterizations of capitalism, what follows examines the ways in which these class antagonisms have (re)created the conditions necessary for maintaining and advancing determinate social formations (Gibson-Graham, Resnick, and Wolff 2001; Resnick and Wolff 1987). Overall, *Still Dying for a Living* explores the relationships between the discursive and extra-discursive, particularly how certain discourses are taken up by, and interpreted through, law-state-economy processes.

Methods and Sources

To critically examine the constitution of Canada's corporate criminal liability legislation, the study draws upon the qualitative tradition of discourse analysis (Fairclough 1992; Fairclough et al. 2004). In general, this investigation involves situating language within its broader social context or what Bernard McKenna (2004, 10) suggests is the "intersection of language, discourse and social structure." A key element of contextualizing discourse is determining what gives certain discourses their "truthfulness" or "appropriateness." Particular discourses become privileged because of the strategies that certain (powerful) agents or groups employ in the process of reproducing social relations. This privileging should not be read as an automatic or determinative process but, rather, as an ongoing and fluid exchange of renewal and transformation (Fairclough, Jessop, and Sayer 2002, 5-6). From this point, we can explore the imbrications of discourse in the (re)production of social relations, how discourse "constructs and maintains relations of power in society" (McKenna 2004, 15).

Contextualizing discourses of corporate crime and corporate criminal liability will help to illuminate the extra-discursive factors that inform the selection and retention of particular discourses as well as how these discourses help stabilize, reproduce, and transform the capitalist social formation (Jessop 2004, 159). *Still Dying for a Living* accomplishes this methodological endeavour by examining a range of data sources, including verbatim transcripts from Canada's Parliament, semi-structured interviews with individuals with insight into issues of corporate criminal liability, and a sample of Internet-based materials in relation to the Westray bill. It also includes information about what has happened since the introduction of Canada's corporate criminal liability provisions, including any charges laid, emerging case law, and new safety measures developed for corporations in response to the legislation.

Outline of Chapters

The emergence of corporate criminal liability legislation offers a new and symbolically important way to speak of corporate wrongdoing. Its mere introduction represents a departure from previous regulatory approaches to corporate offences that, in recent decades, have dominated the legal and political landscape. *Still Dying for a Living* therefore provides an important opportunity to critically explore the constitution of corporate criminal liability in contemporary society. The story begins in Chapter 2 with the history of corporate criminal liability, including the development of criminal liability and the corporate form, the identification doctrine, and the circuitous route that the Westray bill took through Canada's Parliament to become law. It also describes some of the charges and convictions registered under the law since it took effect in 2004 as well as the methods and sources used to critically examine the Westray bill's evolution. The reasons for the law's introduction and subsequent lack of enforcement raise important questions about the constitution of corporate criminal liability and the capacity to hold corporations to account for their harmful and illegal acts.

Chapter 3 situates the book within the corporate crime scholarship and details the empirical and theoretical influences that inform the research. First, it explores how traditional studies of crime and deviance gloss over the corporate criminal in favour of individualistic accounts of crime and disorder. Second, it examines the corporate crime scholarship that attempts to overcome this myopic view of crime, sketching out some of the key debates regarding the "proper" definition of corporate crime and the best way to regulate the corporate form. Finally, it outlines the book's main theoretical influences, building from the corporate crime scholarship with roots in critical socio-legal studies (for example, Pearce and Tombs 1998; Snider 2000; Tombs and Whyte 2007). A key focus is how this literature situates the constitution of corporate crime within its broader social, political, and economic context.

Chapters 4 through 6 critically examine the reform process in Canada's Parliament that has led to the Westray bill's enactment. These chapters interrogate the legal, economic, and cultural discourses that in various uneven and contradictory ways have animated the development of this legislation.

Chapter 4 examines the factors that propelled corporate criminal liability onto the legislative agenda and examines the legal discourses that converged around discussion and debate regarding corporate criminal liability to limit the reform options that received serious consideration. It demonstrates the special status accorded to law throughout the reform process – the privileging of legal discourses, traditions, and rules – when it comes to contemplating measures to hold corporations to legal account (Comack 1999).

Chapter 5 considers the impact of economic discourses on the reform process, including the commitment to neo-liberal common sense that provided a dominant frame to evaluate and speak about corporate crime and corporate criminal liability. As we shall see, despite the absence of corporate actors from the reform process (at least in terms of making public pronouncements about the law), dominant corporate perspectives were well represented in Canada's Parliament, raising questions about the negative impact of corporate criminal liability legislation for both corporations and the economic well-being of the nation. Chapter 5 also explores how neo-liberal perspectives of workplace safety – that is, the dominant notion that workers are responsible for their own safety and protection – permeated the reform process.

Chapter 6 explores the ways in which culturally embedded notions of crime and its control animated the Westray bill's development and enforcement. Dominant voices argued that crime is about the street-level violence that strikes fear in everyone, not about corporations that, but for the rogue few, are comprised of good, law-abiding citizens. However, even if corporations provide a social benefit (at least theoretically) that street criminals do not, this benefit should not deny the arbitrary and socially constructed distinctions between these offences – distinctions with roots in a dominant ideology that downplays the seriousness of corporate harm and wrongdoing in favour of punishing the most marginalized and disadvantaged members of society (Pearce and Tombs 1990). Chapter 6 also reveals that, despite a lack of charges and convictions, many respondents suggested that the Westray bill has encouraged corporations to improve their safety policies and practices. However, a closer look at some of the training and education offered in response to the new law suggests that these initiatives are more about making money to keep corporations and corporate actors out of the criminal justice system than about embracing the value of protecting workers' safety. In this respect, the Westray bill has produced what I refer to as a crime *(un)control* industry, whereby lawyers and consultants stand ready to help corporations (at least those who can afford their services) avoid getting caught and convicted for workplace injury and death.

Chapter 7 summarizes the book's main findings and considers some of their empirical and theoretical implications. It argues that a series of relatively autonomous, yet "mutually reinforcing," discourses have animated the evolution of Canada's corporate criminal liability legislation (Tombs and Whyte 2007, 69). Although these discourses were not part of a consciously orchestrated campaign against the introduction of corporate criminal liability legislation, they nevertheless converged to downplay the seriousness of safety crimes and limit the reform options that received serious consideration. In addition to raising questions about the potential of holding corporations to criminal account for workplace injury and death, it argues that the production of corporate crime and corporate criminal liability effectively (re)enforced and (re)produced the capitalist social formation.

Overall, *Still Dying for a Living* aims to provide an in-depth understanding of corporate crime law reform, therein contributing to discussion and debate regarding the nature and extent of the regulation and control of corporate harm and wrongdoing. It also addresses the ideological bias of law and its enforcement, particularly in that these processes frequently underestimate the seriousness of corporate crime and overlook the arbitrary distinction between regulatory and criminal offences or between "real" and "quasi" crimes (Snider 1993, 17-18). It is a troubling reality that we rarely question why we have laws to punish "murderers," while questions of this nature are the norm when discussing the appropriateness of corporate crime law reform (Wells 1993, 14). As Steve Tombs and Dave Whyte (2003, 4) argue, researching corporate crime lays bare the ability of those in positions of power to avoid the crime control web: *"One of the key features and effects of power is the ability to operate beyond public scrutiny and thus accountability"* [emphasis in original]. It also challenges mainstream examinations of crime and deviance that focus predominantly on crimes of the powerless (Snider 1993, 18). Although there is an important and critical body of literature that examines issues of corporate crime, it pales in comparison to the veritable mountain of research concerning traditional street crimes (Reiman 2004).

Finally, *Still Dying for a Living* attempts to address the fact that many studies of crime and its control overlook processes of law making in favour of examining law's effects.[11] As a result, what remain largely untouched are questions about the constitution of particular laws, the reasons why they are drafted, and the ways they are subsequently enforced or not. As Stanley Cohen (1996, 492, as cited in South 1998, 444) observes, "a major part of criminology is supposed to be the study of law making – criminalization – but we pay little attention to the driving forces behind so many new laws: the demand for protection from abuses of 'power.'" What follows, therefore, takes Cohen's challenge seriously by critically examining the development of legal measures to address the abuses of power by the most dominant institution in contemporary capitalist society.

2

Criminal Liability and the Corporate Form

Bill C-45 constitutes a fundamental change, if not a revolution in corporate
criminal liability.

– Todd Archibald, Kenneth Jull, and Kent Roach (2004, 368)

The history of the corporate criminal law is defined by only the pretense and
rhetoric of a benign big gun.

– William Laufer (2006, 198)

Introduction

The day of 7 November 2003 was historic in Canada's Parliament. Assembled
in the upper house were politicians from both the House of Commons and
Senate, joined by union officials, former Westray miner Vern Theriault, and
Allen and Debbie Martin, representing the families of the victims of the
Westray mine disaster. Their purpose was to witness Her Excellency, the
Governor General of Canada, give royal assent to Bill C-45, *An Act to Amend
the Criminal Code of Canada (Criminal Liability of Organizations)* (Westray
bill).[1] The government argued that the Westray bill represented a fundamental
reform to the *Criminal Code*, significantly "expanding the circumstances in
which an organization can be held criminally responsible for the actions taken
in its name by its representatives" (Paul Harold Macklin, Liberal, Hansard,

27 October 2003).[2] New Democratic member of parliament (MP) Alexa McDonough, a vocal supporter of corporate criminal liability legislation, suggested that the new law "brings us one step closer to ensuring that corporations are held liable for irresponsible working conditions that end up costing workers their lives" (Hansard, 7 November 2003). However, despite its legislative significance, the passing of the Westray bill was a slow, difficult, and, at times, controversial process. It was almost thirteen years after the disaster occurred and more than six years after the conclusion of the Westray inquiry before the law's enactment – not exactly a record-breaking pace for such purportedly important legislation!

This chapter outlines the history of corporate criminal liability legislation as well as the methods and sources used in the research. The first part explores the evolution of corporate criminal liability law, including the history of criminal liability and the corporate form, the identification doctrine, and the circuitous and protracted route that the Westray bill took through Canada's Parliament to become law. It also describes the charges and convictions registered under the new law since it took effect. The reasons for the law's introduction and subsequent lack of enforcement raise important questions about the constitution of corporate criminal liability and the capacity to hold corporations to account for their harmful and illegal acts.

The second part of the chapter details the research methods and sources. The research has methodological roots in critical discourse studies, an approach chosen to situate dominant discourses of corporate crime and corporate criminal liability within their broader social-political-economic context (Fairclough 1992; Fairclough et al. 2004; McKenna 2004). The research strategy also draws upon the tradition of triangulation, which encourages the use of different methods and sources to study social phenomena. Fostering diversity within the research agenda helps guard against any particular biases that may emerge through a specific method or source (Creswell 1994, 174). It also recognizes that any piece of information is only an "imperfectly mirrored reflection" of the phenomenon that it attempts to describe or explain (Palys 1997, 225).

Employing a range of methods and sources contributes to a diverse pool of information from which the researcher can develop an "in-depth understanding of the phenomenon in question" (Denzin and Lincoln 1994, 2). The "information pool" (Palys 1997, 225) developed for this study helps to reveal the complex and contradictory array of factors that contributed to the introduction of the Westray bill. In addition to verbatim transcripts from Canada's Parliament, this investigation includes semi-structured interviews with twenty-three individuals with knowledge of and insight into the issues of corporate criminal liability, relevant case law since the law's enactment, and Internet resources regarding its introduction and enforcement (or lack thereof).

Criminal Liability and the Corporate Form

Although the history of group liability dates back to twelfth-century England, when criminal sanctions applied to collectives or groups, the predominant criminal law approach emerged during feudal times when responsibility and sanctions were conceptualized as individualistic (Slapper and Tombs 1999, 22-23). As a result, historically, the corporation was largely beyond the purview of criminal law. The eighteenth-century First Baron Edward Thurlow, lord chancellor of England, purportedly stated that the corporation "had no soul to damn and no body to kick" (cited in Slapper and Tombs 1999, 26). From a criminal law perspective, it was anathema that there was not one individual to hold to account for corporate wrongdoing and that it was impossible for the corporation to defend itself in court (Glasbeek 2002, 128).

Despite a general reluctance to apply criminal law to corporate wrong-doing, most Western democratic nations today have at their disposal various methods, either through legislation or case law, to hold corporations to account for their harmful and illegal acts (Wells 1993, 1). These strategies offer a range of options to impute the "intent, knowledge or willfulness" of individuals to the corporation (Geis and Dimento 1995, 72). In the late nineteenth century, courts started assigning responsibility to corporations, albeit on a case-by-case basis and without any "conscious or overall direction," spelling out the parameters for attributing corporate criminal liability (Bernard 1984, 3; Department of Justice Canada 2002b).

The history of corporate criminal liability legislation has important links to the development of the corporate form (Bakan 2004). It was not until the mid-nineteenth century that the corporation emerged as the dominant means to undertake significant entrepreneurial ventures (Glasbeek 2002, 32-33). The modern corporation in Canada is a "creature of statute" with its own "legal existence" that is separate from those who invest in it (Yalden et al. 2008, 133). In essence, it is a natural, independent person, regardless of whether one or more individuals own shares in the company (135), with all of the attendant legal "capacities and powers" (Glasbeek 2004, 8). As Christopher Nicholls (2005, 3, 5; as quoted in Yalden et al. 2008, 32) notes,

> the corporation is an abstract concept. One cannot touch a corporation, photograph it, or draw a picture of it. We "see" a corporation only through

the effects it has on the world in which it operates ... In fact, the separate
existence of a corporation is formally recognized in law in a way that the
existence of a club or other unincorporated organization is not. A corporation
can own property in its own name: it can enter into contracts; and it can sue,
and be sued, too. It is, for legal purposes, a single, distinct, entity. Yet as a
practical matter, there are living, breathing people behind the entity.

A vital aspect of the corporation is limited liability. With some exceptions
(discussed later in this chapter), the primary risk for the individual investor is
the money that he or she provides to the venture (Snider 1993).

The forerunner to the limited liability corporation was the regulated company, which first emerged in the thirteenth century as a corporation formed by
"the grant of a charter from the Crown." Its purpose was to facilitate the introduction of a "grantee and repository of monopoly trading rights on behalf of
merchants" (Yalden et al. 2008, 217-18). It was from this basis that the joint stock
company emerged during the seventeenth century, constituting the most common method of conducting business until the introduction of the limited liability corporation. The classic joint stock venture was the East India Company,
first created as a monopoly to trade with the Indies but eventually evolving into
a company that permitted subscription members. Rules relating to partnerships
developed through common law and, later, through statutes that set out the
parameters for business agreements between partners and third parties (216-18).
The notion of limited liability was not part of these joint stock ventures (14).

The corporation's separate legal personality developed gradually, culmin-
ating with the English *Companies Act* in 1862 as well as with the watershed
English case, *Salomon v Salomon and Company* (1892) (Yalden et al. 2008,
135).[3] Rapid economic development in the nineteenth century resulted in
greater demands across the business world to pool economic resources to
encourage new businesses and generate capital (Clarke 2004, 2; Snider 1993,
22). For example, in the United Kingdom, during the late eighteenth and early
nineteenth century, the development of transportation systems (canals and
railways) required "massive amounts of capital" that far outstripped the ca-
pabilities of individual investors (MacPherson 2005, para. 11). Although the
joint stock company enjoyed considerable success during this period, there
was a general and growing hesitation on the part of investors who voiced
concern about what would happen with their "personal fortunes" in "unincorporated joint stock companies with unlimited liability" (Clarke 2004, 2). It was
within this context that pressures mounted for the state to recognize the limited
liability corporation.

The limited liability corporation brought with it important economic and practical benefits.[4] In contemporary terms, it facilitates the pooling of diverse resources for the creation of economically and (potentially) socially productive corporate ventures. At the same time, those who invest in the corporation have few risks beyond their monetary contribution, which, in turn, stimulates economic growth by encouraging as many investors as possible to participate in the marketplace. Although some investors risk more wealth than others (that is, some individuals spend considerable resources in one corporation), there is an overall incentive to spread individual contributions across different firms to reduce risk levels (Easterbrook and Fischel 1985; Yalden et al. 2008, 149-51). In addition, investors are not saddled with monitoring the day-to-day matters of the corporation, although this situation has shifted somewhat in the face of recent corporate scandals and the rise of the shareholders' rights movement (Soederberg 2010). Since most investors are involved in many different ventures, it is neither efficient nor desirable for them to be actively involved in monitoring the corporation, something that falls to those with major investments in the firm and to creditors whose investments are integral to the bottom business line (Yalden et al. 2008, 153). The limited liability corporation therefore represents a tremendous outcome from a "market capitalism perspective" (Glasbeek 2004, 9).

Despite these benefits, some observers question the divide within the limited liability corporation between owners (shareholders) and those charged with managing the enterprise, a process that first emerged with joint stock companies (Clarke 2004, 2). Historically, many economists, including Adam Smith (1937, 700), expressed concern over the potential for inefficiencies given that managers did not have the same economic interests as owners and, therefore, lacked similar incentives to watch over the operation with the same "anxious vigilance" (see, by way of comparison, Clarke 2004, 2-3). Adolf Berle and Gardiner Means (1967, 312) labelled this development as a fundamental shift in the structure of corporate ownership, effectively surrendering the right to operate the organization solely with ownership's interests in mind (see also Chandler 1977). From this perspective, the "visible hand of management" effectively replaced the "invisible hand" of market forces (Clarke 2004, 33).

Other observers have suggested that contemporary laws have created a fiduciary duty for the corporation to consider whether society generally benefits from its financial prosperity (Greenfield 2005; cited in Yalden et al. 2008, 51-54).[5] For instance, according to Anita Anand and Jessica Penley (2005, 942), the *Canada Business Corporations Act* states that corporate directors and officers must act in "good faith" and with the "care, diligence and skill" of a "reasonably prudent person."[6] In addition, in *Peoples Department Store Inc. (Trustee of) v Wise*, the Supreme Court of Canada stated that the "best interests of the corporation" are not automatically nor necessarily the "best interests of shareholders."[7] A board of directors might therefore consider a broad range of perspectives in its decision-making process, including "shareholders, employees, suppliers, creditors, consumers, governments and the environment" (see, by way of comparison, Yalden et al. 2008, 57). However, Paul Paton (2006-07, 236-37) notes that the *Peoples* case also produced considerable ambiguity in that the court stated the fiduciary responsibility of directors is to act in the best interests of the corporation – not to be confused with the interests of other stakeholders – which he sees as signalling a "clear distinction between shareholders and stakeholders."

Although the concept of fiduciary responsibility suggests that corporations do not always act in their own best (economic) interests, this does not negate the fact that the bottom line – namely, the maximization of shareholder value – continues to inform the corporation's decisions and actions. A revealing example is the attempt by corporations to include workers as stakeholders or partners in the organization. Partnerships, it is claimed, will ensure the corporation remains competitive and viable. Unfortunately, according to Harry Arthurs and Claire Mumme (2007, 8), this commitment is more apparent than real: "The current north American 'stakeholder' discourse seems to be designed largely to convince workers that their interests are fundamentally aligned with those of the corporation" (see also Soederberg 2010). Whether or not it is expressly thought and articulated, corporate actors continue to seek ways to improve the corporation's productivity and profitability, a process that ultimately benefits majority shareholders and not the interests of "outsiders."

Notwithstanding the uneven contours of the limited liability corporation, what is clear is that its evolution is the result of political decisions (Yalden et al. 2008, 16). Although the desire for economic prosperity was an essential catalyst behind the modern corporation, it does not make the choices that followed inevitable (MacPherson 2005, para. 6). The emergence of the limited liability corporation during the late nineteenth and early twentieth century was to the economic benefit of everyone involved, including owners, managers, and workers (para. 14; see also Micklethwait and Wooldridge 2003). However, this progress came at a cost, benefiting some more than others and harming many workers who were victimized by the corporation's "success" (Glasbeek 2004).

An important factor to consider is that, despite some historical variations in the general purposes of the corporation, its main motivation remains profit maximization (Clarke 2004; Glasbeek 2004). Except for some "tinkering around the edges," the modern corporation remains essentially unchanged from its original purpose first established more than 150 years ago, including "separate legal personality for the corporation, limited liability for shareholders, freedom for executives in making business decisions in the best interests of the corporation" (MacPherson 2005, para. 28).[8]

For many observers, it is noteworthy that the notion of limited liability was originally a privilege bestowed by the state, a vehicle from which corporations could serve the public interest. However, this privilege soon turned into an unassailable right once governments realized the potential of corporations as a significant revenue-generating mechanism (Snider 1993, 22; see also Bakan 2004; Glasbeek 2002). In Canada, for example, the corporation gained such importance that it quickly evolved from an entity formed through acts of Parliament to a process of incorporation through registration, an almost automatic approval process that simply requires adherence to particular statutory processes (Yalden et al. 2008, 217).[9]

The corporate form therefore expanded significantly, pushing the limits of production in the pursuit of profit, bringing with it frequent and serious injury and death in the workplace (Slapper and Tombs 1999, 25). For instance, working conditions deteriorated throughout the 1800s to the extent that it threatened "the very survival of the capitalist system" (Snider 1993, 95), prompting legislators and the courts to consider new rules to improve workplace safety (Carson 1980). In the United Kingdom, new laws soon followed that limited the length of the working day, eliminated child labour, and mandated meal breaks (Snider 1993, 94-95).

Despite growing concerns with workplace safety, including recognition of its importance by some of the privileged class, corporations were generally successful in lobbying against the reforms that they perceived to be overly stringent. Underpinning this resistance was the notion that corporations were private property and that, therefore, what went on within a company was the owner's private business. In addition, workers were thought to "freely" enter into working arrangements and, by logic, could leave any workplace that they believed to be dangerous (Snider 1993, 97). Regardless, as time passed, there was a growing recognition of the social and economic damages that corporations were capable of inflicting in the absence of accountability. It was from here that, in 1915, the British House of Lords found that a corporation could be civilly liable for damages, a ruling that paved the way for similar reasoning within the realm of criminal law (Glasbeek 2002, 127-28; see also Ferguson 1998, 5).[10]

A series of United Kingdom cases in 1944 provided further criminal law inroads by introducing the identification doctrine, which assigned responsibility to the corporation by equating the *mens rea* of certain employees with that of the company itself (Slapper and Tombs 1999, 28-30).[11] The legal test that emerged from these cases assigned responsibility to the "controlling officer," the individual who effectively acted as the company. The problem, however, was figuring where responsibility lay in serious and complex matters. As Gary Slapper and Steve Tombs (31) note, for cases involving manslaughter, the courts found it difficult to convict corporations given the distribution of responsibility throughout the corporate body, making it a challenge to single out one responsible individual.

Prior to the Westray bill, Canadian courts relied upon English common law to define corporate criminal liability.[12] The standard-setting case is *Canadian Dredge and Dock Company v The Queen,* in which the Supreme Court of Canada introduced the "identification doctrine."[13] In this case, the court argued that attributing liability involved tracing the crime to a senior employee(s), namely the "directing mind" of the corporation. A person was deemed to be a directing mind when he or she was responsible for a particular department or unit and when the crime benefited the corporation in some way (Department of Justice Canada, 2002a). Since the identification doctrine only applied to "high-level managers with decision-making authority," and since lower-level managers are often the people interpreting company policies, tracing responsibility up to senior management frequently proved impossible, particularly when seeking criminal convictions (ibid). Increasingly, vocal critics argued that this approach obviously failed to "reflect the reality or complexity of corporate decision-making in large, modern companies" (Cahill and Cahill 1999, 154).

Although the identification doctrine provided the legal groundwork that made it possible to hold corporations criminally accountable, it remained (and remains) commonplace for corporations to avoid responsibility for their social, environmental, and economic wrongdoing (Pearce and Tombs 1998). For Harry Glasbeek (2002, 130), this conundrum indicates that "the corporate hand may have been twisted into shape to fit inside the criminal glove, but it still seeks to revert to its original, ill-fitting shape." The Westray bill represents the most recent attempt by legislators to see if they can make the criminal glove fit. As Tombs and Dave Whyte (2007, 110) suggest, it constitutes an attempt to "assimilate" corporate wrongdoing into the realm of criminal law.

The Westray Bill's Evolution

The contemporary underpinnings of Canada's corporate criminal liability legislation arose shortly after the Westray mine disaster. As outlined in Chapter 1, in 1993 both the Standing Committee on Justice and Human Rights (Justice Committee)[14] and a white paper published by the Minister of Justice Canada (1993)[15] recommended legal reforms relating to the criminal liability of corporations. Although these proposals were not directly in response to the Westray disaster, they nonetheless signalled recognition of the need for improved legal measures to hold corporations to account for their harmful and illegal acts.

Corporate criminal liability law reform gained additional momentum with the release of the Westray inquiry's report (Richard 1997). In cataloguing the range of workplace health and safety violations that led to the disaster, the inquiry's chair, Justice K. Peter Richard, criticized the company's management and labour officials for failing to ensure that the mine's operations complied with provincial safety regulations (Glasbeek 2002, 62; Richard 1997, 605).[16] Of particular concern was the fact that the mine management were unqualified, ignored input from workers regarding the mine's working conditions, and failed to ensure that workers received proper training in mine safety and operations (Richard 1997, 611). As the report notes of the working culture that permeated the Westray mine,

> the many instances of hazardous and illegal practices encouraged or condoned by Westray management demonstrate its failure to fulfill its legislated responsibility to provide a safe work environment for its workforce. Management avoided any safety ethic and apparently did so out of concern for production imperatives. (612)

Even in situations that required obvious and immediate safety measures, such as neutralizing the excessive build-up of explosive coal dust through its removal or by the spreading of stone dust, management chose not to respond (617).

In addition to outlining safety measures for all mining operations, including better safety training for workers, management, and operators, the Westray inquiry's report called for improved internal and external regulation of the mining industry (Richard 1997, 631-32). However, since the inquiry was a provincial government initiative, and criminal law is federal jurisdiction, issues of corporate criminal liability were largely beyond its mandate (600-1). Nevertheless, building from the outrage over the fact that the mine's owners were never held to legal account for what happened at the Westray mine, the United Steelworkers of America (Steelworkers) pressed the matter with Justice Richard. As the union representing the Westray workers – the workers unionized shortly after the disaster – the Steelworkers had intervener status during the inquiry's proceedings (Comish 1993; Jobb 1994; Richard 1997).

The Steelworkers' efforts to lobby for corporate criminal liability during the inquiry contained three elements. First, they pushed Justice Richard to recommend a criminal offence imposing liability on "directors or other responsible corporate agents for failing to ensure that their corporation maintained an appropriate standard of occupational health and safety in the workplace." Second, they argued for the inquiry's report to recommend an offence of "corporate killing." Third, they lobbied for additions to the *Occupational Health and Safety Act* to "broaden the liability of directors and officers for offences under the act."[17] In recognizing the "weakness in our system" to hold corporate executives to legal account, and straying slightly beyond his mandate, Justice Richard (1997, 600-1) recommended that the government of Canada introduce corporate criminal liability provisions. Recommendation 73 of the report reads as follows:

> The Government of Canada, through the Department of Justice, should institute a study of the accountability of corporate executives and directors for the wrongful or negligent acts of the corporation and should introduce in the Parliament of Canada such amendments to legislation as are necessary to ensure that corporate executives and directors are held properly accountable for workplace safety. (600-1)

The seeds of reform were sown, and it was now up to the federal government to decide whether to heed Justice Richard's advice. However, despite the Westray inquiry's encouragement, and as we shall see later in this chapter, there was little sense of urgency on the part of the federal government to introduce changes to the law.

The Westray Bill in Canada's Parliament

Several overlapping and notable events in Canada's Parliament preceded the enactment of corporate criminal liability legislation – during the six years falling between the Westray inquiry's report and the Westray bill.[18] In February 1999, two years after the Westray inquiry's report, the New Democratic Party (NDP) tabled the first of four private members' bills aimed at holding corporations, directors, and officers to account for unsafe working conditions.[19] Then, in April 1999, Progressive Conservative (PC) Party MP Peter MacKay, who represented the riding in which the Westray disaster occurred, tabled a private members' motion requesting that the government amend the *Criminal Code* "or other appropriate statutes" to ensure that "corporate executives and directors are held properly accountable for workplace safety."[20] In February 2002, Bill C-284, *An Act to Amend the Criminal Code (Offences by Corporations, Directors and Officers)*, the NDP's third private members' bill, reached second stage reading in the House of Commons and was then withdrawn from the order paper and referred to the Justice Committee for its study and review (Hansard, 19 February 2002, 17:55).[21] Throughout the spring of 2002, the Justice Committee received written briefs and heard testimony from, and asked questions of, thirty-four witnesses representing a range of opinions about corporate criminal liability legislation. The Justice Committee's final report, tabled on 10 June 2002, recommended that the federal government introduce corporate criminal liability legislation.[22] Finally, on 12 June 2003, in response to the Justice Committee's work and in the face of continued pressure from the NDP to introduce corporate criminal liability legislation, the Minister of Justice Martin Couchon introduced Bill C-45, *An Act to Amend the Criminal Code (Criminal Liability of Organizations)* – the Westray bill (Hansard, 12 June 2003, 10:10).

These developments have contributed to the empirical focus of this study and are discussed in further detail later in this book. For the purpose of this chapter, the discussion focuses on outlining the different events and processes that preceded the Westray bill's enactment – information about how the bill became law. The chapters that follow explore in greater detail the ways in which these activities helped characterize and animate the law's development.

The NDP's Private Members' Bills
The NDP was a key advocate in Canada's Parliament for the introduction of corporate criminal liability legislation, tabling a series of private members' bills aimed at holding corporations and corporate executives to legal account. The first two efforts (both in 1999) failed when the bills died on the order paper.[23] However, when the House of Commons resumed in late January 2001, NDP MPs continued questioning the government about its intention to table new legislation (for example, see Pat Martin, NDP, Hansard, 2 February 2001, 11:05). Soon thereafter, on 7 February 2001, NDP MP Alexa McDonough introduced Bill C-418, *An Act to Amend the Criminal Code (Criminal Liability*

of Corporations, Directors and Officers). As with previous versions of the NDP's legislation, the bill aimed to establish the "criminal liability of corporations and of their executives and officers with respect to health and safety practices, of which they were aware or should have been aware, that put their workers at risk" (Hansard, 7 February 2001, 15:05).

A little more than two weeks later, NDP MP Bev Desjarlais introduced Bill C-284, *An Act to Amend the Criminal Code (Offences by Corporations, Directors and Officers)*, arguing that it was necessary to table a second private members' bill given that the government had yet to table its own legislation, despite promises otherwise (Hansard, 26 February 2001, 15:10).[24] On 20 September 2001, Desjarlais brought her bill forward for second-stage reading in the House of Commons and, per normal parliamentary procedure, to be referred to a parliamentary committee for study and review (Hansard, 20 September 2001, 17:30). On 19 February 2002, in agreement with the governing Liberal Party, Bill C-284 was withdrawn from the order paper and referred to the Justice Committee (Hansard, 19 February 2002, 17:55).[25]

The NDP-sponsored private members' bills marked a significant departure from the common law identification doctrine. The bill proposed criminal offences for directors and officers when staff of a corporation committed an offence and corporate management "knew or should have known of the act or omission or condoned or was wilfully blind to it." No longer would the directing mind test be the sole or primary means of proving management accountability. In addition, the burden of proving that the act or omission was "unauthorized" or "not tolerated" was put to the corporation, not the Crown, and it criminalized the failure to provide safe working conditions. Of particular note, it incorporated the concept of corporate culture, an initiative pioneered by the federal government of Australia in 1995, wherein senior management was criminally liable if a corporate culture allowed or encouraged law violation or facilitated law avoidance. The Australian legislation defined corporate culture as an "attitude, policy, rule, course of conduct or practice existing within the body corporate generally or in the part of the body corporate in which the relevant activities take place" (Department of Justice Canada, 2002a). In addition to implying a collective responsibility for corporate crime, for allowing criminogenic conditions to become dominant, the concept of corporate culture officially recognizes that in any profit-making business there is always ample motivation to justify or ignore unsafe working conditions (ibid).[26] As we shall see, however, the government's legislation differed significantly, the reasons for which constitute an important focus of this study.

The PC Party's Private Members' Motion

Around the same time the NDP tabled its first private members' bill, the PC Party launched its own corporate criminal liability initiative in the House of Commons. On 23 April 1999, PC MP Peter MacKay tabled a private members' motion requesting that the federal government respond to the Westray inquiry's report by amending the *Criminal Code* "or other appropriate statutes" to ensure that "corporate executives and directors are held properly accountable for workplace safety" (Hansard, 23 April 1999, 12:15). MacKay's motion explained

> that in the opinion of the House, the Criminal Code or other appropriate
> federal statutes should be amended in accordance with recommendation
> 73 of the Province of Nova Scotia's public inquiry into the Westray disaster,
> specifically with the goal of ensuring that corporate executives and directors
> are held properly accountable for workplace safety. (Justice Committee,
> 6 June 2000, 10:12)[27]

MPs debated the motion on a number of occasions and ultimately accepted it on 21 March 2000 and, as a matter of parliamentary procedure, sent it to the Justice Committee for its consideration.[28]

The Justice Committee met on one occasion to examine MacKay's motion. The meeting started with a presentation from MacKay, who noted the difficulty of lifting the corporate veil to hold directors and managers to account for workplace injury and death (Justice Committee, 6 June 2000, 10:20). In referring to the broad support for enacting corporate criminal liability law, MacKay cited a poll commissioned by the Steelworkers in which 85 percent of Canadians surveyed favoured changes to the law to ensure that corporate executives are held to account for criminal wrongdoing (Justice Committee, 6 June 2000, 10:25). MacKay also noted a suggestion from other MPs that his motion be merged with the NDP's private members' bill, given that together they would provide a significant contribution to the legislative agenda (Justice Committee, 6 June 2000, 10:30 and 11:00).

Despite questions and concerns regarding the concept of corporate criminal liability, the Justice Committee agreed with the motion and amended it to include reference to the NDP's proposed legislation. The Justice Committee's recommendation, tabled in the House of Commons the following day, stated: "The Minister of Justice and the Department of Justice bring forward proposed legislation in accordance with the said motion and the principles underlying

... [the first NDP's bill] ... for consideration by the Standing Committee on Justice and Human Rights" (Justice Committee, 6 June 2000, 12:40).[29]

Per parliamentary standing orders, the government had 150 days to respond to the Justice Committee's recommendation, although the committee encouraged the government to respond as quickly as possible (Justice Committee, 6 June 2000, 11:35). However, by October 2000, just days before the end of the 150-day period, and with a federal election call looming, the government had yet to respond. The government's inaction prompted NDP MP Peter Mancini to request in the House of Commons "to move concurrence" on the Justice Committee's report (Hansard, 5 October 2000, 10:10). Mancini's concern was about losing the bipartisan work of the Justice Committee if the House prorogued for an election, therein bringing the administration of justice into disrepute (Hansard, 5 October 2000, 10:20). As Mancini argued in the House of Commons,

> accidents can happen as a matter of chance, but when they happen because a corporation has determined that the lives of its workers are not a factor in determining the balance sheet, then it is time for us to say that it is a crime. It is time for us to say that when a corporation knowingly determines to send men and women possibly to their deaths and it has the means to prevent that and does not, it is time for us to say that it is a crime. I rise today on this motion because we said that in the justice committee. We sent it to the minister and asked for a bill to be brought back that would make it a crime for those directors and corporations to kill their workers. (Hansard, 8 October 2000, 10:25)

MPs passed Mancini's move for concurrence (Hansard, 8 October 2000, 11:05). However, soon after, the House of Commons dissolved for a federal election, leaving the private members' motion and the Justice Committee's report to die on the order paper.[30]

The Justice Committee and Bill C-45

The next significant event in the development of the Westray bill was the Justice Committee's examination of the NDP's private members' bill. The Justice Committee began hearing from witnesses on 2 May 2002, and tabled its final report on 10 June 2002 (see Appendix A for a list of Justice Committee members at that time).[31] As noted in Chapter 1, the committee's inability to reach an agreement on the appropriate model of corporate criminal liability meant that its final report simply requested that "the Government table in the House legislation to deal with the criminal liability of corporations, directors, and officers."[32] This impasse allowed the government's law writers (the legislative drafters at the federal Department of Justice) to "draw [their] own conclusions" from the hearings (Department of Justice Canada 2002b). The government agreed with the Justice Committee's position that reforms were necessary to determine responsibility within modern, complex organizations (ibid).

It would be another year before corporate criminal liability law would progress further in Canada's Parliament. On 10 June 2003, expressing frustration with the government's inaction, NDP MP Bev Desjarlais asked in the House of Commons when the government would finally table new legislation (Hansard, 10 June 2003, 14:15). Two days later, Minister of Justice Martin Couchon introduced Bill C-45, An *Act to Amend the Criminal Code (Criminal Liability of Organizations)* (Hansard, 12 June 2003, 10:10). The following day, Parliament recessed for the summer, and returned on 15 September 2003, at which time Bill C-45 was read for the second time in the House of Commons.

The House debated Bill C-45 at second reading on 15 and 20 September 2003. In launching the debate, the parliamentary secretary noted to the minister of justice and attorney general, Paul Harold Macklin from the Liberal Party, the unanimous consensus over the need for "fundamental reform" in this area.[33] At the debate's conclusion, MPs moved to refer the legislation to the Justice Committee, per parliamentary procedures. The Justice Committee met on only one occasion (22 October 2003) to examine the bill, and tabled its report in the House of Commons the following day, with minor amendments to the bill (Hansard, 23 October 2003, 10:50).

Bill C-45 was returned to the House of Commons for further consideration on 27 October 2003. Liberal MP Paul Harold Macklin once again spoke of the broad-based, non-partisan support for legislation and added that its mere development was already encouraging many organizations to re-think their health and safety strategies. As Macklin argued,

> I understand that officials of the Department of Justice have met with the
> Canadian Chamber of Commerce and with the occupational health and
> safety committee of the Canadian Manufacturers and Exporters to explain
> the potential impact of Bill C-45. They have also participated in a panel on
> Bill C-45 and the implications of proposed amendments to the Criminal
> Code as part of the Health and Safety Law Conference 2003 held in Toronto.
> All members should be encouraged by these signs that corporations and
> other organizations are considering their policies in the light of this new
> duty. (Hansard, 27 October 2003, 17:25)

In addition, NDP MP Alexa McDonough noted the hard work and dedication of the Steelworkers in pushing for the law's enactment. As she submitted, the union "poured their heart and soul, blood and guts into pressing for the kind of changes in law, the changes in health and safety practices in Nova Scotia and across the country, that would ensure never again would there be an occurrence permitted in this country such as what happened at Westray" (Hansard, 27 October 2003, 17:45).

Bill C-45 was then read for the third time, passed, and then sent to the Senate, where it was read for the first time on 27 October 2003 and passed after the third reading on 30 October 2003. Senate members generally supported the legislation and wanted it passed as expeditiously as possible (Senate Committee, Hansard, 29 October 2003). Per Senate procedures, the bill was referred to the Senate Standing Committee on Legal and Constitutional Affairs (Senate Committee) for its consideration (Senate Committee, Hansard, 29 October 2003, 16:50). The Senate Committee heard only from representatives of the Department of Justice Canada, who provided members with an overview of the legislation. Donald Piragoff, senior general council with the Department of Justice, noted the difficulties of establishing *mens rea* and *actus reus* in the context of a corporation as well as the general difficulty of reforming the criminal law. As Piragoff stated, "it is always difficult to make changes in the criminal law. The stakes are very high, and many will fear that the changes will expose them to the stigma of a criminal conviction for actions that were legitimate under the existing Criminal Code" (Senate Committee, Hansard, 30 October 2003, 16:50). After further discussion, the Senate Committee moved directly to a clause-by-clause consideration of the bill. Although some members expressed concern about not following normal procedure by hearing evidence from witnesses, they decided to proceed based on assurances from the Department of Justice representatives that they had consulted various stakeholders and incorporated many of their concerns into the final version of the bill (Senate Committee, Hansard, 30 October 2003). The Senate Committee therefore adopted Bill C-45 without amendment.

Bill C-45: The Final Steps

After taking a protracted and circuitous route through Canada's Parliament, the Westray bill received royal assent on 7 November 2003. The new law differed from the NDP's proposed legislation in several significant ways. First, it substituted corporations with organizations, defined as a "public body, body corporate, society, company, firm, partnership, trade union or municipality" (Department of Justice Canada 2003, 4). This substitution paved the way for charges against trade unions, charitable organizations, or non-governmental organizations. As Todd Archibald, Kenneth Jull, and Kent Roach (2004, 375) state, "the explicit reference to [these bodies] in this legislation sends a green light to policing bodies and private complainants that they may now become potential targets."

Second, it shies away from corporate culture in favour of individual liability, better reflecting the individualistic aspects of the common law standard of the directing mind. In comparison to the NDP's corporate culture approach, the Westray bill affixes culpability to the senior officer, defined as the individual(s) with important roles, who are "setting policy or managing an important part of the organization's activities." It also introduces the concept of representative, which refers to a "director, partner, employee, member, agent or contractor" (see also Department of Justice Canada 2003, 5).[34] Although these definitions widen the scope of the law and increase its flexibility – prosecutors can go beyond a particular job title to establish corporate criminal liability (Archibald, Jull, and Roach 2004, 368) – it remains focused on establishing individual fault.

Third, the Westray bill creates different methods for holding organizations criminally accountable. For offences based on negligence, an organization can be found guilty if the Crown can prove that "employees of the organization committed the act and that a senior officer should have taken reasonable steps to prevent them from doing so" (Department of Justice Canada 2003, 6). This change makes it possible for the corporation to be held accountable for "collective action," such as when the separate actions of several employees combine to result in a negligent act (Archibald, Jull, and Roach 2004, 386). What is essential is that the senior officer must depart "markedly" from standards that could reasonably be followed to prevent the employee(s) from committing the offence (385).[35]

For subjective intent offences – offences requiring intent, knowledge, or proof of fault – there must be evidence that the harmful actions of senior officers somehow benefited the organization (Department of Justice Canada 2003, 70).[36] A corporation can therefore be held accountable for the actions of someone (namely, a senior officer) who is not necessarily the directing mind of the corporation, taking corporate responsibility beyond the boardroom to the operational decisions of senior managers: "While this is not pure vicarious liability (as it only applies to senior officers), it borders on that principle" (Archibald, Jull, and Roach 2004, 376, 381). Some legal observers suggest that this change is significant in that, if a senior officer knew or allowed a representative to fail in their legal duties – to commit or become a party to an offence

– then the corporation can be found guilty. As Archibald, Jull, and Roach (2004, 380) argue, this provision has the potential to spread the "stigma" of subjective intent offences throughout the organization, "even if only one part of the corporation was at fault."

The notion of vicarious liability is commonly associated with corporate criminal liability standards in the United States. Under this doctrine, a corporation can be held criminally liable for the acts of "its *officers, agents or servants* who are acting within the scope of their employment and for the benefit of the corporation" (Department of Justice Canada 2002a [emphasis added]). Once *mens rea* is established, responsibility is "imputed to the corporation itself" (ibid). For many commentators, this doctrine minimizes the principle of *mens rea* by transferring the guilt of the individual too easily onto the company (Department of Justice Canada 2003, 5).[37] The term senior officer represents a classic Canadian compromise – broader than the directing mind but narrower than vicarious liability.

Finally, the Westray bill provides a new sentencing regime for organizations.[38] In addition to outlining factors for courts to consider during sentencing (issues such as "moral blameworthiness," "public interest," and "prospects of rehabilitation"),[39] it introduces fines of up to one hundred thousand dollars for summary conviction offences (fines for indictable offences are already unrestricted in the *Criminal Code*),[40] and outlines probation orders for organizations – for example, restitution, new policies to prevent further offending, notification of the offence to the public, and any other "reasonable condition" that the court deems necessary (Department of Justice Canada 2003, 9; see also Archibald, Jull, and Roach 2004, 389-92).[41]

The Westray Bill in Action

Since the Westray bill became law in 2004, there have been only a handful of charges and convictions.[42] The first charge was laid on 19 April 2004.[43] Domenico Fantini, a sixty-eight year-old owner/supervisor of a small construction company was charged with one count of criminal negligence causing death after a trench collapsed at the site of a private house renovation, killing one employee, Ameth Garrido (Brown 2004; York Regional Police 2004). Garrido was crushed to death when the walls of the trench he was working in gave way (Saint-Cyr 2005). Ontario's *Occupational Health and Safety Act* required that the trench be properly sloped or shored to prevent the collapse.[44] What is more, the homeowner, who worked in construction, had "specifically directed the defendant to slope the excavation of the trench at a 45 degree angle slope to prevent the collapse."[45] Criminal charges against Fantini were eventually dropped when he pleaded guilty to provincial regulatory offences (Saint-Cyr 2005). He was fined $50,000 and ordered to pay a $10,000 victim surcharge.

The second charge, and first conviction, was against Transpavé, a manufacturer of concrete patio blocks, after a machine that stacks concrete stones onto wooden pallets crushed a worker to death (Edwards and Conlin 2006; Keith and Walsh 2008).[46] On 11 October 2005, Steve L'Ecuyer, who was "not performing his regular job and was acting as a replacement for an employee who was on break," entered the machine's stacking area to remove a jam when he was grabbed by a mechanical arm and crushed (Edwards and Conlin 2006, 1; Hamilton 2008). An investigation by the Commission de la santé et de la sécurité du travail, Quebec's occupational health and safety authority, revealed that the machine's light curtain system, a safety device that stops the machine from operating when someone enters the stacking area, was purposely disabled at the time of the incident (Hamilton 2008; Edwards and Conlin 2006). The investigation also revealed that the company lacked appropriate training procedures and failed to inspect the machine to ensure its proper functioning (Edwards and Conlin 2006, 1).

In December 2007, as part of a plea agreement between the Crown and defence lawyers, Transpavé pled guilty to criminal negligence causing death. The sentencing hearing took place on 17 March 2008, at which time the judge accepted the joint sentencing submission of the Crown and defence and ordered the company to pay a fine of $100,000, plus a $10,000 victim surcharge (Canadian Human Rights Reporter 2008; Keith and Walsh 2008). Factors in the judge's decision included the company's size (he described it as a small, family-run business, not a large multinational) and the fact that they had spent more than $500,000 since the incident to improve workplace safety (Cherry 2008, A8; Emond and Harnden 2008; Keith and Walsh 2008).

The plea bargain and punishment outraged the victim's family and union representatives. L'Ecuyer's mother expected the fine to be "in the millions" and that someone would be sent to prison (Canadian Press 2008; Cherry 2008, A8). The Quebec Federation of Labour (QFL), who actively lobbied the Crown to pursue criminal charges in the case, argued that the Crown "botched the case" in describing the company's health and safety record as "exemplary" (Edwards and Conlin 2006, 1). According to the QFL, health and safety had been an issue at Transpavé for years (Daily Commercial News and Construction Record 2008). The president of the Canadian Labour Congress, Ken Georgetti, suggested that the ruling "sends the wrong message to employers and corporations that nothing's changed and they can still afford to put their workers' lives at risk without any personal consequences" (Canadian Labour Congress 2008). Meanwhile, in response to suggestions that the fine was insufficient, legal observers noted that occupational health and safety fines were typically much lower in Quebec than in other provinces, such as Ontario and Alberta (Emond and Harnden 2008; Millan 2008).

The third charge occurred in February 2010 after a crane fell into an excavation pit in Sault Ste. Marie, Ontario, crushing a worker to death. After a lengthy investigation, the police charged Millennium Crane Rentals, along with its owner and a crane operator, with criminal negligence causing death (Edwards, Todd, and Warning 2010). However, the Crown dropped these charges in 2011 after an engineer's report was unable to conclude whether the crane's braking system was sufficient to prevent it from falling into the excavation. The report's findings left the Crown with insufficient evidence to proceed criminally. Charges against the company under the province's health and safety regulations are presently before the courts (O'Ferrall 2011).

The fourth charge and second conviction came in March 2011 when Pasquale Scrocca, the owner of a small landscaping company, was found guilty of criminal negligence causing death.[47] Scrocca was operating a backhoe in June 2006 when it pinned one of his workers, Aniello Boccanfuso, against a wall, crushing him to death. Investigators found that the backhoe's front brakes were non-functional and that the machine was poorly maintained. Scrocca received a two-year conditional sentence, which was to be served in the community (Workers' Health and Safety Centre 2011).

In August 2010, police charged Metron Construction Corporation and three company officials with four counts of criminal negligence causing death and criminal negligence causing bodily harm. The charges stemmed from an incident that occurred on Christmas Eve 2009 in which five migrant workers plummeted thirteen floors when the "swing-stage" scaffold that they were working on to repair the outside of a Toronto apartment building broke in half. Four of the workers died from the fall, while a fifth suffered serious injuries (Keith 2011a). The case continues to make its way through the courts.

Finally, in early 2010, in a move reflective of a growing frustration with the lack of Westray bill charges and convictions, the Steelworkers launched a private prosecution in relation to the death of a sawmill employee in New Westminster, British Columbia. Lyle Hewer died on 17 November 2004 when he was smothered to death while cleaning debris from a machine that converts wood to chips – a grinding machine referred to as a hog. Managers of the sawmill, owned by Weyerhaeuser, instructed Hewer to clean out the backed-up machine despite knowledge of the dangers of undertaking such work. The Crown decided against proceeding with a criminal prosecution, despite recommendations to the contrary by the provincial regulator, Worksafe British Columbia, and the local police. It was at this juncture that the Steelworkers launched a private prosecution (Lau 2011; Sinclair 2011).

In August 2011, a lower court judge approved the Steelworkers' case against Weyerhaeuser, which alleged that the company was criminally negligent for Hewer's death (Canadian Labour Reporter 2011; Lau 2011). Once again, the Crown declined to proceed with criminal charges (private prosecutions ultimately require the Crown's approval), concluding that the required "charge assessment standard" had not been met and that the evidence did not "provide a substantial likelihood of conviction against the company" (British Columbia Criminal Justice Branch 2011). The Steelworkers reacted angrily, arguing that the case involved obvious negligence that cried out for Westray bill charges. Union officials added that the failed prosecution meant that they would turn their attention to lobbying the federal government to take the necessary steps to ensure the Westray bill's enforcement (United Steelworkers of America 2011).[48]

None of these cases looks to be a precedent-setting decision that will have corporate moguls quaking in their boots, much less usher in a new era of corporate criminal liability. They are hardly what critics had in mind when they pointed to the limits of the identification doctrine in tracing the chain of responsibility throughout large and complex corporate structures (Cahill and Cahill 1999). On the contrary, *R v Fantini* and *R v Scrocca* involved small, independent contractors, while *R c Transpavé inc* involved a family-owned company with less than 100 employees (Conlin 2008).[49] In addition, given that Transpavé pled guilty, the *Scrocca* case involved easily proven negligence, and other cases continue to make their way through the courts, there is still little case law to indicate how and under what circumstances the courts will interpret the new law. As a result, the question remains whether these cases will be ultimately harbingers or anomalies.

Research Methods and Sources: Examining a Long and Protracted Route

As the preceding discussion illustrates, the Westray bill's enactment was anything but expeditious. It took several iterations of the NDP's private members' bills, a private members' motion from the PC Party, parliamentary committee hearings, and much political discussion and debate for the government to introduce corporate criminal liability legislation. And despite political rhetoric about the importance of the law, there have been only a few charges and convictions since its introduction.

In order to delve deeper into the history of the Westray bill, the study draws upon the qualitative tradition of discourse analysis. The decision to employ discourse analysis stems from the goal to critically analyze the discourses that have animated the introduction of the Westray bill – the ways in which they "simultaneously sustain, legitimize and change" the nature and scope of the law (Fairclough et al. 2004, 2). As part of this examination, the study subscribes to the argument that one's approach to data collection is intricately related to broader issues of theory and methodology – to how we conceptualize the object of inquiry (Frauley and Pearce 2007). As such, the next chapter details the analytical lens that informs my approach to discourse analysis – one that draws from both Foucauldian and neo-Marxist perspectives. Michel Foucault's notion of discursive formations uncovers the dominant voices that characterize corporate crime and corporate criminal liability – the knowledge claims that are taken for granted, treated as natural, logical ways to describe corporate crime. Neo-Marxism situates these discourses within their broader social-economic-political context. In this respect, the research considers how discourse and discursive relations are inculcated in the capitalist mode of production, albeit in non-linear, unpredictable, and often contradictory ways.[50]

The study's methodological framework also draws inspiration from a growing cadre of critical discourse scholars interested in the links between post-structuralism and neo-Marxism. This investigation involves examining language within its broader social context or what Bernard McKenna (2004, 10) suggests is the "intersection of language, discourse and social structure." For example, Norman Fairclough, Bob Jessop, and Andrew Sayer (2002, 3; see also Jessop 2004) put "semiotic processes into context" by interrogating how semiosis interacts within the social and material world.[51] Of particular interest is the "mutual implication of critical realism and semiosis" or how critical realism's concern with the "reproduction and transformation" of social relations can benefit from the analysis of "intersubjective production of meaning" within critical discourse studies (Fairclough, Jessop, and Sayer 2002, 2).[52] As they argue,

semiosis – the making of meaning – is a crucial part of social life but it does not exhaust the latter. Thus, because texts are both socially-structuring and socially-structured, we must examine not only how texts generate meaning and thereby help to generate social structure but also how the production of meaning is itself constrained by emergent, non-semiotic features of social structure. (3-4; see also Jessop 2004, 163)

Semiosis informs the social structure in that certain discourses represent, or give meaning to, and therein maintain or transform, social phenomena. Certain discourses are retained, passing through different filters to become privileged ways of referring to, or representing, social phenomena. *Vide* Foucault ([1972] 2001), discourse and discursive formations provide the possibilities from which particular statements are made. As McKenna (2004, 14) suggests, "this is the constructedness of discourse."

A key element of contextualizing discourse is determining what gives certain discourses their "truthfulness" or "appropriateness." There is a privileging of particular discourses because of the strategies that certain (powerful) agents or groups employ in the process of reproducing social relations. This is not an automatic or determinative process – semiotic processes can both secure and "militate against" social reproduction – but, rather, an ongoing and fluid exchange of renewal and transformation (Fairclough, Jessop, and Sayer 2002, 5-6). From this process, we can explore the imbrications of discourse in the (re)production of broader social relations – how discourse "constructs and maintains relations of power in society" (McKenna 2004, 15).

Contextualizing discourses of corporate crime and corporate criminal liability will illuminate the extra-discursive factors that inform the selection and retention of particular discourses as well as how these discourses help stabilize, reproduce, and transform the capitalist social formation (Jessop 2004, 159). In addition, by exploring how discourses work in conjunction with the extra-discursive, the study guards against "rationalist or ideologist" views of social relations that conceptualize discourse *qua* discourse, thereby ignoring the importance of extra-discursive factors (Fairclough, Jessop, and Sayer 2002, 9). The goal is to eschew "pure social constructionism," which claims that individuals create social reality – they can "will anything into existence" – in favour of exploring the "materiality of social relations" and the constraints or limits of various social processes that "operate 'behind the backs' of the relevant agents" (Jessop 2004, 161). In this respect, as Bob Jessop (2004, 164) reminds us, it is important to consider the "dialectic of discursivity and materiality" in the (re)production of political economies.

Several data sources provide the basis for critically examining the various discourses that animate Canada's corporate criminal liability legislation (see Appendix B for a detailed description of these data sources). These sources include approximately thirty-five hours of Hansard documents; verbatim transcripts of various proceedings from Canada's Parliament;[53] verbatim transcripts from the Justice Committee's meetings relating to their study of corporate criminal liability (see Appendix C for a list of witnesses who appeared before the Justice Committee);[54] the results of twenty-three semi-structured interviews, conducted to gain insight into the varied constitution of corporate criminal liability throughout the reform process; the knowledge claims that helped frame the Westray bill (see Appendix D for a list of research participants and Appendix E for the interview schedule);[55] and the Internet to glean additional details regarding the Westray bill. The next chapter situates this research focus within the corporate crime literature and outlines the empirical and theoretical influences that inform this study. As we shall see, the study's approach to discourse analysis is grounded in a theoretical integration of Foucauldian and neo-Marxist perspectives.

3

Theorizing Corporate Harm and Wrongdoing

> One measure of the growing ideological and structural influence of the
> dominant corporation is that when corporate actors commit crimes they are
> rarely charged; if charged, they are rarely convicted; and if convicted they
> are rarely punished severely.
>
> – Harry Glasbeek (2002, 118)

> In our view, capitalism as a class structure is itself a moral and ethical outrage.
> Beyond that it contributes to a host of social ills (inequality of wealth, political
> power, health, ecological sustainability, and access to culture).
>
> – Stephen Resnick and Richard Wolff (2006, 4)

Introduction

There is considerable evidence from recent decades of the immense, virtually
inconceivable, social and economic harm caused by corporations (Friedrichs
2010; Glasbeek 2002). The massive corporate frauds associated with the 2008
global financial crisis (Resnick and Wolff 2010); the corporate debacles of
companies such as Enron, WorldCom, and Parmalat in the early 2000s (Tillman
and Indergaard 2005); the deadly chemical explosion in Bhopal, India, that
killed "at least 1,700 and as many as 10,000 people" immediately after the
disaster (Pearce and Tombs 1998, 197); and the foreseeable and preventable

killing of twenty-six miners at the Westray mine (Richard 1997) are just a few tragic reminders of the devastating effects of corporate wrongdoing. And although a significant number of these harms contain a criminal element, they are rarely treated as such, effectively ignored by those in the position of authority, dealt with outside of the formal criminal justice system and defined away as mere accidents or the necessary by-product of capital's march to success (Snider 2008). As William Carson (1980, 41) notes in his examination of early corporate crime-related legislation,

> proscribed by law, it is often substantially tolerated in practice, although commentators never tire of pointing to the extremely high social price which it exacts. While it is statutorily defined as crime, moreover, it is frequently dealt with through administrative agencies that are discontinuous in origin and far from the normal machinery of criminal justice.

What is more, as both a concept and in law, the priority accorded to corporate crime, harm, and wrongdoing pales in comparison to the long-standing concern with street crimes (Snider 2008).

Gary Slapper and Steve Tombs (1999, 85-108) argue that the invisibility of corporate crime in law and order-speak – what Steven Box (1983, 16) refers to as a "collective ignorance" – has its roots in a series of "mutually reinforcing" social and economic ideologies that reproduce dominant notions of crime and disorder. An important element of this equation is academic studies of crime and deviance – examinations that fixate on the transgressions of individuals, fuelling the belief that what constitutes "real" crime are the street-level criminal activities that preoccupy contemporary law and its enforcement. As Michel Foucault (1979, 254) notes, the study of crime provides these acts with an ontological reality: "The act 'scientifically' *qua* offence and above all the individual *qua* delinquent." This explanation does not suggest that corporate crime is totally absent from the academic agenda – there is an established tradition of exposing crimes by the privileged and powerful – but that it occupies a marginal position within crime and deviance research (Friedrichs 1992, 6). How we study or do not study corporate crime matters; it shapes how we understand and respond to such acts, both as a social priority and in law.

This chapter situates the study within the corporate crime literature and outlines its empirical and theoretical influences. The first part considers how traditional studies of crime and deviance gloss over the corporate criminal in favour of individualistic accounts of crime and disorder. The second part of the chapter examines the corporate crime scholarship that attempts to overcome

Theorizing Corporate Harm and Wrongdoing   **39**

this myopic view of crime. It also considers some key debates within the corporate crime literature, including those regarding the most effective way to regulate the corporation.[1]

The third part of the chapter builds from the corporate crime scholarship to outline the book's theoretical underpinnings. The influence here is from the corporate crime scholarship with roots in critical socio-legal studies (Pearce and Tombs 1998; Tombs and Whyte 2007). Of particular interest is how this literature transcends the focus of traditional criminological and sociology of deviance studies – with their attendant focus on individualistic and positivistic accounts of crime – to situate the constitution of corporate crime within its broader social, political, and economic context. With this literature as its reference, the study draws its theoretical inspiration from Foucauldian and political economy studies to interrogate the constitution of corporate criminal liability.

Excluding the Corporate Criminal

Before delving into the corporate crime scholarship, it is important to briefly situate this body of work within the broader examinations of crime and deviance. Although it is beyond this chapter to examine the complete range of academic studies within the criminology and sociology of deviance, we will explore some of their general contours here to highlight how they are "bound up with modernity" (Sumner 1994, 3). Although modern culture shapes how we understand and respond to crime and deviance, these dominant conceptualizations also shape the world in which we live (3-4; see also Foucault 1972). As Colin Sumner (1994, x) argues,

> in the social sciences, the world we study changes, partly because of the knowledge we provide about it and because of our "scientific" interventions within its politics; and that, in turn, transforms the way we look at the world. In our case, that is certainly what has happened. We have changed the world that gave rise to the sociology of deviance and those changes have altered the way we look at the old world. The sociology of deviance no longer expresses our vision in the very new world ... In that sense, it is dead. Its voice cannot speak.

In this respect, there are links between the broader social context and the criminological and sociology of deviance literatures, a relationship historically preoccupied with the individual transgressions of traditional street criminals (Reiman 2004).

A related point is that criminology and the sociology of deviance is relatively inhospitable to studies of corporate crime (Tombs and Whyte 2007) and more generally inhospitable to "crimes of the powerful" (Pearce 1976). As Alexander Liazos (1972, 111) suggested almost forty years ago, the dominant trajectory of the sociology of deviance has been "the sociology of nuts, sluts and preverts," a comment that still aptly applies today. From this perspective, crime and deviance are ideological constructs, void of any essence beyond their socially defined parameters. Deviance, as Sumner (1994, 229) suggests, "is a series of normative divides or ideological cuts, cuts made in social practice – and the dominant cuts in our society are those made by the rich, powerful and authoritative." Accordingly, corporate crime scholarship remains a significant "blind spot" for many criminologists and sociology of deviance scholars (310).

Perspectives of deviance trace back to the demonic ages when deviance was equated with sin, and those who committed sins were either tempted by evil or possessed (Pfohl 1985, 20-21). Systematic examinations of crime and deviance first emerged through the classical school, most notably Cesare Beccaria ([1764] 1986) and Jeremy Bentham (1789), for whom crime was a problem of hedonism, a rational choice by individuals who wanted to "maximize pleasure and minimize pain" (Pfohl 1985, 49). Later in 1876, Cesare Lombroso ([1876] 1911) argued that criminals were evolutionary throwbacks – atavistic, born criminals (see, by way of comparison, Pfohl 1985, 85). As Steve Tombs and Dave Whyte (2007, 198) note, "various forms of individual positivism that emerged after the heyday of the eighteenth- and nineteenth-century classicist theories sought to identify the 'abnormalities' that either propelled individuals into crime, or ensured that they were more predisposed to committing crime than the general population." Crime's aetiology resided in the individual, causing certain people to stray beyond socially ascribed norms; crime was a disease-like problem, and it needed a cure (Morrison 1995, 9).

Alternative perspectives of crime and deviance gradually developed alongside of, and in response to, classical accounts. For instance, the sociology of deviance, with ties to the work of Émile Durkheim (1966), first emerged during the twentieth century as a "liberal version of criminology" (Sumner 1994, 301). Although Durkheim did not set out to form the sociology of deviance, nor did he explicitly address this subject, his work provided the conceptual frame for deviance scholars to ply their trade. Durkheim (1966, 70) argued that a certain amount of crime – individual differentiation – was a normal part of society and that the social conscience determined the appropriate degree of censure. Laws were an expression of the moral majority, a dividing line between acceptable and unacceptable behaviour (Deflem 2008). In North America, Durkheim's ideas flourished within a "political-intellectual context" concerned with what to do about the "socially inadequate" (Sumner 1994, 38-39).

Although the advent of the sociology of deviance shifted discussion of the causes of crime from the individual to the social, the focus remained individualistic in that it centred on the impact of the social environment for the individual (Pfohl 1985). In this regard, if criminology was guilty of individual positivism, then the sociology of deviance constituted a form of sociological positivism (Tombs and Whyte 2007, 198). Whether it was Robert Merton's (1938) strain theory that lower class individuals turn to crime out of frustration with their inability to realize legitimate social goals; Edwin Sutherland's (1939) theory of differential association that crime is a learned behaviour; or Travis Hirschi's control theory that crime results from loose bonds between an individual and his or her social groups (for example, family, school, or peer groups), criminals were considered to be a product of criminogenic contexts, or "normal" people who responded to difficult environments in socially unacceptable ways (Sumner 1994, 43). Crime was a "normal" and empirically identifiable fact within society, and, consequently, law reflected the will of the moral majority (Morrison 1995, 139). Implicitly accepted within this body of work were official definitions of crime and deviance, definitions that pertained to crimes of the powerless (street crimes), not the powerful (corporate crimes) (Pfohl 1985, 275). A range of contemporary crime and deviance studies have followed the path forged by these traditional criminological and sociology of deviance scholars; this dominant paradigm reinforces the idea that crime is an individualistic problem.[2]

Despite the dominance of these traditional perspectives, they are far from the only explanations of crime and deviance. There is a broad range of critical perspectives that are beyond the scope of this discussion that attempt to transcend individualistic accounts of crime.[3] For instance, early conflict and Marxist theories challenged consensus-based perspectives of crime and deviance, arguing that "official" definitions of crime and deviance were the result of conflict within capitalist society and that law reinforced the interests of the capitalist class (Taylor, Walton, and Young 1973). This critical scholarship garners important influence for many contemporary examinations of crime and its control – critical scholarship that reveals the socially constructed nature of crime and the ways in which law differentially impacts individuals and groups based on their social location(s) (for example, Hillyard et al. 2004; Taylor 1999). As we shall see, various aspects of this critical work inform a range of contemporary corporate crime research.

For the purpose of the current discussion, however, what matters is that the dominant focus within the criminological and the sociology of deviance has been, and remains, street crime and that corporate crime is relegated to the margins (Friedrichs 2010; Slapper and Tombs 1999). This does not suggest that traditional studies of crime and deviance are without merit – as Left realists argue, we should not underestimate the serious material and psychological harm that street crimes impose on society's most marginalized people (Lowman and MacLean 1992). And it does not mean that these perspectives have no relevance for the study of corporate crime. For instance, John Braithwaite (1989) and James Coleman (1987) integrate mainstream criminological theories to explain the motivations and opportunities of corporate criminals.[4] However, it does remind us of the ideological dominance of individualistic perspectives of crime and deviance. The ideological table has been set, and while corporate crime scholarship is on the guest list, more often than not it sits at the kid's table.

Enter Corporate Crime

Despite the relative paucity of corporate crime scholarship, there is an important body of work that defines and studies this phenomenon. A range of terms has been used over the years to characterize crimes committed by corporations and their actors or representatives: white-collar crime (Sutherland 1940 and 1949), corporate crime (Braithwaite 1984), elite deviance (Simon and Eitzen 1986), crimes of the powerful (Pearce 1976), economic crimes (Edelhertz 1970), occupational crime (Green 1990), and safety crimes (Tombs and Whyte 2007).

Corporate crime is generally categorized in two ways: financial corporate crime, including insider trading, fraudulent bookkeeping, and price fixing; and social corporate crime, encompassing offences against the environment (air and water pollution) and occupational health and safety crimes (Snider 1993). *Still Dying for a Living* deals with a subset of corporate crime – occupational safety, or what Tombs and Whyte (2007) refer to as safety crimes.[5]

Edwin Sutherland pioneered the definition of white-collar crime through a series of lectures and papers in the 1940s.[6] Sutherland (1983, 7) defined white-collar crime as "a crime committed by a person of respectability and high social status in the course of his occupation." His contribution was to challenge the notion that crime was a distinctly lower-class phenomenon – that in reality businessmen and professionals routinely committed serious harm and wrongdoing (Slapper and Tombs 1999, 3).

Critics, such as Paul Tappan (1947), argued that Sutherland was wrong to speak of criminals without a legal finding of guilt – that doing so was merely a form of normative or moralistic jockeying – and that fundamental differences existed between business crimes and criminal offences (Slapper and Tombs 1999, 5-6). What Tappan failed to appreciate, however, is that Sutherland had revealed the ideologically based distinction between criminal, civil, and administrative laws – that there is nothing inherent about the behaviours captured within these respective categories to warrant their legal designation (Snider 1993, 15). In doing so, Sutherland identified the range of actions that potentially fall under the banner of white-collar or corporate crime, including acts of omission and commission, the different victims of these crimes, the factors contributing to the illegality, and the ability of powerful members of society to resist legal detection (Slapper and Tombs 1999).

Despite Sutherland's contributions, Gary Slapper and Steve Tombs (1999, 14-15) assert that his definition of white-collar crime anthropomorphizes the corporation (it conceives the corporation as resulting from the conscious intentions of individual actors), which concomitantly means that corporate crime is an individual act or choice to transgress the law. It thus fails to shed light upon the organizational and socio-economic factors that shape corporate crime, including why it occurs and how the state responds. They assert that the definition of corporate crime should transcend humanist terms to conceive it as a "structural problematic" (Slapper and Tombs 1999, 17). This does not mean that individuals are without fault but, rather, that structural factors – such as the "pressures of profitability" – influence actions (McMullan 1992, 45).

Many critical scholars have therefore turned to definitions of corporate crime that account for the broader context and that include acts of omission and commission within the organizational context (Slapper and Tombs 1999). The influence here is from Steven Box (1983, 20-22), who defined corporate crime as "illegal acts of omission or commission of an individual or group of individuals in a legitimate formal organization, in accordance with the goals of that organization, which have serious physical or economic impact on employees, consumers ... the general public and other organizations" (see, by way of comparison, Tombs 1995, 132). Building from this perspective, corporate crime scholars such as Frank Pearce and Steve Tombs (1998, 107-10) define corporate crime as

> illegal acts or omissions, punishable by the state under administrative, civil
> or criminal law which are the result of the deliberate decision making or
> culpable negligence within a legitimate formal organization. These acts or

omissions are based in legitimate, formal, business organizations, made in accordance with the normative goals, standard operating procedures, and/or cultural norms of the organization, and are intended to benefit the corporation itself. (See, by way of comparison, Tombs and Whyte 2007, 2)

This definition respects Sutherland's contribution that legal distinctions between administrative, criminal, and civil law are "conventional, time-bound social products without an intrinsic substantive meaning that transcends their social or historical contexts" (Tombs and Whyte 2007, 3). In addition, as Tombs (1995, 133) notes, it challenges us to focus on acts prescribed by law so that we do not become trapped within an endless debate about "moral blameworthiness." Further, by including both acts of omission and commission, it avoids the need for determining a guilty mind to establish the occurrence of a corporate crime. In addition to anthropomorphizing and individualizing corporate crime, the expectation of establishing *actus rea* and *mens rea* implies a simple causal link between "an act or omission and its consequence" (Tombs and Whyte 2007, 3). In the process, it obscures the "organizational production" of corporate crime, the fragmentation, decentralization, and contradictory goals within the modern corporation that foster the situations, and the conditions that are conducive to occupational health and safety offences (Slapper and Tombs 1999, 14). As Tombs and Whyte (2007, 3) argue,

[corporate crime] can be produced by an organization's structure, its culture, its unquestioned assumptions, its very modus operandi, and so on. Thus to understand such phenomena must not obscure human agency, but does require a shift from abstracted, atomized individuals to account for agency in the context of structures.

The debates over the definition of corporate crime are important for us to consider here because, as the chapters that follow argue, definitions (including legal ones) should transcend narrow, individualistic notions of corporate harm and wrongdoing. Simply put, they need to recognize that corporate crime is much more than simply about individual fault – that at its roots lie complex structural matters (McMullan 1992). They are also important for reminding us that there is nothing inherent to corporate crimes that dictate whether they are different from, or similar to, traditional criminal offences – that is, legal definitions of corporate crime do not unfold in a vacuum (Lacey 1995; Tombs and Whyte 2007). In this respect, as Slapper and Tombs (1999, 12) suggest, it is essential to consider aspects of law in the definition of corporate crime, "the coverage and omissions of legal categories, the presence and absences within legal discourse, the social constructions of these categories and discourses, their underpinnings of, treatment within and development through criminal justice systems." As such, this book argues that, if the goal is to ensure that legislative responses to corporate crime effectively address the harms caused by these offences, we need to better understand the many different and contradictory factors that shape law and its enforcement.

Regulating Corporate Crime

How we conceptualize and define corporate crime matters – it shapes, but does not determine, how the state responds through law. Definitions that imply individual motivations lend themselves well to the formulation of traditional legal rules regarding individual guilt. Likewise, definitions of crime that differentiate corporate offences from traditional street crimes lend themselves well to the use of non-criminal or administrative responses to corporate harm and wrongdoing (Snider 1993, 8-15).

A "bifurcated model of criminal process" best describes the history of corporate crime control (Tombs and Whyte 2007). According to Tombs and Whyte, governments have responded to corporate wrongdoing in two distinct, yet related, ways: attempts to *assimilate* corporate deviance into traditional criminal law by amending the mainstream criminal process to respond to corporate offenders, and efforts to *differentiate* corporate deviance from traditional crime by responding to it through a separate regulatory framework (110). Historically, criminal law measures, such as Bill C-45, *An Act to Amend the Criminal Code (Criminal Liability of Organizations)* (Westray bill), have been overshadowed by regulatory responses that differentiate corporate wrongdoing from traditional crime control strategies (Tombs and Whyte 2007).[7] That is, corporate offences have been, and continue to be, dealt with primarily within a regulatory framework and, more specifically, within a compliance model of regulatory enforcement (Gray 2006). In general, regulation involves "state imposed limitation on the discretion that may be exercised by individuals or organizations, which is supported by the threat of sanction" (Stone 1982, 11; as quoted in Simpson 2002, 80).[8] It emphasizes the use of persuasion and education to ensure organizations comply with regulations, such as occupational health and safety rules, relying on punishment only as a last resort (Simpson 2002, 93). Regulatory approaches stem from the belief that, on the whole, individuals are "reasonable, of good faith, and motivated to heed advice"

(Braithwaite 1989, 131) – that corporations and corporate actors are not criminal. As Sally Simpson (2002, 49) notes, "regulatory offences are not immoral in their own right but rather are illegal because they are prohibited by law."

Commonly associated with this school of thought is the work of John Braithwaite (1982, 1985, 1989; Braithwaite and Fisse 1985, 1987). Based on rational actor theory, Braithwaite employs the notion of a pyramid of regulation to advocate a persuasion-first policy, a strategy that provides corporations with the opportunity to learn from their mistakes and take the necessary corrective action to avoid future offences. The purported benefits of this strategy include that it does not assume all corporations are potential offenders, that it reduces the defensiveness and resistance of corporations through education and persuasion, and it does not conceive criminal law as being the hallmark of the state's response to corporate wrongdoing (Braithwaite 1989, 132-33). Although Braithwaite (1989, 150) does not abandon punishment strategies, he cautions against a criminal law-first approach given the state's poor enforcement and the apparent failure of criminal law to deter offenders.

Regulating Health and Safety

Eric Tucker (1995, 245) isolates three waves of occupational health and safety regulation in Canada: market regulation (1830-80), weak command and control (1880-1970), and partial self-regulation (1970s on). The premise of market regulation was that workers and employers entered freely into contractual arrangements and negotiated all of the terms and conditions of employment, including safety. From this perspective, workers "knew what they were getting into" and freely accepted certain levels of risk (246). During the second period, government standards and regulations that attempted to balance workplace risks with safety were introduced. Legislation guaranteed certain rights and minimum safety protections for workers, but the prevailing assumption was that workers could only expect the implementation of safety measures that were "reasonably practicable in the circumstances" (246). As Tucker notes, safety inspectors typically interpreted compliance in ways that "did not significantly impair profitability or interfere with managerial prerogative. They also relied primarily on persuasion to achieve compliance. Prosecution was a last resort" (247).

The third wave brought reforms intended to give workers legal rights to participate in occupational health and safety decisions. In particular, changes were made to both internal responsibility systems and external responsibility systems. Within the workplace, workers gained rights to participate in decisions related to health and safety, most notably through joint health and safety committees. Unfortunately, organizational issues (for example, they were poorly organized) and structural factors (for example, the unequal distribution of power between employers and workers) constrained these efforts (Tucker 1995, 256).[9] Meanwhile, external systems – provincial laws in the Canadian case – suffered from weak and underfunded enforcement, which was characterized more by persuasion than enforcement (262-63).

Underpinning this entire history is the assumption that all workplaces include an element of risk and that employers and employees can freely agree about what constitutes acceptable risk levels and what does not (Tucker 1995, 246). A second assumption is the belief that corporate crimes are different than traditional street crimes because they are accidents, while street offences are predatory and deliberate. Celia Wells (1993, 6) characterizes occupational health and safety offences as *"inchoate"* in that they focus on attempts rather than on results and, in the process, obscure the severity of safety crimes. For instance, we rarely refer to workplace deaths as homicides, Wells notes, but instead describe them as "accidents" or "incomplete acts" (such as the failure to provide proper safety protections), which are somehow distinct from "true" crimes (12).

The history of occupational health and safety regulation is also based on a tradition of resistance from corporate owners and managers who argue that safety measures cost too much, interfere with management's right to develop "effective" production strategies (which do not always equate with the safest production methods), and give workers and unions too much power and control over working conditions (Noble 1995, 268). For instance, Laureen Snider (1993, 104-5) documents the business community's resistance to the *Ontario Factories Act,* which was introduced in 1884 in response to concerns among an increasingly vocal working class about their lack of control in the workplace.[10] During this time, it was common for workers to endure sixty-hour workweeks, poor wages, and unsafe working conditions, regardless of gender and age (women and children were a source of cheap labour). Although reforms were eventually implemented and improvements to working conditions realized, the reform process was anything but expeditious, with the close relationship between the political and business elite resulting in laws that favoured the interests of business (Snider 1993, 105).[11]

This recognition does not suggest that corporate owners absolutely resisted legal reforms but, rather, that, historically, they supported such efforts primarily in cases where it served their interests by minimizing the long-term impact on "capital accumulation and profits" (McMullan 1992, 87). Laws restricting the length of the working day, for instance, helped to ensure a rested and durable workforce and created a level playing field in terms of what companies were expected to do regarding occupational health and safety. They limited competition from businesses that were only too willing to take whatever advantage was possible of workers (Snider 1993, 99-100). As Snider (1993, 100) notes, "if all firms were forced by government fiat to behave ethically, not hire children, or provide safe environments, manufacturers would be able to be socially responsible without suffering economically." In this respect, reforms rarely emerged on the basis of humanitarian or moral grounds but, instead, followed the economic interests of the corporate elite (Slapper and Tombs 1999, 159).

Successful corporate resistance to laws intended to curb corporate wrongdoing has been, in many respects, endemic. For example, despite recent government claims to "crackdown" on corporate scandals in the United States (Enron and WorldCom, for instance) and Canada, there is evidence that new laws have benefited the interests of corporate capitalists by restoring confidence in the marketplace and ensuring that the free market continues to operate smoothly (Snider 2009; Tillman and Indergaard 2005). Robert Tillman and Michael Indergaard (2005, 246) note that, despite the get-tough message on corporate crime contained in the *Public Company Accounting Reform and Investor Protection Act of 2002 (Sarbanes-Oxley Act),* there was little evidence of a significant increase in prosecutions.[12] For them, the government was more concerned with "damage control" than they were with actual "crime control" (251). Snider (2009, 183) arrives at similar conclusions from her examination of Bill C-13, *An Act to Amend the Criminal Code (Capital Markets Fraud and Evidence Gathering),* which criminalized "improper insider trading" (maximum penalty of ten years), doubled penalties for "market manipulation," and created the offence of "tipping," "knowingly convey[ing] inside information ... to another person, knowing [they might] use the information to buy or sell, directly or indirectly, a security."[13] Since the introduction of this legislation in 2004 its enforcement has been sporadic and, in many respects, non-existent, despite the creation through the Royal Canadian Mounted Police (RCMP) of inter disciplinary Integrated Market Enforcement Teams (IMETs) with fenced funding. As Snider (2009) notes, IMETs have produced few charges and even fewer convictions, with most cases bogged down in complex legal proceedings.

Co-operation and Self-Regulation
Since the early 1980s, regulation based on a co-operative model has dominated responses to corporate offending. In particular, a self-regulatory approach has largely replaced state regulation, which was thought to be ineffective and overly

intrusive for business (Snider 2001, 123). Fuelled by neo-liberal beliefs that the market is the most efficient means of dealing with corporate wrongdoing – that "reputation" and market forces would prevent misdeeds (Tillman and Indergaard 2005, 15-16) – there has been a gradual and pronounced erosion of "formal rules of law and regulation" (28).

Within the market realm, the corporate form became the most important and efficient way to "organize production" and accumulate capital (Pearce and Tombs, 1998, 5-6). As a result, corporate harm and wrongdoing became less and less of a government priority, giving way to the belief that the corporation is an inherent social and economic good (Snider 2000). Snider (2000, 192; 2001, 112) argues that this shifting mentality has meant that corporate crime effectively disappeared as both a concept and in law – "today, potentially profitable acts cannot be wrong." Propelled by the neo-liberal belief in minimal government interference in the free market economy, governments in most Western capitalist democracies bought into the idea that criminal law (deterrence) was ineffective in dealing with "crimes of the powerful," preferring various forms of self-regulation. This perspective starkly contrasts with the massive increase in punitive measures introduced by these same states during the same period for individuals guilty of traditional street crimes (Garland 2001).

Compliance strategies emphasize "persuasion and bargaining" or the idea that corporations need guidance and do not respond well to chastisement and deterrence (Slapper and Tombs 1999, 165-69). Unlike state-centred regulation, self-regulation trusts corporations to "monitor and control their own compliance with the law under a minimalist regulatory framework" (Tombs and Whyte 2007, 166, n. 14). The role of regulators, then, is to co-operate with corporations to build consensus regarding the most effective forms of regulation. As Tombs and Whyte (2007, 153) note, "from this perspective, corporations have the capacity to act as good corporate citizens, capable of responsible and moral decision-making." The ascendancy of self-regulation as it applies to corporate offences has spawned an industry of compliance scholars dedicated to understanding how best to apply these rules to the corporate realm (Bardach and Kagan 1982; Hawkins 1984, 1997, 2002; Hutter 1988). Braithwaite's (1982) work is (again) influential for proponents of self-regulation. Although he does not advocate a model of pure self-enforcement, he does see it as part of an effective regulatory strategy (Ayres and Braithwaite 1992; Braithwaite and Fisse 1987). In what he refers to as "enforced self-regulation," the author advocates a "carrot-and-stick" approach in which outside (government) regulators force corporations to develop new policies and rules in cases where self-regulation fails. Punitive measures are only to be used in situations where non-compliance continues. According to Simpson (2002, 100), "enforced self-regulation combines the benefits of voluntary self-regulation with the coercive power of the state."

Punishment versus Compliance

The dominance of the compliance model has produced considerable debate about the most effective way to regulate the corporation. On one side, compliance scholars support co-operative models rooted in persuasion, education, and self-regulation. On the other, critical scholars argue for criminal law strategies that are sufficiently punitive and strongly enforced.[14] At the heart of the debate lie fundamental differences of perspective regarding the nature of corporate crime and how to respond through law (Gray 2006).

Compliance school advocates argue against strict legal enforcement, suggesting that it produces what Eugene Bardach and Robert Kagan (1982) refer to as "legalism" or assigning a uniform set of regulatory requirements when they are not always necessary (see, by way of comparison, Kagan and Scholz 1984, 73). From this perspective, punishment instils resistance or a lack of co-operation from corporate actors, who become defensive and unresponsive to regulatory measures and may in fact co-ordinate efforts to lobby government for even less state intervention (73). Criminal law approaches also cause more harm than good as the act must progress far enough along the causal chain of events to collect sufficient evidence. A further suggestion is that the cost of full criminal law enforcement is both impossible and prohibitive (Snider 1990, 376). In support of their perspective, compliance scholars argue that corporations will co-operate with regulators to ensure compliance (Hawkins 1990, 451).

For some critical corporate crime scholars, self-regulation strategies do not work. In addition to the fact that corporations simply will not self-regulate in the absence of external pressures, corporate executives will falsify records to deceive regulators and will only use self-regulation symbolically and under limited conditions (McMullan 1992, 89-96; Slapper and Tombs 1999, 184). Further, the compliance school argument that strict enforcement does not work is purely hypothetical since it has never occurred (Tombs and Whyte 2007, 156), underscored by the fact that compliance scholars do not demonstrate how compliance strategies actually work, just how the alternatives are ineffective (Pearce and Tombs 1991, 422). Compliance scholars therefore confound the way things are with the way things should or must be. As Pearce and Tombs (1990, 429 [emphasis in original]) argue, "their work is limited because *the legitimacy of a capitalist system and the illegitimacy of its being policed are in fact starting-points for their analysis."*

Although co-operative models are touted as flexible and consistent with market efficiency, in practice they work predominantly to the advantage of powerful corporate interests (Noble 1995, 271-72). Compliance scholars fail to account for the element of power in this respect (Tombs and Whyte 2007, 156), arguing that resistance to regulations by corporations are the exception, not the rule. Meanwhile, history illustrates considerable resistance to new laws by corporate actors. Further, in assuming that corporations are inherently good, compliance scholars ignore the fact that the imperative to accumulate profit sometimes takes precedence over safety concerns (156-57). Finally, given the prevalence of corporate power, compliance scholars underestimate the relevance of regulatory capture – that regulators will co-operate too closely with corporations and, in the process, "institutionalise corporate influence" (160).

Critics of the compliance model call for strict enforcement of criminal law, along with innovative regulatory strategies that introduce formal sanctions at earlier stages of offending (Pearce and Tombs 1991, 423). They argue that, unlike traditional street crimes, deterrence strategies have an important role in the corporate context. In comparison to street crimes, corporate offences "tend not to be one-off acts," and, hence, the identification of the act and offender is relatively unproblematic (Pearce and Tombs 1997, 92). Further, since corporate crimes do not pose the same detection problems as traditional crimes, "then greater regulatory resources *would* increase detection" (93 [emphasis original]). The symbolic message of punishment also applies easily to corporate offenders given there is little risk that the corporation will not receive or understand the message. Finally, unlike criminal sanctions against traditional crimes, punishing corporate offenders will not produce greater social inequality (92-94).

In the end, while compliance scholars "condone violations" in the hope of preventing further offences, deterrence advocates want to prevent future violations through effective laws and consistent enforcement (Wells 1993, 28). At the heart of the matter are different views about the nature of the corporate form. Compliance scholars believe that corporations are motivated to be good and law abiding and that only some of them (the "bad apples") will transgress the law (Bardach and Kagan 1982). Deterrence scholars argue that corporations are amoral calculators with a mandate to "prioritize profit maximization" (Pearce and Tombs 1997). And it is because of this amoral calculation that we need "rigorous enforcement by regulatory agencies" (Pearce 1990, 424).[15]

Building from Pearce and Tombs (1998, 99), this study departs from compliance scholars who are disinterested in the distinction between criminal law and regulation, treating both as natural or pre-determined. As Tombs and Whyte (2007, 155-56) note, theories of compliance "tend to reflect the dominant themes in 'official' doctrine and policy on controlling safety crime. As a result, we might say that consensus theories analyze the regulatory process from a perspective that incorporates many of the assumptions that governments, regulatory officials and businesses use to inform policy." Compliance advocates ignore the fact that it is corporate power that renders regulatory agencies and measures ineffective, "not the measures themselves" (Snider 1990, 380).

Overall, an important factor that limits discussion and debate about the introduction of corporate criminal liability is the primacy accorded to regulatory responses. However, in recent years, there has been growing evidence of a desire to develop criminal law strategies to hold corporations to account for their harmful actions and to deter wrongdoing. After all, the state is not simply a "tool of corporate capital" – there is relative autonomy of the state, meaning there are times when it must act against corporate interests (McMullan 1992, 108). It is within this context that we witness attempts to assimilate corporate deviance into traditional criminal law through the introduction of the Westray bill (Tombs and Whyte 2007).

Theoretical Links to the Corporate Crime Literature

The first part of this chapter situated the study of corporate crime within broader considerations of crime and deviance as well as within some of the main issues and claims from the corporate crime literature. However, there is also a rich body of scholarship that situates the study of corporate crime and corporate crime law reform within its broader social-political-economic context. Of particular interest is how this literature distinguishes itself from more deterministic approaches that treat law as the mere expression of ruling class interests and from liberal legal perspectives that see law as reflecting the consensus of the moral majority (Pearce and Tombs 1998; Tombs and Whyte 2007). Instead, as Tombs and Whyte (2007, 109) argue, law is not a "naked instrument of power that is always used to control subordinate groups, but ... a complex and often contradictory system of rules and practices that ultimately aims to maintain and stabilise the existing social order."

Critical corporate crime scholars argue that, to understand corporate crime law reform, it is important to examine the modern corporate form, the most prominent vehicle for organizing corporate capital in contemporary society (Glasbeek 2002). It is significant that Canada's new corporate criminal liability legislation – the Westray bill – emerged within traditional bourgeois law, and yet corporations have consistently shown themselves unable to adhere to such laws (Slapper and Tombs 1999, 19). As several critical scholars note, the incessant demand for profit maximization within the corporate form – a perspective that sees corporations as amoral calculators – is a significant factor in shaping corporate criminality (Glasbeek 2002; Pearce and Tombs 1998; Tombs and Whyte 2007).

The critical corporate crime literature also points to the importance of not individualizing corporate crime law reform. This does not suggest that individuals do not matter but, rather, that their actions must be placed within the broader social and economic context (Slapper and Tombs 1999).[16] As Pearce and Tombs (1998, 281) suggest, corporate crime law is "never simply the result of some 'programmer's dream.'" Although this approach does not "absolve individual actors of any responsibility," it emphasizes the importance of understanding the complex relations that help constitute corporate crime legislation, the processes that produce legal regimes (Slapper and Tombs 1999, 17). This perspective underscores the need to examine the politics of corporate crime law reform – the open, fluid, and contested relationships between different political actors and groups – including the language used to constitute corporate crime and corporate criminal liability.

For instance, Tucker (1995b, see also Tucker 2006) contextualizes the discourses and decision making of individuals through his examination of the politics of causation as it relates to the Westray mine disaster. In addition to noting that establishing causality helps to determine "moral, legal, economic or political" responsibility, he states that identifying causal factors is a complex and highly contested process, characterized by considerable disagreement about the "significance of the many events that are causal in some sense" (Tucker 1995b, 94-95). Tucker argues that those charged with determining causality operated within a particular social and economic context: "The terrain on which judges and other public officials operate is shaped by prevailing political-economic conditions, dominant ideological assumptions and the particular institutional context in which the causal question is addressed" (95). As we shall see, a similar terrain characterizes the processes of constituting the state's response to the disaster, the Westray bill.

Finally, critical corporate crime scholars remind us that although the state plays an important role in defining and responding to corporate crime through law, it does not determine its nature and scope (Haines and Sutton 2003, 10-11;

Tombs and Whyte 2007, 207). Positing an all-powerful state that always gets its way is empirically incorrect as well as theoretically blind.[17] Critical scholars working within a neo-Marxist framework have moved beyond narrow, instrumentalist approaches that espouse a one-to-one relationship between the state and capitalist interests (the claims that the state merely reflects and reinforces capitalist and corporate interests), and now conceptualize the state as one of many mechanisms within society that play an important, but not automatic, role in (re)producing capitalist market conditions (Jessop 2002, 2008). As Bob Jessop (2002, 41) notes, the state is both "operationally autonomous" and "institutionally separate" from the capitalist market, meaning there is no *a priori* guarantee that the state will either advance or challenge the interests of capital.

For example, while analyzing Ontario's occupational health and safety laws of 1850 to 1940, Tucker (1990) uses a neo-Marxist perspective to illustrate that those who owned the means of production – the structurally privileged – resisted overly stringent health and safety regulations. The author suggests that the state is dependent on corporate capital to stimulate the economy and contribute to the tax base, thereby placing it in a difficult and complex position when it comes to legislating and regulating corporate offences. Tucker avoids a simplistic, instrumental Marxist approach, suggesting that capital's privileged position is not automatic, that "conflict and contradictions in the private accumulation process will often be displaced into the political-administrative system where they are mediated in complex ways" (7).

The operational autonomy of the state is evidenced by the fact that, in addition to helping valorize the capitalist mode of production, the state also has the "overall political responsibility for maintaining social cohesion in a socially divided, pluralistic social formation" (Jessop 2002, 21). For instance, the introduction of the Westray bill to protect workers' safety stands in contrast to the economic subsidies given by the state – subsidies that made the extraction of coal from the Westray mine for profit-making purposes possible in the first place (Glasbeek 2004; McMullan 2005; Tucker 1995b). This contradiction reminds us that there is nothing inherent to the logic of capitalist accumulation that stipulates it will "inevitably subordinate other institutional orders [including the state] or colonize the lifeworld" (Jessop 2002, 30). There are times when economic logic imposes its hegemonic will upon the extra-economic realm, but these cases are not automatic or predetermined. Instead, as Jessop (2002, 30) argues, it "depends on the outcome of political and ideological struggles around political projects and hegemonic visions as well as on the ecological dominance of the circuit of capital."

Overall, the critical corporate crime scholarship challenges us to situate issues of corporate crime within their broader social-political-economic context. In doing so, it transcends the narrow confines of traditional crime and deviance studies, with their attendant focus on the individual causes and consequences of crime, to better appreciate the ideological basis of (corporate) crime and its control (Pearce and Tombs 1998, 280). Accomplishing this goal involves stepping outside criminology and the sociology of deviance to embrace social theory and political economy perspectives. The next section outlines this theoretical framework as it applies to the current study.

Theoretical Considerations

Building from the critical corporate crime scholarship, the theoretical framework for *Still Dying for a Living* combines Michel Foucault's ([1972] 2001) analysis of discursive formations with a non-deterministic, anti-essentialist (re)reading of Marx (Althusser 1969, 1971; Althusser and Balibar 1968).[18] Of particular interest is Louis Althusser's notion of aleatory materialism, the idea that no particular social phenomenon can be reduced to one identifiable and determining cause. Aleatory materialism is a philosophy of history that considers chance to be an essential ingredient in the politics of renewal and change (Datta 2007, 275; Ferretter 2006, 5). It reminds us that the socio-economic context shapes, but does not determine, the social world. Combining elements of Foucault and Althusser offers a rich analytical lens to examine the relationships between discourse and social structures. It combines Foucault's focus on the "how" of "economic exploitation and political domination" with neo-Marxist concerns with the "why" of "capital accumulation and state power" (Jessop 2007, 40). It also illuminates the complex relationship between Foucault and Marx, something that many of Foucault's interlocutors fail to acknowledge (Dupont and Pearce 2001).

Discourse and Discursive Formations

For Foucault ([1972] 2001, 31), it is important to examine "relations between statements," particularly how different statements converge at certain junctures of history to speak about a particular object (for example, madness). At different times, statements form regularities, what Foucault refers to as discursive formations, thereby constituting the dominant knowledge claims about an object. As Foucault notes, whenever one can describe, between a number of statements, such as system of dispersion, whenever, between objects, types of statement, concepts, or thematic choices, once can define a regularity (an order, correlations, positions and functionings, transformations), we will say, for the sake of convenience, that we are dealing with a *discursive formation*. (38 [emphasis in original])

Foucault argues that the relationships between discourses and the emergence of discursive formations produce "positivities" or that statements made by certain individuals constitute the "correct" way to understand and describe the social world at a particular time (Pearce and Tombs 1998, 144). For example, he illustrates how discourses of the church, law, and medicine converge to delineate psychopathology during the nineteenth century (143).

Discursive formations emerge within certain conditions, or rules of formation, which Foucault (1972, 38) refers to as "surfaces of emergence" (for example, social institutions), "authorities of delineation," or authorized "knowers" (for example, professionals) as well as the relations between these elements (see, by way of comparison, Pearce and Tombs 1998, 143). Foucault also refers to "grids of specification," "which are most usefully thought of as ways in which the production and functioning of discursive formations comes about" (143). Every element has its own "genealogy and internal logic" and therefore does not develop in any linear or predictable manner. At the same time, however, changes to discourse influence, and are influenced by, the extra-discursive. As Pearce and Tombs (1998, 143) note, "Foucault's interest was in how 'statements, as events, and in their so particular specificity, can be articulated to events which are not discursive in nature, but may be of a technical, practical, economic, social, political or other variety.'" Different discourses are defined by their relationship with each other, thereby forming a discursive relation while also helping shape, and being shaped by, the extra-discursive.

Foucault's ([1972] 2001) notion of discursive formations helps to explore the dominant knowledge claims in relation to corporate crime and corporate criminal liability. Whose knowledge claims had legs when it came to defining the nature and scope of corporate crime and corporate criminal liability (Snider 2000)? It also helps to explore the relationship between discourse and the extra-discursive. What are the "conditions of existence" that both shape and are shaped by discourse on corporate crime and corporate criminal liability (Foucault 1972, 38)?

Suggesting that Foucault's notion of discursive formation lends itself to considerations of the extra-discursive is not common within neo-Foucauldian studies. Following the lead of Norman Fairclough, Bob Jessop, and Andrew Sayer (2002, 4), the current study departs from interpretations of Foucault that conceptualize discourse as a catalyst of social meaning – a form of "discourse imperialism" that equates language with "strong social constructionism." Instead, it attempts to explore Foucault's discursive formations in relation to his (underdeveloped) reference to broader structural issues (4; Dupont and Pearce 2001).

Two examples from the critical corporate crime literature exemplify the importance of examining the complex relationships between discourse and the broader structural context. For instance, Nob Doran's (1996, 524) research considers "modern power's discursive constitution" through an examination of occupational health and safety in the early nineteenth century. Doran examines how official definitions of workplace accidents – "disembodied statistics" – usurped workers' voices, muting their knowledge and experiences concerning workplace health (527 and passim). By using a theoretical lens that combines elements of Smith's "relations of ruling" with Foucault's analysis of power and knowledge, Doran provides a framework for considering "the complex relationship between class and power/knowledge ... largely ignored in Foucault's own work" (524).[19]

A different relationship between discourse and power emerges in Pearce and Tombs' (1998) examination of corporate crime in the chemical industry, which draws from Antonio Gramsci's (1971, 1975) notion of hegemony and Foucault's (1979) work relating to governance and discursive formations (Foucault [1972] 2001). Gramsci provides the analytical lens for examining the role of capitalist hegemony in reinforcing ruling-class interests, albeit in contradictory, uneven ways that are susceptible to counter-hegemonic movements (Pearce and Tombs 1998, 35-38). Foucault's notion of discursive relations provides insight into how certain discourses dominate within "various conditions of existence," including how different discourses converge at particular (hegemonic) moments to create "truths" (38, 142-44). Using the tragic example of the Union Carbide chemical disaster in Bhopal, India, Pearce and Tombs examine how the "destructive nature" of the chemical industry is effectively downplayed and ignored, defined away as non-criminal acts (ix). The dominance of this perspective stems from the struggle between how the chemical industry is understood and defined and the privileged position of the corporation within the capitalist (neo-liberal) economy. The current study builds from this research to examine how discourses that characterize corporate criminal liability are constitutive of the broader capitalist social formation.

Extra-Discursive Considerations

Building from Althusser's notion of aleatory materialism, some Marxists have jettisoned notions of "necessity" – that is, the "laws of motion" that are essential to the reproduction of the capitalist system in its totality – to embrace postmodern notions of "contingency and particularity" (Gibson-Graham, Resnick, and Wolff 2001, 1-4). Others, while not expressly employing an Althusserian framework, have followed a similar route and moved beyond characterizing Marx in crude economic terms, in which the economy was thought to directly cause or determine the social realm (for example, see Pearce and Tombs 1998; Tucker 1990, 1995a, 2006). In this respect, they provide the space to consider how discourse and discursive relations have become inculcated in the capitalist mode of production, albeit in non-linear, unpredictable, and often contradictory ways. Certain aspects of Althusser's work are fruitful for developing this line of inquiry.[20]

For Althusser, Marx had a paradoxical attitude toward bourgeois society. The young Marx was influenced by Georg Hegel's notion of the history of society as indistinguishable from its genesis – society as a "result produced by a history" (Althusser and Balibar [1968] 1997, 64). Marx considered society to be a complex combination of relations that unfolded differently in varied contexts. Here we can see that Marx went beyond Hegel's linear notion of history to embrace the relative and productive nature of social relations (41). Therefore, according to Althusser, society is both a particular "result" and a particular "society," the effect of certain mechanisms that make a society possible (65).

In attempting to rid Marxism of its teleological tendencies, Althusser and Balibar ([1968] 1997, 52) consider various factors outside the mode of production that help constitute the social. Evidence of this consideration emerges through their discussion of the "problem of knowledge" and the multifarious interests that are constitutive of ideological spaces. For Althusser, the formulation of ideology occurs outside the production of knowledge, the "extra theoretical" factors (for example, religious, ethical, and political) that shape how we understand the social world. This is where we find Althusser's aleatory underpinnings in that he conceives knowledge production to be more than the result of a single determining cause.

Since Althusser and Balibar ([1968] 1997, 98) believe ideological formations emanate from diffuse sources, they consequently and necessarily argue that there can be no dominant structure that is reducible to the "primacy of a center." Instead, they recognize different "structured levels" – including the political, economic, and ideological – which can in no way be thought of as a "model of continuous and homogeneous time," but it may nonetheless converge at different moments to produce particular social formations (99). Different structures have their own genesis and separate timelines in terms of their individual production, the same of which applies to their relationships to other structures. Each structured level is therefore "relatively autonomous and hence relatively independent" (99). For Althusser, this theory reflects Marx's anti-essentialist work in *The Poverty of Philosophy,* wherein Marx questions how society could contain any logical formulation or sequence when it is the result of numerous relations that, in Marx's words, "coexist simultaneously (gleichzeitig) and support one another" (as quoted at 64-65).

Althusser therefore argues that the economic is not a given since what constitutes the economic differs within each mode of production and that, in each case, the levels of the social (political, ideological, and so on) relate to the economic in uneven and unpredictable ways. As Antonio Callari and David Ruccio (1996, 24) note, Althusser stressed that "action, movement, praxis, process cannot be reduced to any one (single or complex) idea, cannot be motivated by a posited end, but is rather characterized by contingency, by 'history.'" Social phenomena are much more than the result of one (economic) encounter – each circumstance must be viewed as the result of an array of encounters, producing their own unique form of "causality or effectivity" (Althusser 1994, 564; Read 2002, 32; 2003). The economic is not a homogeneous field or smooth space that exists on an "infinite plane" but, instead, a "deep and complex" phenomenon, a different understanding of causality that is nonlinear and anti-essentialist, what Althusser ([1968] 1997, 183-84) considered to be "determination by a structure."

In Althusser and Balibar's ([1968] 1997, 65 [emphasis original]) terms, society is much more than just a result – it is "*this* particular result, *this* particular *product,* which functions as a *society.*" Contemporary society is the result of a particular structure, but one in which the structure is not reducible to its history – we cannot theorize bourgeois society as simply being the genesis of this result (65). It is therefore important to understand the mechanism that shapes contemporary society, the multiple means upon which society, as a particular result, becomes possible (66).

A crucial point herein is that no single mode of production assumes responsibility for the ways in which societies function. Just as there is no logical sequence to history, there is similarly no "production in general" (Althusser and Balibar [1968] 1997, 108). The society effect therefore differs within and between different modes of production (108-9). The exploration of these different and specific society effects necessitates the unveiling of the mechanism that gives rise to them, without "pre-judging" the constitutive elements of these effects (66).

The Canadian Social Formation

Stemming from Althusser's society effect, an important consideration for the current study is the Canadian social formation – an integral part of the political-economic-ideological space, or extra-discursive realm, that shapes, but does not determine, different discourses about corporate crime and corporate criminal liability. Within Canada, this space includes links between the state, law, and the mode of production (economy). The main form of economic organization in Canada, as with other countries within the Organisation for Economic Co-operation and Development, is capitalistic (Pearce and Tombs 1998). In theory, this organization involves a commitment to a market economy based on private property in which goods and services are bought and sold between economic agents. The economic organization, or limited liability corporation, is the primary vehicle for producing the goods and services that are sold to consumers (Pearce and Tombs 1998, 3-4; Yalden et al. 2008).

A staples industry that exploited the nation's raw materials for export to various metropolitan centres historically shaped the Canadian mode of production. Commercial staples, such as "fish, fur, placer gold and square timber," were sent to European markets, while "industrial ones (pulp and paper, minerals, energy)" were destined for the United States (Clement 2001, 2). This resource base gave Canada a strong mixed economy with a significant blend of private and public investment. However, with the ascendancy of neoliberalism during the 1980s, the privatization of many public institutions significantly altered Canada's mixed economy. During this time, the Canadian government "sold off all or part of forty governmental organizations" (Mosco 1989; Pearce and Snider 1995, 25). As Pearce and Snider (1995, 25) note,

> this process of privatization in traditionally mixed economies has of course provided new market opportunities for many firms, particularly in the financial, manufacturing, and service sectors. Since, increasingly, the only way of producing and distributing goods and services is by capitalist enterprise in a global market economy, the world now looks like a more "rational" place.

Although these changes have transformed the Canadian social structure, the state remains a vital component of the Canadian economy, such as through state involvement in "provincial power companies" (Clement 2006, 147) and as a prominent employer for many Canadians (Fudge 2002, 86).[21] Nevertheless, the Canadian economy rests primarily in the hands of the minority of the population – corporate Canada is heavily oligopolistic and monopolistic in that giant companies dominate it and wealthy families represent a majority of its economic elite (Clement 2006, 147; Glasbeek 2002, 31; Pearce and Snider 1995, 20).[22]

In recent decades, capitalism's globalizing efforts have consumed the Canadian economy.[23] As a result, the economic focus has shifted from domestic investment to international opportunities. While foreign direct investment in Canada has dropped precipitously, "Canadian foreign investment abroad has exploded." In the context of free trade, this shift has resulted in a greater presence of multinational corporations within Canada, including considerable US presence through the operation of branch plants (Clement 2006, 147-48). Meanwhile, the country's traditional dependence on raw material exports became increasingly vulnerable to the conditions of global business (Fudge and Cossman 2002, 13), particularly as economic priorities shifted from production to distribution and sales (Taylor 1999, 11) and the state became more concerned with attracting global capital (Fudge and Cossman 2002, 17). Corporations thus gained unprecedented power within this global economy, with some of the largest economies in the world no longer belonging to countries but, instead, to multinational corporations (Pearce and Snider 1995, 21).[24]

A number of developments within Canada's social formation underscore the impact of recent neo-liberal and global capital ideals. Most notable is the significant shift in the nature of work over recent decades. While previous generations of workers experienced strong unionization and relatively stable employment, the situation is very different today, evidenced by the declining role of unions under the pressures of profitability (Glasbeek 2002, 83).[25] For many Canadians, particularly women and visible minorities, work is now less about employment for life and more about temporary, part-time, and contract work, which are susceptible to the whims of the market economy (Cranford et al. 2005; Taylor 1999).

In addition, the once prominent model of the single breadwinner is a thing of the past (Fudge and Cossman 2002, 15). Starting in the 1970s, real wages began to plateau – even fall slightly – while production levels continued to rise, fuelled by a consumer culture that became the neo-liberal basis for determining personal success and fulfillment. This shift meant that workers received no greater remuneration for producing more and working longer hours (Resnick and Wolff 2010, 175-77). As Judy Fudge and Brenda Cossman (2002, 15) note, by the 1980s "it took between sixty-five and eighty hours of work each week for a family to earn what it took a single breadwinner, typically a man, to earn in a forty-five hour work week in the mid-1970s."[26] To help make ends meet, workers took on unprecedented levels of debt. By 2008, as the global economy entered the worst downturn since the Great Depression, the average Canadian household owed $1.40 "on every dollar of income" (Yalnizyan 2009, 7), and by 2010 Canadians held more than $1 trillion in mortgage loans (Allen 2010-11). Clearly, the neo-liberal ideal worked only for the privileged few, while the majority struggled to maintain an increasingly unattainable standard of living.

A related point is that, despite these transformations, both the state and law continue to play an important role within the Canadian social formation. In the past, Keynesian welfare principles have fuelled the actions of the Canadian state, embracing (at least theoretically) the benefits of "full employment" and "universal welfare" (Fudge and Cossman 2002, 10). However, the emergence of neo-liberalism following the Second World War marked the death of state socialism, cautioning against "government overreach and overload" rather than espousing the virtues of welfarism and state responsibility for addressing social and economic problems (Barry, Osborne, and Rose 1996; Rose and Miller 1992, 198). As Nikolas Rose and Peter Miller (1992, 199) note,

> neo-liberalism re-codes the locus of the state in the discourse of politics. The state must be strong to defend the interests of the nation in the international sphere, and must ensure order by providing a legal framework for social and economic life. Within this framework autonomous actors – commercial concerns, families, individuals – are to go freely about their business, making their own decisions and controlling their own destinies.

A neo-liberal state is thus committed to fostering optimal conditions for the flourishing of economic competition and an entrepreneurial spirit (Barry, Osborne, and Rose 1996, 10; Mahon 2005). The market thus became the most natural, efficient means to accumulate wealth, which is in everyone's best (economic) interests (Glasbeek 2002, 20).

Beginning in the 1980s, when the federal Conservative government declared that Canada was "open for business," the state systematically disassembled the welfare state (Snider 1990, 131). This trend continued throughout the 1990s as the Liberal government introduced crippling cutbacks to unemployment insurance and provincial transfers for "welfare, social services, and post secondary institutions" (Fudge and Cossman 2002, 15-16). Key to this approach was a move away from the idea of dependency on the state for help and support to one of self-reliance. Today, most Western capitalist states virtually trip over themselves to promote their liberal, market-friendly efficiency (Mahon 2005, 9).

The dominance of capital does not mean that the state (and, through it, law) is a mere tool in the economic process. On the contrary, the (Canadian) state and law are both relatively autonomous and "variously interventionist" (Woodiwiss 1997, 101). However, state and legal institutions do play an integral role in providing the political-economic-ideological space for capitalism to prevail, even if the outcome of this support is far from predetermined. We cannot overlook, for instance, that the state promotes the free market through the introduction of laws relating to securities and mutual funds (Fudge and Cossman 2002, 19). While previous Canadian governments were more directly and blatantly involved with individual capitalists, the priorities of contemporary governments are more ideologically aligned with free market interests on a global scale (Panitch 1999, 32). In Althusserian terms, this is what provides Canada's social formation with its unique shape and form – the extra-discursive considerations in relation to initiatives to tighten the criminal liability of corporations.

(Re)considering Class

Despite Althusser's contributions to neo-Marxism, we must reconcile certain limitations to his work, particularly his inability to shed certain Hegelian tendencies. According to Barry Hindess and Paul Hirst (1975, 7), Althusser replaces economic determinism with structural determinism, one that conceives modes of production as the result of a reproducing structure, and history as the expression of a determinate idea or a particular mode of production. Jessop (2002, 23) is also critical of the idea that the economic is determinative of the "extra-economic" (or ideological superstructure) in the "first, last or any intermediate instance." For the economic to fulfil such a deterministic role would mean that the capitalist mode of production has to be entirely "self-contained and self-reproducing," what Jessop refers to as "a cause without a cause." It would also entail a causal relationship between the economy and all other relations within society. Neither premise holds true when confronted with the reality of the "interdependence of the economic and the extra-economic" (23).

To avoid this essentialist trapdoor, Hindess and Hirst (1975, 9) return to what they argue is the essence of Marxist theory: "the role of class struggle in history." For them, we need to interrogate how class struggles (re)produce determinate social formations, arguing that the social formation corresponds to a complex array of social relations in which the economic, political, and ideological levels are determined by the economy (13). However, while the mode of production sets limits to the structure of these different levels, it can only persist if its conditions of existence are supported, maintained, and transformed (14-15). These conditions are not predetermined but, instead, must be produced through class struggle, what Hindess and Hirst refer to as a *conjuncture*:

> The economic, political and ideological conditions of existence of the mode of production are secured, modified, or transformed as the outcome of specific class struggles conducted under the particular conditions of the economic, political and ideological levels of the social formation. The particular structure of economic, political and ideological conditions in the social formation determines the possible outcomes of the class struggles conducted under such conditions. Such a structure will be called a *conjuncture*.
> (15 [emphasis in original])

Returning to Marx's fundamental concept of class has proven analytically fruitful for neo-Marxists interested in moving beyond essentialist and teleological accounts of the capitalist economy (Gibson-Graham, Resnick, and Wolff 2001; Resnick and Wolff 1987, 2006). For Marx, the fundamental exploitation of capitalism flows from the difference between necessary and surplus labour. Necessary labour represents the time that is necessary to "produce the consumables customarily required by the producer to keep working." Surplus labour is the additional labour time performed beyond what is necessary and is appropriated by "someone other than the producer" (Gibson-Graham, Resnick, and Wolff 2001, 6-7; Resnick and Wolff 1987, 155; 2006, 91-92). In capitalist societies, each worker performs enough labour in a day to theoretically sustain themselves, a process made possible through the provision of wages in exchange for a worker's labour. Any extra or surplus labour performed by the worker in a day is "appropriated by the individual capitalist or by the board of directors of the capitalist firm" (Gibson-Graham, Resnick, and Wolff 2001, 7). The capitalist who owns the corporation and controls the means of production realizes and consumes the appropriation of surplus labour in the form of profits (Resnick and Wolff 1987, 150). As J.K. Gibson-Graham, Stephen Resnick, and Richard Wolff (2001, 7 [emphasis in original]) note, "the exploitative process in which surplus labour is produced and appropriated is for Marx a *class* process, and the positions of the producer and appropriator are *class* positions."

Beyond this fundamental exploitation, Marx identified subsumed class processes (Gibson-Graham, Resnick, and Wolff 2001, 7-8) – the distribution of surplus value once appropriated by the individual capitalist or firm. Subsumed class processes occur on a variety of levels, both within the corporation (for example, in the form of salaries to owners, managers, and employees) and across the economy (for example, in payments to government, financial institutions, landlords, and merchants) (7). This thinking takes us beyond the fundamental aspects of the exploiter-exploited to consider the varied distribution of surplus values throughout society and, in turn, how this process of distribution becomes implicated in society's organization in support of the capitalist social formation. It is therefore not only class positions and the ability to exploit surplus labour that is important from a Marxist perspective but also the "social ramifications of class" (8).

An examination of subsumed class processes illuminates how surplus labour is distributed in a diversity of ways that are necessary for the (re)production of the capitalist enterprise. In particular, it reveals how the distribution of surplus value through subsumed class processes is vital to the longevity of the corporation via the distribution of fundamental surplus value within the organization. As Resnick and Wolff (1987, 178) note in discussing subsumed class processes beyond the corporation, "taxes are paid to the state by industrial capitalists – a subsumed class process – for economic, political, and cultural processes performed in and by the state ... All of these social processes and still others provided by the state make possible the existence of the industrial enterprise's appropriation of surplus value." Subsumed class processes therefore help create the conditions for those who own the mode of production to continually extract surplus labour from the individual worker. This exploitation is not a pre-ordained fact but, rather, something produced and reproduced through different class processes.

A final aspect of Marx's notion of class involves the association between productive and unproductive labour. Workers who produce commodities are directly involved in the production of surplus labour. However, those who do not produce commodities, such as marketing firms or financial institutions, are still implicated in capitalist processes, albeit in unproductive ways: "Unproductive laborers are paid out of surplus value if they are employed by capitalist firms engaged in commodity production (thus, they are recipients of subsumed class payments) and receive non-class forms of remuneration if they are otherwise employed" (Gibson-Graham, Resnick, and Wolff 2001, 8). In some respects, the difference between productive and unproductive labour is artificial in that all forms of labour can be said to contribute to the appropriation of surplus value (Resnick and Wolff 2006, 104). Notwithstanding, it reminds us that class processes extend beyond the fundamental extraction of surplus labour and are imbued within the entire social formation.

Outside Marx's fundamental and subsumed class process, according to Resnick and Wolff (2006, 94) lie "all other natural and social processes," which he referred to as non-class processes. In addition to the fact that all fundamental class processes have unique conditions of existence, including the economic, political, and cultural factors that are constitutive of the fundamental class process, non-class processes may provide a constituent element of other class processes. Resnick and Wolff refer to the example of educating children as being a non-class process, which is an important component of the fundamental class process (94). The same could be said of law, which does not receive surplus value for either fundamental or subsumed class processes but which nevertheless forms a key element of the broader social formation.

These different aspects of class are important for understanding the processes in which class unfolds and has particular effects. These class elements include distinct implications for the capitalist enterprise in that each forms part of its overall configuration (Gibson-Graham, Resnick, and Wolff 2001, 13). For example, the state, as a recipient of subsumed class benefits, can influence the enterprise through various initiatives, such as the imposition of taxes or the introduction of a new law (such as the Westray bill) that implicates corporate activities (13). Further underscoring the importance of class processes are the limitations of analyzing class positions within a two-class focus (that is, dominant and subordinate class) (Resnick and Wolff 2006, 91). Employing a two-class perspective assumes that capitalism is an all-encompassing structure that "governs political identity and constrains political possibility" (Gibson-Graham, Resnick, and Wolff 2001, 17). Within this rigid analytical space, the focus becomes trying to place individuals into their appropriate social "grouping," a task that is increasingly difficult in the face of multiple "class categories and contradictory class locations." It is therefore materially relevant to consider how different class processes are constitutive of the appropriation of surplus labour. As Gibson-Graham, Resnick, and Wolff (2001, 18) argue, "individuals may participate in a variety of different class processes and inhabit a number of different class positions, simultaneously and over time."

In this respect, we need to consider how class processes (re)create the conditions necessary for the valorization of the capitalist economy (Jessop 2002, 31). This perspective means looking beyond traditional struggles over "wages and working conditions" to consider struggles regarding different modes of regulating the economy, forms of competition, and various "economic and social policy regimes." In short, it means thinking beyond class consciousness to examine the class relevance of different struggles. As Jessop argues, "there is certainly no univocal correspondence between the declared class belonging (i.e. location, affiliation or membership) and the actual class impact of particular social movements or forms of struggle" (31). Class struggles and politics are not closed spaces that are omnipresent and difficult to challenge but, rather, are productive and open, effecting politics, not simply determining them (Gibson-Graham, Resnick and Wolff, 2001, 18-19).[27]

Class politics focuses our attention on an ongoing process of extracting surplus labour through the capitalist mode of production. From a Marxist perspective, class is therefore an "adjective, not a noun" (Resnick and Wolff 1987, 159). As a result, various other social processes "that comprise the social totality" implicate economic processes. It flows from this point that individuals are shaped by, and reflect, the different social processes within which they participate, whether it is, for example, the state, home, a corporation, or the education system. As Resnick and Wolff note, "human beings are sites of specific subsets of social processes" (159). Individuals are therefore more than simply containers of economic ideologies; they instead express a range of class and non-class positions that they occupy in life. To reduce individuals to their class position is to fall victim to an essentialist analysis of the economy: "Classes, then, do not struggle or do anything else for that matter. The term *class struggle* must refer to the object of groups struggling, not the subjects doing the struggling" (161 [emphasis original]).

Class Relevance

When it comes to examining the constitution of the Westray bill, this Marxist understanding of class reminds us that individuals involved in the reform process do not represent a universalistic version of capitalist (or any other) interests. As Bruce Norton (2001, 44) notes, Marx argued that capitalists do not always act "as capital personified" but, instead, are subjects that are "constructed under particular social and discursive conditions." A Marxian class position also illuminates how various knowledges and discourses, both economic and non-economic, are implicated in the production of power and, in particular, in the production and reproduction of particular class processes

(20-21). The essence of this idea is that class does not unfold in a vacuum; instead, it is constitutive of different relationships in society that produce "particular sets of processes" (Resnick and Wolff 2006, 93).

The Westray bill has class relevance in that it constitutes an object of struggle that implicates the nature and scope of workplace safety and, hence, who controls the means of production or the methods for extracting surplus labour. In particular, the law emerged in response to the killing of twenty-six miners, an incident that resulted from the decision to push production levels to maximize surplus value extraction and beyond the capacity of safety. The government responded by introducing legislation that imposes a duty on employers to provide safe working conditions and penalizes those who fail to do so (at least it does so theoretically). A duty of care has the potential to impact upon class processes, such as through additional costs to the corporation through the creation of policies and practices to ensure safety compliance. Punishments also implicate class processes in that they reduce the surplus value of the corporation, such as through fines or the imposition of probation orders.

The chapters that follow therefore draw from a fundamental aspect of Marxism – class antagonisms – to consider the extent that class processes are implicated in the (re)production of the capitalist mode of production. Through this theoretical integration, the remainder of the book explores how dominant notions of the capitalist mode of production constitute, and are constituted by, the various discourses that characterize corporate crime and criminal liability. Again, of particular interest is the relationship between the discursive and extra-discursive, for, as Gibson-Graham, Resnick, and Wolff (2001, 20) suggest, discourse is "implicated in and constitutive of power" and is an "important medium through which other social processes are constituted."

This perspective does not mean searching for class politics and struggles as exercised by consciously acting individuals but, instead, looking for the relations that unfold at the political, economic, and ideological levels – that is, through the law-state economy nexus. What are the various discourses that run through these relations that help to characterize corporate criminal liability? How do these characterizations support or challenge dominant notions of political economy? How do they reflect class struggles to define or control the means of production? What are their class relevance and effects?

As the chapters that follow illustrate, a key consideration to answering these questions is my neo-Marxist-inspired claim that the economic is not a given but, instead, a social relation that must be constantly (re)produced to maintain its ideologically dominant position within contemporary capitalist

Theorizing Corporate Harm and Wrongdoing

society. This reproduction occurs through class struggles at the economic, political, and ideological levels that are constitutive of the capitalist mode of production and unique to each social formation (Hindess and Hirst 1975). The Westray bill is an ideal example of such struggles in that it represents an object around which relatively autonomous discourses converge to animate its development, content, and enforcement – discourses that also inform the broader social formation. We now turn to critically examine the dominant legal, economic, and cultural (ideological) discourses that shaped the Westray bill and contemplate the extent to which they reinforce the corporate capital status quo.

4

Constituting the Corporate Criminal through Law

> It is important to acknowledge that the usage of the term "law" operates as a claim to power in that it embodies a claim to a superior and unified field of knowledge which concedes little to other competing discourses which by comparison fail to promote such a unified appearance.
>
> – Carol Smart (1989, 4)

> As a mechanism of power, legal discourse has material effects on people's lives.
>
> – Elizabeth Comack (1999, 67)

> The way the state responds to safety crimes shapes the way that those crimes are tolerated from the boardroom to the workplace.
>
> – Steve Tombs and Dave Whyte (2007, 207)

Introduction

The next three chapters (Chapters 4-6) critically examine the discursive formations that in various uneven and contradictory ways have animated the development of corporate criminal liability legislation in Canada. Throughout the reform process, both individuals and groups who advocated for, or raised concerns about, the introduction of this legislation faced contradictory messages about the importance of regulating workplace safety. On the one hand, there was official, broad-level support for developing federal measures to ensure adequate protections for workers, particularly insofar as a (supposed) hallmark of liberal democratic societies is the protection of life and liberty. On the other hand, there was significant reference and deference to various other considerations that oftentimes were incongruent with the goal of protecting workers – discourses that mitigated the seriousness of safety crimes and the nature and scope of corporate criminal liability legislation. These contradictory messages were not part of an orchestrated campaign against corporate criminal liability law but, instead, reflected a convergence of different discursive formations that permeated the reform process to produce particular effects.

Three mutually constitutive discursive formations influenced the development of Bill C-45, *An Act to Amend the Criminal Code (Criminal Liability of Organizations)* (Westray bill): legal, economic, and cultural.[1] State discursive formations also played an integral role in that state institutions and actors facilitated the different discourses that constituted this legislation. As Elizabeth Comack (1999, 67 [emphasis original]) reminds us, "the state could be said to *condense* the relations of power in society, and one of the ways it does so is through discourse." Although these discourses overlapped and, at times, occupied the same discursive spaces, the chapters that follow discuss them separately so that we might appreciate their unique genesis and specific contributions to the Westray bill's reform process. The conclusion (Chapter 7) considers the cumulative impact of these discourses, particularly how they converged to inform the development and enforcement of corporate criminal liability law as well as their constitutive role in (re)enforcing and (re)producing the capitalist and class-based social formation.

The first part of the chapter considers the factors that propelled corporate criminal liability onto the legislative agenda – the arguments in support of the Westray bill. The second section begins to critically examine the discursive formations that informed these reform efforts, focusing on the role of law and legal discourses. Of particular interest is the special status accorded to law throughout the reform process – in particular, law's position as a specialized form of knowledge with unique rules and parameters and a "T" truth with scientific-like status (Smart 1989). Those who attempted to speak to the issues of law were subjugated to its discourses, traditions, rules, and methods and were expected to adhere to these qualities in order to be recognized as authorized and credible voices (Comack 1999). This dynamic surfaced most prominently through references to the importance of establishing individual responsibility, or *mens rea*, when assigning criminal fault to the corporation. It also emerged through suggestions that only certain, credible voices understood corporate criminal liability law and through suggestions that law is infallible. It is the human component of law – enforcement – that is problematic, not the law itself (Smart 1989, 9-14). Legal discourses thus set parameters for the introduction of the Westray bill, framing the debate within "acceptable" legal confines and limiting the reform options that received serious consideration.

Realizing the Westray Bill: The Importance of Life and Liberty

Various factors propelled the introduction of corporate criminal liability legislation, including the Westray mine disaster and the inquiry's report; broader societal concerns with corporate power and wrongdoing; official political rhetoric in support of law reform; and, significantly, lobby efforts pressuring the federal government to introduce new legislation. The recommendation of the Westray inquiry's report that the federal government introduce new *Criminal Code* legislation pertaining to workplace safety was in and of itself insufficient to ensure the enactment of a new law.[2] In this respect, it is important to understand the elements that made it possible (perhaps unavoidable) for the Westray bill to come to fruition. Noteworthy are the lobby efforts of the New Democratic Party (NDP) and the United Steelworkers of America (Steelworkers), both of whom worked diligently to ensure that corporate criminal liability remained on the political agenda and that the federal government responded to the Westray inquiry's report by amending the *Criminal Code* accordingly.

This section details the influences that encouraged the introduction of corporate criminal liability law in Canada. In addition to providing an understanding of the impetus for reform, it illustrates that powerful interests that favour the corporate form are not automatic – the state is not always an instrument of capital, the economy is not omnipresent, and implementing laws to protect workers is not impossible (Tombs and Whyte 2007). To think otherwise would be to ignore the fact that corporate criminal liability law is now part of the *Criminal Code* and that, as a consequence, some corporations and corporate actors will be (and have been) held to account for their harmful and illegal acts (Archibald, Jull, and Roach 2004; Bittle and Snider 2006). At the same time, however, if not for the efforts of pro-labour politicians and representatives from the union movement, this law may never have seen the light of day. The reform process was, from the outset, a struggle over the meaning of corporate wrongdoing and, more specifically, about how to regulate safety and control the workplace. As we shall see – both in this chapter and in those that follow – in juxtaposition to the official support of, and lobbying for, corporate criminal liability law were various discourses that resisted, or raised questions about, the appropriateness of such measures.

The Westray Inquiry's Report

The Westray disaster and its aftermath played a vital role in bringing the issue of corporate criminal liability to the fore. The failed criminal prosecution, blatant and obvious negligence uncovered during the public inquiry, and Justice Peter Richard's recommendation that the federal government examine options for introducing corporate criminal liability law all provided important motivations for reform. These factors created the space within which it became possible to discuss and debate measures to better protect workers and punish corporations and corporate executives for workplace injury and death. As one union representative noted,

> there had to be something on the books ... this event [Westray] resonated far and wide, I mean not just in Canada. This thing was reported on around the world, right, just because of the nature of the tragedy itself, not just because you killed twenty-six people, but just why it happened was just so blatantly negligent. There had to be something happening as a result of that, as a result of Richard's report and everything, that couldn't just be left there as another report put on the shelf of the library at the House of Commons. So there were a lot of expectations everywhere from a whole host of people that something had to be done, that it couldn't just be left.[3] (Union representative, Interview 13)

In this respect, the Westray tragedy provided an important backdrop to the introduction of corporate criminal liability legislation. The gravity of the negligence associated with the killing of twenty-six miners made it difficult for legislators to ignore calls for corporate criminal liability law reform.

In addition to the Westray disaster, the broader social context provided an important ingredient for reform. After all, Westray was not the first time workers had been killed on the job as a result of unsafe working conditions – particularly in the mining industry – nor was it the first time that a corporation and its executives had escaped criminal responsibility for a safety crime (Tombs and Whyte 2007; Tucker 1990). And while some of these tragedies produced reforms to better protect workers' safety – for example, various regulations introduced over the years to protect mine workers, despite their overall ineffectiveness – they did not reach the point of resulting in corporate criminal liability provisions in the *Criminal Code* (Barnetson 2010; Tucker 1990).

The decade prior to the Westray bill witnessed growing concern with the damage caused by corporate wrongdoing – a concern that continues today in the wake of ongoing corporate financial scandals, including the 2008 collapse of the global financial system (Eagleton 2010; Wolff 2010a). Fuelled by a series of high profile corporate disasters, it became more and more acceptable to consider measures to punish corporations for their harmful and illegal acts. In particular, after the stock market technology bubble burst in 1999-2000, revealing a series of high profile corporate crimes, it became apparent that the profits of many highly respected corporations (for example, Parmalat, Enron, and WorldCom) were built on corruption, dishonesty, and fraud (Laufer 2006). In 2002, the United States government declared war on corporate crime in the *Public Company Accounting Reform and Investor Protection Act of 2002 (Sarbanes-Oxley Act),* with new regulations and increased penalties on everything from insider trading to accounting fraud (Tillman and Indergaard 2005).[4] Since the Canadian economy is hugely dependent on the United States, this declaration had a major impact on the politicians and citizens of Canada, leading to the enactment of new laws dealing with "improper" insider trading (Snider 2009).

Shortly before these corporate debacles surfaced, the Canadian public was outraged when neo-liberal initiatives privatizing public water-testing facilities and decimating the Ontario Department of the Environment were implicated in a water poisoning disaster that killed seven people and sickened 2,300 (Snider 2004). Thus, for the first time in two decades, criticizing anti-social corporate acts became acceptable. Westray, Walkerton, Enron, and the like were interpreted by many as cautionary lessons, illustrations of the "dangers of industrialization [and financialization] when it is beyond democratic control" (Pearce and Snider 1995, 26). As a criminal lawyer noted in discussing the Westray bill, this shift in societal attitude toward corporations – a general concern with issues of corporate power and responsibility – fuelled debate concerning corporate criminal liability (Criminal lawyer, Interview 5). A representative from a non-profit organization offered a similar observation, suggesting that there was a certain "mood" at the time that something needed to be done to hold corporations to account for their harmful and illegal acts (Non-profit representative, Interview 10). In short, it became politically feasible (even necessary) for the federal government to call corporations to account.

Political Support for Corporate Criminal Liability

Another motivating factor behind the introduction of corporate criminal liability legislation was the lobby efforts of key individuals and groups. At the political level, this activity included the NDP's private members' bills and, to a lesser extent, the Progressive Conservative (PC) Party's private members' motion, which urged the federal government to act upon Justice Richard's recommendation. Each measure helped keep the issue of corporate criminal liability on the political radar.

The NDP and the PCs both had political stakes in championing new legislation in that each party figured prominently in the region of the country where the Westray disaster had occurred. As Canada's pro-labour party, the NDP had (and has) significant roots in eastern Canada, a region of the country that relies heavily on the primary resource (staples) industry, including mining and fishing, for its economic well-being. With the ascendancy of neoliberalism and the concomitant demise of these industries, this part of the country has experienced its share of economic and labour woes. It is within this context that the NDP's pro-labour platform resonated well with the electorate, at times accounting for a large number of the party's seats in the House of Commons.[5]

In tabling different private members' bills, the NDP provided some of the moral and political inspiration for the introduction of corporate criminal liability legislation. Underscoring this contribution were the various comments made by NDP members of parliament (MPs) in the House of Commons regarding the party's bill. For example, NDP MP Bev Desjarlais urged MPs to vote for her legislation in principle so that it might be sent to the Standing Committee on Justice and Human Rights (Justice Committee) for further consideration. In support of her efforts, Desjarlais referred to initiatives in the United Kingdom to introduce corporate manslaughter legislation, the essence of which she argued applied equally to the Canadian context:

> It is murder. It is murder when someone's life is knowingly put at risk. We accept in our country that managers and directors in workplaces have control over the workers to the point that in sexual harassment cases we hold them seriously accountable because the workers are controlled by those bosses. They are controlled because they need that income to support their families or controlled because often those people are in a vulnerable position. That is the situation in so many workplaces. (Hansard, 20 September 2001, 17:45)

Another NDP MP also employed the discourse of killing and murder in support of the private members' bill, drawing a link between drinking and driving and workplace accidents:

> [W]hat happens when someone drinks a bottle of whiskey, hops in a car, runs someone over and kills them. That is criminal. That is murder. That is not just a traffic violation. The person is guilty of murder if he or she is convicted under the Criminal Code of Canada. It is not just a workplace safety and health issue when someone is killed due to criminal negligence on the job, it is murder. (Pat Martin, NDP, Hansard, 3 March 2000, 13:35)

At the same time, however, as an indication that this mode of thinking was anything but unanimous, an MP responded by arguing that it was wrong to equate the "tragic events" of Westray to murder, particularly while the issue was, at the time, still before "various tribunals" (John Bryden, Liberal, Hansard, 3 March 2008, 13:35). In many respects, as we shall see, this comment indicates some of the resistance toward the notion of corporate criminal liability.

The PC Party also had a direct link to this region of the country in that Peter MacKay was the MP in the riding where the Westray mine is located, and his father, Elmer MacKay, was the MP of this riding at the time of the disaster.[6] Beyond this connection, however, the relationship between the PCs and the Westray mine becomes considerably more complex. In particular, it was Elmer MacKay who lobbied the federal government extensively in support of Curragh Resources's bid to re-open the mine. Elmer MacKay convinced Brian Mulroney, leader of the PC Party and then prime minister, of the mine's political and economic saleability, despite warnings of the dangers associated with extracting coal from that particular seam (Glasbeek 2002, 61-66; Glasbeek and Tucker 1993, 16; Richard 1997).[7] As Dean Jobb (1994, 13; see also Comish 1993) points out, it was MacKay, along with the then premier of Nova Scotia, Donald Cameron, who backed Westray "to the hilt." After the mine began production, and as working conditions deteriorated, some observers suggested that these same politicians failed to see the writing on the wall, warnings that something disastrous was about to happen (Glasbeek and Tucker 1993; Richards 1997). Although Peter MacKay should not be held to account for the "sins of his father," as one politician suggested, and we should not undermine his sincerity in wanting to address workplace safety, this complex history constitutes an important backdrop to the PC Party's private members' motion (Politician, Interview 20).

Regardless of the PC Party's history with the Westray disaster, MacKay's motion helped keep corporate criminal liability on the political agenda. In forwarding this motion, the MP spoke of the importance of workplace safety and the need to introduce new legislation so that the Westray miners who lost their lives would not die in vain. As MacKay argued,

> it alarms us all to no end that such tragedies can occur and that no change results. The circumstances of the Westray mine cannot be forgotten and the lessons learned. To take it one extension further, the efforts made with respect to the tabling of the Westray inquiry only to sit idle on a shelf and to not be adopted or at least examined further ... is again an abdication of a responsibility that exists within the federal parliament. It is painful and I would suggest puzzling to suggest that we will do nothing further at this time. (Hansard, 23 April 1999, 12:20)

MacKay's motion encouraged MPs to realize their responsibility to ensure workplace safety by enacting appropriate and stringent laws, which he argued were necessary given the difficulty of establishing proof of criminal intent in cases such as Westray:

> I suggest quite strongly that knowing criminal sanctions or other disciplinary acts of retribution exist is the most direct way to ensure that those with the implicit responsibility for ensuring safety will abide. This would lead to a higher level of accountability among executives, CEOs and management in companies that directly benefit from what might be phrased expediency over safety in the workplace. (Hansard, 23 April 1999, 12:15)

MacKay further argued that the moral duty of legislators to protect Canadian workers was a sufficient imperative for reform:

> We are faced with an issue of complete moral duty when we talk about protecting lives and workplace safety. It is something so fundamental. When people get up in the morning and go out the door to their workplace, whether it is into a factory or on a trawler or in the woods or into a mine or an office building, it is not too much for them to expect or hope that they will be able to return to their homes safely that evening to be with their loved ones. Surely that is not something which should be too much for any Canadian to expect. Yet we are tasked in this place with trying to ensure that is just what happens. (Hansard, 5 October 2000, 10:35)

Other MPs also expressed support for MacKay's motion, directly challenging the legal and political status quo. For example, New Democrat MP Michelle Dockrill argued that the motion would ensure adequate accountability and punishment of corporations who "run their businesses in unsafe ways" (Hansard, 18 February 2000, 14:10). During a different House of Commons debate, another NDP MP argued that "it is too bad we have to plead with the government to pass a law that any person in charge of a company should not have a licence to run an industry unsafely and jeopardize the lives of workers" (Pat Martin, NDP, Hansard 3 March 2000, 14:00).

The PC Party's motion also acknowledged the underlying dynamics of unsafe workplaces, including the notion that profits can take precedence over safety. As Peter MacKay noted, in any enterprise, "corporate executives sometimes seem less interested in the merits of workplace safety and simply in the pursuit of profit" and that the pressures of production deadlines and looming threats of shutdowns oftentimes mean that safety suffers:

> It stands to reason that when weighing business goals versus those of safety, sometimes businesses find themselves on the horns of a dilemma. They have to make production deadlines. They have to produce and shutting an operation down obviously has huge financial consequences. That is where the human element and the safe discretion must be exercised. If we need to remind executives and management and CEOs of this through legislation, I say we do it.[8] (Hansard, 23 April 1999, 12:30)

Recognition of the negative pressures of profitability also came from NDP MP Pat Martin, who argued: "There is no production schedule in the world that justifies injuring, butchering, maiming, poisoning or killing Canadian workers" (Hansard, 3 March 2008, 13:35).

At one point, a PC MP criticized other parliamentarians who questioned the need for reform, arguing that safety was a priority over the economic security of corporations:

> Those people who have been persuaded that jobs and votes are higher priorities than life enter into a clear conflict of interest and it must stop. Many well-intentioned business executives agree with this motion because it provides safety legislation in the workplace. However there are still some who do not. Sadly the benefits of their behaviours accrue only to those executives and those people involved, while the workers, their families and ultimately the Canadian taxpayer pay for their gain. (Bill Casey, PC, Hansard, 13 March 2000, 11:05)

From these accounts, there appeared to be strong support, at least at the level of political rhetoric, for the idea that workplace injury and death is a serious matter that needs to be addressed through the introduction of corporate criminal liability legislation. However, as we shall see, this support was anything but unanimous, and even those who acknowledged the need for reform argued that there were certain extenuating circumstances that needed to be accounted for when considering different reform options.

Steelworkers' Lobby for Reform

In addition to the support from some politicians, the Steelworkers proved a vital component of the reform process. To fully understand the Steelworkers' contribution, we need to consider their role in the union-organizing efforts of Westray workers prior to, and following, the deadly explosion; their involvement in the Westray inquiry, particularly their role in ensuring that the final report recommended the introduction of corporate criminal liability legislation; and their subsequent lobbying of parliamentarians to enact such legislation.

Almost from the time that the Westray mine opened in the fall of 1991, working conditions were of such poor quality that most workers feared for their safety and lives each time they descended the mine at the start of a shift (Comish 1993; Jobb 1994; Richard 1997). From the company's viewpoint, the mine had seriously underperformed and, as a result, workers were expected to increase coal production to meet the (unrealistic) commitments that the company had made as part of its financing agreement with the provincial and federal government and its private investors. As revealed by the Westray inquiry's report, coupled with a cavalier attitude toward workplace safety by management, the mine's working conditions were ripe for serious injury and death (Richard 1997). It was within this context that some workers began exploring opportunities to unionize in the hopes of improving their working conditions. Fear of job security in a region of the country with high unemployment levels and a negative reaction by management to workers who had previously vocalized concerns about workplace safety (those who complained too loudly were singled out for harassment by management, including some who were later fired) meant that organizing efforts were undertaken without management's knowledge (Comish 1993, 28-29). It also meant that the Westray workers were far from unanimous in their support of unionizing, with many fearing being labelled as troublemakers and fired. As former Westray worker Shaun Comish wrote after the tragedy, a lot of people ask me why we kept working there [despite the safety concerns]. I guess the only answer I can give is that nowadays when you have a job it is very scary to quit and hope to get a job somewhere else. I often felt that maybe things would get better someday. Some guys who worked at Westray didn't really know anything else but mining. That's all they had ever done and probably all they ever will do. The promise of fifteen years of steady work weighed heavy on your mind. (28)

The workers' first efforts at organizing in the fall of 1991 failed. A second attempt brought the Steelworkers into the picture, efforts that were still underway when the deadly explosion occurred (Jobb 1994, 25; Comish 1993). As Jobb (1994, 222) notes, "membership cards were being sent out at the time of the blast, and some widows received them in the mail within days of their husbands' deaths." After the explosion, the Steelworkers continued their association with the Westray workers, providing support to grieving families and offering legal advice and support to workers (222). Efforts to unionize continued, and, shortly thereafter, the Westray workers officially certified (Comish 1993, 49; Jobb 1994, 222). Although this achievement came too late for those killed in the explosion, the hope for those remaining was that organizing would help in the event that they returned to work as well as help them try and make sense of the disaster and hold those responsible for the explosion – particularly management and owners – to account (Jobb 1994).[9]

Following the Nova Scotia government's announcement of a public inquiry, the Steelworkers sought successfully to gain intervener status in the proceedings. In doing so, the union worked extensively to ensure that the inquiry proceeded (Jobb 1994), and once the inquiry was underway they tabled a number of items for Justice Richard's consideration. In particular, the Steelworkers pressed Justice Richard to pursue "three rather bold initiatives": to recommend a criminal offence imposing criminal liability on "directors or other responsible corporate agents for failing to ensure that their corporation maintained an appropriate standard of occupational health and safety in the workplace"; to recommend the offence of "corporate killing"; and to recommend additions to the *Occupational Health and Safety Act* that would "broaden the liability of directors and offices for offences under the act" (Richard 1997, 600-1).[10] While Justice Richard appreciated the union's position, noting that the lack of accountability indicated a "weakness in our system," he found that their recommendations were beyond the scope of the inquiry's mandate (600-1). Notwithstanding, the Steelworkers eventually convinced Justice

Richard to recommend to the federal government that it amend the *Criminal Code* to make it easier to hold corporate executives and directors to legal account for workplace safety.

Following the release of the Westray inquiry's report, the Steelworkers continued their corporate criminal liability campaign by lobbying federal politicians to adopt Justice Richard's recommendations. In June 2000, after the NDP introduced its first private members' bill and the PC Party had tabled its private members' motion, the Steelworkers sent thirteen of its members to Ottawa for two weeks to lobby MPs to support the proposed legislation. During this time, representatives from the Steelworkers appeared before the Justice Committee at its examination of the PC Party's private members' motion, even though the committee was not hearing testimony from witnesses at that time. The Steelworkers used this opportunity to urge the government to act upon Justice Richard's recommendations. Unfortunately, these efforts were cut short with the dissolution of Parliament, effectively bringing an end to both the private members' motion and bill.

Following this initial lobbying, the Steelworkers sent a second, larger group to Ottawa in April and May 2002 to lobby MPs to support another version of the NDP's bill. In addition to lobbying various politicians about the importance of this issue, the union's representatives made another appearance before the Justice Committee, this time in relation to the committee's examination of the private members' bill. The union once again urged the government to introduce new legislation to better protect workers' safety and hold corporate management, executives, and board members to account for their harmful and illegal actions. As the national director of the Steelworkers argued before the Justice Committee, "corporate officers, directors and corporations need to be held accountable according to their responsibility. In this sense, we are asking for nothing more than to make corporations and their officers and directors accountable, as every other person in Canada is" (Lawrence McBrearty, Justice Committee, 8 May 2002, 15:40).

From the perspective of many research participants, the Steelworker's efforts, described as dogged and determined, were instrumental in bringing the Westray bill to fruition. As one union representative noted,

> once the lobbying started and the Private Members' bill went in, I think
> the politicians knew deep down that the Steelworkers were like a dog with a
> bone and they weren't going to let go, and they were going to be there no
> matter what. (Union representative, Interview 12)

The union's efforts were noteworthy in that they restarted their campaign on a number of occasions after the legislation failed to progress through Parliament because of prorogation or dissolution for an election. After each interruption, there was a risk that the government would dominate the political agenda with other issues and priorities, therein limiting the opportunity for corporate criminal liability to become part of the political agenda. There was also a risk that newly elected MPs, both in opposition and government, would not support the legislation, preferring instead to focus their energies on other issues. As one politician noted in describing the process that all MPs must negotiate when contemplating legislative reforms:

> It is a very crowded agenda in terms of a government bill, on the Private Members' side it is really just a matter of the luck of the draw. But on the government side it is space ... you're in significant competition with others with the government's agenda. And the system of having bills, particularly ones with a lot of interest, you spend a lot of time on the legislation, and then that exercise is often put at risk by the vagaries of elections. (Politician, Interview 15)

Despite these obstacles, the Steelworkers "had a plan, and they didn't deviate" (Union representative, Interview 12). As part of their efforts, they kept a "score sheet" that tracked every politician they had met with, including when they had spoken with them, what they said, and if they supported the law. As a union representative noted, "they knew they had the votes there when this thing went to a vote. Once it got to a vote at a certain stage, they knew that they had the votes. That's not always the case" (Union representative, Interview 12). As the Steelworkers continued their lobbying, it became increasingly difficult for MPs to ignore their calls for reform. It was too much of a contradiction for politicians to sidestep their responsibility to introduce measures to better protect workers' safety. As a union representative suggested,

> once they [politicians] committed to something like that [corporate criminal liability law], it's not like saying you're going to vote for motherhood and apple pie, or whatever; this was something that people died, they died because of damages. When they committed that they were going to support something, they couldn't back off on that one. They had to follow through with it, or else that would have been taken by the Steelworkers and just turned against them in their home [ridings]. And we're talking workers killed,

Constituting the Corporate Criminal through Law

corporate negligence, you'd never live that one down. (Union representative, Interview 12)

Without the Steelworkers' efforts, there is some question whether there would have been enough support for the legislation to survive the parliamentary reform process. As one politician suggested,

> somebody should write ... [about] ... the magnificence of the United Steel-
> workers of America['s] unselfish devotion to that cause. It cost them, I don't
> know, did you ever ask them what it cost? ... It would be huge, it would be
> huge, and they had no legal obligation, you know, to do it ... Without the
> Steelworkers, and I don't want to sound like I'm a sycophant, because no-
> body's perfect, but without the Steelworkers there never would have been
> a Westray inquiry. (Politician, Interview 20)

At the very least, the union helped keep the issue of corporate criminal liability law on the political agenda, ensuring that momentum was maintained at times when it could have been overtaken by the vagaries of politics and the passage of time. To date, the Steelworkers remain committed to the Westray bill, lobbying for its enforcement and, most recently, initiating a private prosecution in relation to the death of a sawmill worker in British Columbia (a more detailed discussion of this case can be found in Chapter 2).

The Possibilities of Change: Lessons from the Reform Process

As the preceding discussion reveals, despite the seriousness and obvious negligence associated with the Westray disaster, it took several different factors to converge for the Westray bill to come to fruition. The commitment – "virtù" or political will – of the Steelworkers is noteworthy in that it is conceivable that the law would not have made it on, or stayed on, the political agenda without their lobbying efforts (Althusser 1999, 74). At the same time, however, underpinning these factors is the element of chance – "fortuna" (74). The efforts of those individuals involved in the reform process were, to some extent, subject to the whims of politics and the vagaries of Parliament. If other issues had dominated the political agenda (and there was a period when the issue of corporate criminal liability was overtaken by the events of 11 September 2001), if the NDP was not fortunate enough to get their private members' bill on the legislative agenda more than once, or if the politicians who supported the law had lost their seats as a result of the two different elections that occurred during the reform process, then the issue might have been derailed. What is more, as the next section begins to illustrate, interwoven with these different factors were the various competing and contradictory discourses that helped to constitute the nature and scope of the Westray bill. At a minimum, these discourses blunted support for new workplace safety criminal legislation, providing "yes it's a good idea, but" statements at several junctures of the reform process.

Law as Capital "T" Truth

Throughout the Westray bill's development, law functioned as a capital "T" truth, a discursive formation that animated discussion and debate regarding corporate criminal liability. In particular, established legal principles limited the reform options that were given serious consideration; notions of individual responsibility, or *mens rea,* represented the dominant understanding of corporate criminal liability; particular legal experts, or authorized "knowers," were believed to possess the proper credentials to speak to issues of law; and law was conceived as unproblematic – that any difficulties with holding corporations or corporate actors to account resided with the individuals responsible for policing the corporation, not with law itself. These discourses converged around the discussion of the NDP's private members' bill to downplay support of a corporate culture approach to corporate criminal liability. As well, regardless of the fact that no individual had expressly argued against the desire to create safe and secure workplaces, the various legal discourses helped limit the reform options and minimize the nature, scope, and impact of the Westray bill.

The Role of Law in Contemporary Capitalist Societies
In contemporary capitalist societies – particularly those steeped in common law traditions – law is a potent discourse, one that plays a prominent role in ordering relations of power (Fudge and Cossman 2002, 30; Smart 1989). Although not a "homogenous force" that determines how various social relations (gender, race, and class) will unfold, it is a powerful constraining and enabling practice that "plays a significant role in the process of governing life" (Chunn and Lacombe 2000, 14). A key element of this process is law's "internally dominant concern to achieve consistency" (Woodiwiss 1990, 108). In particular, legal method necessitates the establishment of "conceptual consistency" in the development and use of legal discourse. In turn, "legal principles, doctrine, and method provide the normative basis for the authority of the law" (Fudge and Cossman 2002, 30).

Through striving for consistency, law produces its own "will to truth" (Hunt and Wickham 1994, 41-42). Although Western law varies tremendously historically and culturally (slavery, for example, was once justified under US constitutional guarantees; government control over business was excluded under the same legal statutes that now allow it), it is routinely represented as an authoritative, unitary, unchanging entity – a neutral, objective tool (Glasbeek 2002). In reality, law is anything but – it emerges and is interpreted through particular and inherently unequal social contexts. As Wayne Morrison (1995, 213) reminds us, in late modern society "we are not equally located structurally."

The truths produced in law's name often disqualify the knowledge claims of others – those based in women's birthing experiences, for example, or the local knowledges of fishing communities (Comack 1999). Law is a discourse of closure in that the application of certain criteria produces particular meaning (Woodiwiss 1990, 118-19). Under the Anglo-American legal system, the roots of law's right to speak truth stem from its claim to embody key cultural values of fairness, liberty, and equality and its ability to speak in the name of universal human rights (Comack 1999; Naffine, 1990). Law's legitimacy is guaranteed by its monopoly over legal method, seen as an objective but complex path to truth, a methodology only legal "experts" understand, thereby eliminating the subjective by prescribing the one correct, just, fair meaning of text, precedent, and statute law (Morrison 1995, 464; Snider 2004, 169).

Although Western law derives its legitimacy from claims of "fairness, stability and justice" (Woodiwiss 2006, 525), critical legal scholars remind us that law is anything but neutral and fair – an argument that becomes evident when exploring the differences between law as legislation and law as practice (Chunn and Lacombe 2000, 11). As Ngaire Naffine (1990, 24) notes, "the official version of law – what the legal world would have us believe about itself – is that it is an impartial, neutral and objective system for resolving social conflict" (as quoted in Comack, 1999, 21). In reality, however, Western law has its roots in particular gendered, racialized, and capitalist experiences, most notably the liberal belief that law should protect the *"rights and freedoms of the individual"* (25 [emphasis in original]).

The priority accorded to law and legal method does not suggest that law's effects are unidirectional or that there is a complete silencing of counter-hegemonic discourses. On the contrary, "legal and social relations are mutually constitutive." Law is not simply a container of ideologies, capitalist or otherwise, but also "a site where particular ideologies are (re)produced" (Bonnycastle

2000, 65). Law therefore struggles with, negotiates, and mediates various social and legal contradictions (Fudge and Cossman 2002, 4-5). For example, law plays an important role in advancing capitalist ideals, such as through the enactment of laws relating to property, contract, and contract of employment as well as through the constitution of the limited liability corporation (Woodiwiss 1990, 139). Likewise, law facilitates a "climate of free market enterprise" in today's global economy (Fudge and Cossman 2002, 33). At the same time, there are certain (limited) occasions where law rules against capitalist interests (Woodiwiss 1990, 139). Protections for workers through occupational health and safety regulations and corporate criminal liability legislation are two such instances.

Legal discourses within contemporary capitalist societies must therefore be understood as "relatively autonomous" (Woodiwiss 1990, 1997). According to Anthony Woodiwiss (1997, 485), "the foundational and constitutive role of 'consistency' in democratic capitalist law is what gives legal discourse its autonomy." However, this consistency does not exist in a vacuum and, instead, draws from the broader "ideological background" to gain its substantive meaning. Law in contemporary capitalist society is therefore relative – "relative to the economic, political, ideological and class-structural balances defining a particular social formation" (485). It is this relative context that must be kept in mind while exploring the ways in which dominant conceptualizations of law have characterized the introduction of Canada's corporate criminal liability legislation.

Adherence to Established Legal Principles

Adherence to established legal principles is evident through discussion and debate in Canada's Parliament regarding the introduction of corporate criminal liability legislation. On a number of occasions, there was reference to respecting law's internal consistency as a key parameter of the reform process. For example, following a presentation to the Justice Committee by a family member of a victim of the Westray tragedy, a Conservative Alliance MP informed the witness that certain legal principles restricted the committee's work:

> I know you can appreciate that this committee has to do things in accordance with *certain principles*. I'm sure the members of your group want to make sure the laws we pass are effective and just, and that means justice even for people who are accused of a crime. I don't think I've heard anything in your statements here today to suggest that you're seeking some kind of vengeance

that doesn't recognize certain *principles* we have in our Canadian legal system. I think, though, hearing from the victim in that sense is important in having us make sure we balance the interests of victims and the *legal principles* we have to take into consideration. (Vic Toews, Justice Committee, 7 May 2002, 9:45 [emphasis added])

The importance of maintaining legal principles surfaced again at the Justice Committee during a discussion of whether there was, in fact, a need to implement new legislation in response to the Westray disaster. For instance, comments from one witness underscore the dominant notion that legal principles can guide legislative decision making – that law can somehow transcend messy social conflicts to determine if particular matters should be resolved through legal channels:

It may very well be that new legislation is needed for workplace safety. If that's the case, let's say it, but let's not go on to say it looks like or it appears that these disasters mean we can't get the people responsible; therefore, we're going to change the law. In my respectful submission, it is very dangerous. I would ask you to continue to study this, and divide it up into deciding what's really necessary and what may be a reaction to large events. (William Trudell, Canadian Council of Criminal Defence Lawyers, Justice Committee, 23 May 2002, 11:25)

In response to this comment, an MP suggested that enacting new legislation without due respect to core legal principles could result in an unjust situation:

I, too, share some of the concerns Mr. Trudell has indicated in respect of the scope of the law and issues of constitutionality. It would be a great disservice to the survivors of Westray, and the families, if we were simply to pass a law that reacted to the situation without ensuring the *principles were constitutionally sound.* I think the advice you've provided is very important in this respect. (Vic Toews, Justice Committee, 23 May 2002, 11:30 [emphasis added])

In another instance, deference to established legal principles surfaced in relation to the "fairness" of stigmatizing corporations through law. A Justice Committee witness suggested that reference in the private members' bill to "ought to have known" that injury or death might occur as a result of unsafe working conditions was too vague to assign liability for fatalities, that it was incongruent with the principle of proportionality:

A policy consideration is simply when, in Canadian society, we want to stigmatize an individual or a corporation with criminal liability. It might be that the "ought to have known" standard is insufficient in that regard ... it is perhaps unfair and disproportional to stigmatize with criminal conviction and imprisonment on an "ought to have known" basis. (Greg DelBiggio, Canadian Bar Association (CBA), Justice Committee, 23 May 2002, 11:05)

As these comments reveal, reference and deference to law's parameters helped characterize the reform process, setting limits to any expectations of what could be achieved through law reform. Dominant voices planted a seed of doubt as to whether corporate harm and wrongdoing were appropriate matters for law reform – that attempts to legislate against these activities were potentially incongruent with established legal principles. These parameters were reinforced through reference to law's specific qualities and rules that have underpinned its normative authority.

The Predominance of Individual Responsibility

Another conduit for the expression of legal principles was reference to the importance of maintaining individual responsibility, particularly in relation to traditional notions of *mens rea*. A (purportedly) novel aspect of the Westray bill is that it attempts to attribute liability to the corporation, focusing on the organization or entity as opposed to the guilty individual. However, some research participants expressed concern that the new law fails to address the unique aspects of individual liability within the corporate setting. In this respect, the law differs from Justice Richard's recommendation and the position of the Steelworkers, to enact legislation that specifically addresses the accountability of corporate executives and directors. The Steelworkers argued that holding senior executives and board members criminally liable was the most effective way to get their attention and ensure that they addressed workplace safety (Union representative, Interview 9).

Following the Westray bill's tabling, it was clear that the government chose a different direction (Union representative, Interview 7). As one government official admitted, senior officers are at no more risk of personal liability than they were prior to the introduction of the Westray bill (Government official, Interview 1). A corporate lawyer described this decision as "ironic" and "tragic" in its abandonment of Justice Richard's recommendation, pointing out that

it is much more plausible and likely that a foreman, supervisor, maybe a plant manager ... is going to be targeted for Bill C-45 enforcement than a senior executive or somebody in a suite in a public or large private corporation. I just don't think that police on the ground are going to be thinking about what is in Bay street, if there is in a Northern Ontario pulp mill or mine in northern BC somebody injured or killed. You are going to be looking at who is there, who gave direction, who didn't give direction, and why, and was there wanton and reckless disregard for some worker's health and safety? I think it is part of police nature to look for a clear suspect or target and they are going to take recommendations from Crown attorneys, not the other way around. And that's how it is going to play out. (Corporate lawyer, Interview 4)

The basis for not enacting provisions relating to executive and board member liability was that the *Criminal Code* already addresses individual negligence (Government official, Interview 1). From this perspective, an individual can only be held responsible for a crime if they commit the act themselves or are a party to the offence. As a government official suggested,

we don't hold people responsible as individuals for acts that they don't commit or are not party to, and a lot of the recommendations seemed to be in the nature of, "well if you are a CEO of a company, and that company is responsible for the death of 26 miners, then you as a CEO bear a personal responsibility," and that is inconsistent with all the principles of criminal law. (Government official, Interview 1)

The predominance of *mens rea* as it applies to corporate criminal liability, particularly the fact that you need a guilty mind to hold senior executives to personal account, emerged through various comments made by MPs and witnesses during the Justice Committee's hearings. For example, as part of the Justice Committee's consideration of the private members' motion, PC MP Peter MacKay highlighted the difficulty of attributing liability for acts of omission: "It's very onerous to try to attach criminal liability to something a person didn't do, and I think we have to be very careful when we start assigning such a weighty degree of liability for acts of omission" (Justice Committee, 6 June 2000, 10:55). Other MPs expressed similar concerns and wondered about the "empirical evidence" that could be collected to determine director responsibility (Gary Lunn, Reform, Hansard, 18 February 2000, 13:55) or whether it was appropriate to hold someone in a head office to account for something that occurred in another location and as a result of day-to-day operations (John Maloney, Liberal, Justice Committee, 6 June 2000, 11:20). A Liberal MP expressed these concerns in the following manner:

The problem with industrial accidents is that it is very difficult to determine if negligence occurred. Sometimes it may not be negligence at all. It may be that the firm has done everything it thought was correct, but still the accidents occur. The problem is, where do we draw the line between no negligence, negligence and wilful negligence. (John Bryden, Liberal, Hansard, 3 March 2000, 13:45)

Even proponents of corporate criminal liability legislation found themselves subject to traditional notions of individual responsibility, as evidenced by comments from a non-profit representative who expressed his reservations about assigning criminal responsibility for workplace accidents:

You really have to understand who's making the decision and if it was something deliberate by, let's say a supervisor in the field or a line manager who's doing it. The director, I feel, should not be held as liable as that person, and I think the intent of the bill is that you don't have to necessarily charge the director, you can charge the supervisor, the line manager and leave the directors out of it ... I mean, you have a large corporation ... they're putting the money, they've hired the right people and they still have a line manager that's going against the rules just to meet production, whatever. Technically, yes they are running the company, but should they be held as accountable as that line manager? I don't think so. (Non-profit representative, Interview 10)

Recognition of traditional notions of individual responsibility, therefore, raised questions about assigning corporate criminal liability beyond the guilty individual – in the absence of a smoking gun. This line of reasoning produced conceptual difficulties over the prospects of piercing the corporate veil to assign legal responsibility for safety crimes.

How Far Up the Corporate Ladder Can We Go?

Perceived problems with establishing intent within the corporation also framed the discussion and debate about corporate criminal liability. There were numerous comments that questioned whether those individuals in the suites – senior officers, executives, and board members – are responsible for what happens on the company's streets, the corporation's front line. Related to this idea, several commentators questioned whether attempting to establish criminal intent at the top end of the corporate ladder was a constitutionally spurious endeavour. Several examples underscore the conceptual roadblocks that existed when they were considering the criminal responsibility of those in charge of the corporation, those who reap the greatest economic rewards but take the fewest risks, at least in terms of workplace safety. As one member noted during debate of the NDP's private members' bill,

> I believe we must tread very carefully in our legislative endeavours for fear that we may inadvertently alter our legal system in such a fashion as to provide a basis for criminal culpability without criminal intent, which would not be congruent with natural justice ... Directors of corporations tend to deal with issues such as strategic marketing and profit margins, whereas middle management tends to deal with operations on the ground. Is it fair to say that the manager who oversees the safety conditions in the factory is not ultimately responsible for the safety conditions in the factory, whereas the director who spends his or her time studying pie charts relating to relative market share is culpable of corporate killing? (Scott Reid, Canadian Alliance, Hansard, 8 November 2001, 17:40)

Further examples of this reasoning surfaced during the Justice Committee's work, particularly in terms of establishing intent in the corporation in meaningful, legal ways. As a Conservative Alliance MP suggested to a witness,

> I think your position that criminal liability not attach to persons, directors, or officers who do not have the requisite degree of criminal intent is a sound principle, and it's a necessary principle if we're to attach criminal liability. I'm pleased that most members here, if not all members, recognize that there are certain minimum standards of criminal intent that we must see in the legislation. (Vic Toews, Justice Committee, 9 May 2002, 10:05)

Although this MP agreed that there may be workplace safety issues to address in the "context of criminal law," he nonetheless maintained that the "principle of criminal intent, which is necessary for criminal prosecution, needs to be saved" (Vic Toews, Justice Committee, 28 May 2002, 11:35). A witness gave further credence to this perspective in stating:

> When you talk about directors' and officers' liability, and then about life in prison for unsafe working conditions resulting in the death of any person, can I just say – wearing a defence counsel's hat – this is kind of a shocking statement to get us all paying attention. But obviously this flies in the face of everything we know in this country in relation to the presumption of innocence. There are other ways to get the message out in relation to corporate

responsibility. (William Trudell, Canadian Council of Defence Lawyers, Justice Committee, 28 May 2002, 11:35)

Conservative MP Peter MacKay, who supported the introduction of corporate criminal liability legislation, also struggled with assigning criminal responsibility within the corporate form: "How do we hold the corporation responsible for what, in many instances, were omissions, things they didn't do, they should have been responsible for doing, chose not to do?" (Justice Committee, 22 May 2002, 16:05). A short time later, MacKay effectively answered his own question by stating to a witness: "I guess what I'm getting at is this chain of evidence. You're more than aware of the fact there has to be proof of both the act, the *actus reus,* and the *mens rea,* the intent" (Justice Committee, 22 May 2002, 16:10).

One exchange between Liberal MP Derek Lee and a witness, sociologist Susan Dodd, further underscores the perceived difficulties of establishing the intentions of executives and directors. Lee began his intervention by differentiating between "accidents" and "intentional" acts, which are themselves socially constructed categorizations of workplace safety:

The general who was in command of the four Canadian soldiers who died by accident in Afghanistan recently is still on the job. These accidents are not intended. I'm not talking about things that are intended to happen that take life or cause injury, I'm talking about things that are not planned. There may be carelessness, but they're not intended to happen. And whoever was involved in the Westray matter, either as a victim or as a survivor, life goes on there. I don't accept that there has been a total failure of the justice system in the Westray file. (Justice Committee, 22 May 2002, 16:15)

The witness responded by suggesting it was a mistake to refer to cases such as Westray as "accidents" and that the criminal law was an opportunity to hold corporate "agents and directors accountable in the strongest way we know how, which is under criminal responsibility" (Susan Dodd, Justice Committee, 22 May 2002, 16:20). Lee rebutted that it was difficult to hold someone such as a corporate director to account for something that they did not know was happening: "I don't see how we can make the criminal law reach that far, walk in the back door with the criminal law when some person on a corporate basis might have had no idea of what was going on" (Justice Committee, 22 May 2002, 16:20). Another MP continued by suggesting that there were limits to establishing guilt within the corporate setting: "To carry on with what Mr.

Lee suggests, is there a fear of going way too far here?" (Kevin Sorenson, Conservative Alliance, Justice Committee, 22 May 2002, 16:25).

The fear of "going too far" was echoed by those who distinguished the decision-making (and profit-taking) portion of the corporation from the production side of the equation. One MP questioned whether an officer in a head office should be responsible for a workplace accident at a branch plant: "So if we have an officer of a corporation in Winnipeg, the working conditions relate to an issue in Sarnia, and that officer, as a part of his or her responsibilities, has nothing to do with the Sarnia operation, would this not impose criminal liability on the officer in Winnipeg?" (Vic Toews, Canadian Alliance Justice Committee, 8 May 2002, 16:35). Comments from other MPs further underscored the general uneasiness of contemplating the liability of corporate executives and directors:

> How far up the chain do we attach accountability and liability? Some folks
> have said that the directors should be responsible for virtually everything
> done by their employees, and then we get varying degrees of that all the way
> down. I'd just like some opinions. If you're talking about a large corporation
> that may have directors in Vancouver and something happens at a plant
> in Toronto, how liable is the director in Vancouver for what happens in
> Toronto? That's what I'm struggling with. (Chuck Cadman, Canadian
> Alliance, Justice Committee, 23 May 2002, 9:55)

> But if I'm sitting in a corporate boardroom in Halifax or Vancouver or
> Toronto or Montreal, General Motors perhaps, realistically, how can I be held
> liable because a health and safety supervisor in the General Motors plant in
> Oshawa is incompetent or negligent? (John Maloney, Liberal, Justice
> Committee, 22 May 2002, 16:55)

A revealing example of the perceived limits of establishing the criminal intent of corporate executives emerged during an exchange between a Conservative Alliance MP and a witness who supported the corporate culture model. The exchange unfolded as follows:

> *Chuck Cadman (Surrey North, Canadian Alliance):* Thank you, Mr. Chair.
> For me, the crux of this is how far up the line it goes, how many people are
> affected, who's held responsible, and at what level. I worked once in a small
> shop where I wired high voltage electrical control panels. There was a gov-
> ernment inspector who was responsible for coming round and checking

those panels to make sure they were safe on a random basis. This government inspector, I found out later, had a little side business going building little ground fault interrupters and had entered into some kind of deal or arrangement with the shop supervisor – not the owner, not the director, but the shop supervisor – that he would buy some of these things if the guy would just look the other way once in a while. If I'm wiring that control panel and somebody gets electrocuted, I have no knowledge of a fault, because I wasn't the inspector. Is the company owner liable at that point? Is the board of directors liable? You had an inspector that was in collusion with a floor supervisor to look the other way. How far up does the liability extend?

Dr. Susan Dodd: To my mind, it would again have to be determined what one had a responsibility to know.

Chuck Cadman: I just want to know whether you feel the owner of the company or the board of directors, the CEOs, should have been liable at that point, when something has happened way down the chain, close to the bottom, where there was no way for them to know what was going on. In fact, I wouldn't have known it.

Dr. Susan Dodd: I'll make a speculation and say that in that case the board of directors would not be responsible. That's very different from participating in creating a workplace like the Westray coal mine.

Chuck Cadman: I'd say it's similar, it's just a matter of scale. (Justice Committee, Hansard, 22 May 2002, 17:20)

An exchange between another MP and a criminal lawyer also reinforced the prevailing concern with establishing the criminal liability of senior executives. The member suggested that it was important for the committee to consider how far up the chain of command the legislation could apply (Andy Scott, Liberal, Justice Committee, 23 May 2002, 11:35). The witness responded by reiterating the importance of establishing individual liability:

There is a desire expressed by some to try to press liability higher up the ladder. The question that arises is why that desire exists. To go to the 'ought' question, why ought it be the case that liability attaches at the top rather than the bottom or the middle? I don't know that this question can be answered in the abstract. I would suggest that the best way of examining the question is to determine who is responsible for a particular wrongdoing. Maybe it's the top, maybe it's the middle, or maybe it's the bottom. But without more, simply striving to attach liability at the top is perhaps going to invite problems. (Greg DelBiggio, CBA, Justice Committee, 23 May 2002, 11:40)

On the surface, this exchange presents itself as a legitimate legal question that is concerned with establishing an appropriate balance of accountability within the corporation. The problem, however, is that the structure of the modern corporation already favours those in positions of authority and power – those behind the corporate veil – the very basis of the recommendation for law reform.

The various questions raised in relation to establishing criminal intent at the higher end of the corporate ladder received further credence by legal commentators who reminded everyone that criminal intent was a constitutional matter. The testimony of Patrick Healy, recognized by the Justice Committee for his legal expertise, is instructive in this regard. Healy provided a thorough analysis of the private members' bill, expressing concern with the possibility of a "cascade of liability" that it would introduce. The idea that someone might be held liable for an act they did not commit was something that strayed too far from the principles of criminal law for Healy's comfort:

> [The private members' bill] would mean at the end of the chain directors and officers are going to be held liable and exposed to the same level of punishment as a natural person who is proved to have committed the offence with a full degree of fault ... This is a sweeping measure. I understand its purpose; nevertheless, it's sweeping in its scope, and I think there is a very real possibility ... that this measure would be open to constitutional challenge on the basis that the grounds of culpability, certainly so far as directors and officers are concerned, are not of commensurate weight and culpability with the commission of an offence by a natural person. (Justice Committee, 28 November 2003, 11:05)

Additional interventions from Healy shed further light on this concern, and this intent is intricately related to constitutional matters:

> I do think ... when you're talking about the most serious criminal offences, not just homicide, but the top end of fraud and other commercial offences, it's going to be very difficult for the courts to find constitutional validity in legislation that does not preserve some notion of individual fault, rather than a very diffuse form of collective fault. I'm convinced of that, at least to the extent that the courts have said there are offences that require proof beyond reasonable doubt of an element of *mens rea,* by which I mean a subjective mental element of intention or recklessness. (Justice Committee, 28 May 2002, 11:50)

When you move progressively away from the idea of individual responsibility, in my view, it's likely that you would open the legislation to further and further constitutional challenge. That would certainly be a possibility or probability if the corporate culture test were adopted, because, first of all, it would be open to challenge on some ground of vagueness, which is a concern of the Supreme Court under a number of decisions over the last decade, and further, there would be a serious possibility of challenge on the basis that the test for the directors' and officers' liability is not proportional to the offence with which they're being charged. In other words, they're effectively being held responsible for something that they might not have been able to influence or control. (Justice Committee, 28 May 2002, 12:05)

The written submission to the Justice Committee from the CBA, a leading voice of the legal profession in Canada, reinforced the association between criminal intent and constitutional protections:

Long standing principles of criminal law and constitutional protections available for individuals charged with criminal offences must not be compromised or eroded in an overzealous effort to attain social objectives. Constitutional and quasi-constitutional protections, such as the requirements of a criminal intent or *mens rea,* proof beyond a reasonable doubt, the presumption of innocence, and the clarity of criminal legislation must be appropriately transposed. It is no answer to say that these protections are unnecessary when the accused is a corporation. (Canadian Bar Association 2002, 2)

In this respect, in addition to being conceptually difficult for many individuals involved in the reform process to consider the criminal liability of corporate executives and board members for workplace injury and death, it was constitutionally unsound.

It is tempting to conclude that conservative MPs and legal experts working from a traditional, black-letter law perspective did espouse notions of criminal intent – and, in many respects, these were the dominant voices. At the same time, however, the language of intent also had to be reconciled by those advocating for reform. For instance, at a Justice Committee meeting, an MP raised the question of union responsibility for workplace injury and death – that is, if senior executives are responsible for workplace safety, then unions should also be held to account. In response, a union representative noted that "the further you get into the notion of union liability in these cases, the deeper you get into the problem that was previously raised, which is criminal intent" (Andrew King, United Steelworkers of America, Justice Committee, 8 May 2002, 16:45). By responding this way, the witnesses reinforced the importance of criminal intent, even if his comments were meant to protect the interests of unions and avoid the suggestion of equally shared criminal liability (an issue discussed in greater detail in Chapter 5 of this book). In this respect, the reform process was imbued with the language of criminal intent, ensuring that law's parameters were respected by all when contemplating options for reform.

Law and Authorized Knowers

In couching the issue of corporate liability in primarily (exclusively) legal terms, non-legal descriptions by non-legal experts were effectively marginalized. Simply put, corporate criminal liability, and the Westray bill in particular, was described as complex law that only some knowledgeable legal experts ("authorized knowers") could understand. For example, in speculating on the brevity of the Justice Committee's report on corporate criminal liability, one government official suggested that it would be difficult for them to come up with solutions in such a sophisticated area of law. From this perspective, corporate criminal liability was seen as a specialized and unique subset of criminal law that only a select group of criminal law experts would understand (Government official, Interview 1). Other respondents also referred to the particular knowledge or insight that was necessary to understand the law and its implications. As a private sector representative noted when discussing his understanding of the Westray bill:

> I may have been at a bit of an advantage [when it came to the Westray bill] because I'm a lawyer by training, so I'm used to looking at legislative amendments, bills, and I think the most important part of looking at anything like this is to understand what the motivating factors behind it are, what its intention is, and then to measure what the impact is likely to be, or the intended impact, of the legislation. (Private sector representative, Interview 22)

There were also references during the Justice Committee's work to the complexities of corporate criminal liability law and the fact that it took expert, legal knowledge to understand and craft new legislation in a manner that respected core legal principles. The notion of legal expertise gave credence to some voices and disqualified others, especially in that some legal experts were deemed more knowledgeable than other witnesses and members. As one MP commented following a presentation by union representatives:

I'm glad you took this matter to criminal lawyers, who, one hopes, understand constitutional law as well, to take a look at this very important issue. I
think we'd be doing the workers of this country a real disservice if we passed
legislation that didn't meet the requirements of our underlying constitutional obligations. I think that is very important, and I think your assistance in
that respect will be of use to me and my colleagues in their determinations.
(Vic Toews, Canadian Alliance, Justice Committee, 8 May 2002, 15:50)

In some instances, only those with the proper legal training were deemed
"authorized" to speak of these complex matters. For example, following a
comment made by a union representative that he was not a lawyer (which itself
gives special status to legal practitioners), a member thought it was necessary
to refer to his own legal training:

Unfortunately, because I'm a lawyer, I do get into some of the technical things,
but I have to ask these questions. I think, in order to be able to justify this,
not just to myself or my colleagues here, but to the rest of my caucus, there
are some questions I have to ask. (Vic Toews, Canadian Alliance, Justice
Committee, 8 May 2002, 16:30)

One MP excused herself for her lack of legal knowledge: "I'm not a lawyer, so
excuse me if I'm not particularly up to the necessary terms of law" (Hedy Fry,
Liberal, Justice Committee, 22 May 2002, 16:40). After suggesting that there
was a need to introduce rules to criminalize the failure to provide for a safe
working environment, the member added:

Isn't that simple? I don't know, I'm not a lawyer. It seems to me it's so simple
for us to just do that. There's a clear moral issue here: the corporation must
have a moral duty. It can be made into a legal duty to have the knowledge,
and failure to have the knowledge in itself should involve guilt. You shouldn't
be running a company if you don't have the knowledge. That's my argument.
If it is simplistic, I just want to lay it on the table anyway and ask what you
think of that kind of simple way of looking at the problem. (Hedy Fry, Liberal,
Justice Committee, 22 May 2002, 16:40)

Consider, also, the reception accorded another woman and non-lawyer.
This woman appeared before the Justice Committee as a representative of the
Aurora Institute, a critical, non-profit think-tank dedicated to examining the
social and legal status of corporations in Canadian society. The two male legally

Constituting the Corporate Criminal through Law

credentialed witnesses who testified that day were received with enthusiasm – their professional status was outlined and they were asked to expand on their testimony or to tell the committee the best ways to establish *mens rea* and *actus reus*. The representative from the Aurora Institute was asked only one question, and it came after one MP noted that the two male lawyers had been allowed to "run away with the process" (Paul Harold Macklin, Liberal, Justice Committee, 28 May 2002, 12:15). Her comments on the need for strong corporate criminal liability legislation were then rebutted and contradicted, not by an MP but, rather, by one of the witnesses. He reiterated the importance of retaining the legal notion of individual responsibility (directing mind) and argued that there was little demonstrated need for reform. His rebuke continued: "I don't know that corporations are getting away with it [corporate crime]. Charges are happening every day in relation to corporations ... I don't think the void [in law] has been demonstrated. I think there have been some disasters that resulted in unsatisfactory prosecutions" (William Trudell, Justice Committee, 28 May 2002, 12:15 and 12:20).

Law as Neutral/Infallible

Another way in which law functioned as a capital "T" truth was through the perception that law is infallible, so long as the rules of legal method and precise legal language are followed correctly. "The official version of law" – the belief that law is "an impartial, neutral and objective system for resolving social conflict" – was fundamental throughout the reform process (Naffine 1990, 24; quoted in Comack 1999, 21). This belief is maintained by a legal sleight of hand that transforms social conflicts into individual, legal problems and abstracts individuals (and corporations) out of their social contexts, thus allowing law's gendered, racialized, and class-based origins and impact to be ignored (Comack 1999, 23).

Belief in the sanctity of official law is particularly important for the study of corporate crime because law legitimizes the disparity in sanctions between traditional and corporate offenders. Corporate actors who cause injury and death rarely receive sanctions equivalent to those meted out to traditional criminals. Workplace injury and deaths, environmental crimes, and corporate fraud are rarely sanctioned or shamed. And when they are, punishments are much lighter than those received by the street offender who commits comparable acts of theft, fraud, assault, and murder (Glasbeek 2002; Rosoff, Pontell, and Tillman 2005). Clearly, as Laureen Snider (2004, 177) observes, "control is not an equal-opportunity game."

Suggestions that law is a neutral arbiter that will establish the "truth" through its proper application reinforced law's authoritative status. In particular, although corporate criminal liability was seen as complex law, the problem with protecting workers' safety was thought to rest with extra-legal factors (factors beyond the way in which the law was written), including a lack of enforcement and the factual complexities of different cases. One respondent spoke of the complexities of investigating and prosecuting workplace deaths, citing the difficulties of weaving together the various causal factors (Government official, Interview 1). And while rigorous enforcement would help to ensure the law's use, advancing this perspective removes the burden of accountability from the law. Law is not the problem; the problem lies with those charged with its enforcement who fail to understand law's value. In the process, the unequal relations of power imbued in law's constitution are ignored, leaving the impression that law transcends social conflicts. Law remains above human error, a tool that is "fair, dispassionate, disinterested, and – above all – just" (Comack 1999, 23).

Further expression of law's infallibility surfaced through suggestions that the failure to hold Westray managers and owners to account resulted from poor regulatory enforcement before the disaster and an inadequate criminal investigation afterwards. For example, one MP, citing his expertise as a mining engineer, suggested that focusing on the enforcement side of the equation would save implementing legal measures:

> We are perhaps shooting at the wrong target here. The problem at Westray was not governance. The problem at Westray was safety enforcement. Perhaps we might say that line management was guilty but the mine inspection system failed. Any mine inspector should have been able to spot the violations which have been described here which took place in that mine ... Because there was this one particular disaster, let us not talk about revamping a law which has served us well over the years. (Lee Morrison, Reform, Hansard, 13 March 2000, 11:35)

There was also some discussion about the difficulty and complexity of attempting to hold corporations to legal account, a suggestion that again led to debate about whether the problem lay with the law or those charged with its enforcement. As Conservative MP Peter MacKay asked of a witness,

> I guess I have a straightforward question about what you would say, as an expert in this area and having studied this, to the suggestion that the current

Criminal Code provisions are sufficient; that criminal negligence, manslaughter – these types of *Criminal Code* charges that currently exist, that in fact were utilized in the Westray case ... What happened in Westray is perhaps not the best example. That prosecution went completely awry. It went in all kinds of directions. Tactical delays were used. The case died by paper instead of on its merits. (Justice Committee, 2 May 2002, 10:45)

And a representative from the Canadian Council of Criminal Defence Lawyers noted:

I think the proper application of existing legislation, both provincial and federal, will satisfy the need to address environmental protection and workplace safety, etc. ... I don't think we need to really examine the whole corporate structure. What we need to do is look at the tools we have in relation to enforcement. (William Trudell, Justice Committee, 28 May 2002, 11:35)

Law is perfect, while enforcement is imperfect, as expressed through a statement by Liberal MP Paul Harold Macklin:

In listening to your testimony, I get an impression, as from some other evidence we've already heard in this hearing process, that in fact, there were a great many laws available, there were a great many protections available, but the failure was not necessarily in the creation of the laws, but rather in the enforcement process of those laws. (Justice Committee, 7 May 2002, 10:15)

The notion of law as infallible propelled the myth that it provides the method for determining "truth," the belief that legislators simply need to strike the appropriate balance when creating law to ensure that workplaces are safe. Once again, law is not the problem; it is those charged with its enforcement that need discipline and correction:

Was it a failure of law ... there is truth in saying charges were laid, albeit belatedly, and there were issues with the evidence and how it was collected. Charges were laid, the corporation was charged. The corporation then was insolvent, so it became redundant, the owner-operator was not charged, so there is perhaps a gap there that has to be closed. But the real issue then became the process. The process is what failed. The process completely fell down, and there are all sorts of reasons. We know how those men died, we want to know why, about that convoluted conspiracy of circumstances that led to this disaster. (Peter MacKay, Conservative, Justice Committee, 22 May 2002, 17:10)

On the one hand, these comments raise questions about the ineffective enforcement of existing laws, which is a proverbial problem for the policing of corporate crimes. At the same time, however, underpinning these comments is the belief that law is ideologically neutral. The perception of law as infallible decontextualizes legal measures from their social, political, and economic context, suggesting that it is above these messy disputes and that it is a neutral arbiter that can resolve social problems. Meanwhile, law is anything but neutral and fair, working to the advantage of the powerful few, while distributing its "justice" in a manner that disproportionally affects the most marginalized members of society (Comack 2006). In addition, maintaining the myth of law as infallible also casts doubt over the need for law reform, shifting the discussion from the limits of the law to problems with the administration of justice. Why should the law be changed if it will only be (mis)interpreted and (mis)applied by those charged with its enforcement?

Law's Convergence around the Concept of Corporate Culture

Law's capital "T" status factored prominently in the discussion and debate of the private members' bill and its support of a corporate culture approach to criminal liability. Within this context, there was a convergence of the various legal discourses, which were discussed earlier – that is, legal principles, criminal intent, and authorized "knowers" – which raised doubt about the viability of such an approach to corporate criminal liability. These discourses shaped the consideration of the relationship between corporate culture and criminal liability, ensuring that existing criminal law standards were the basis from which to judge all reform proposals.

Considerable support for the corporate culture approach came (predictably) from NDP MPs, whose party introduced the private members' legislation. For example, NDP MP Bill Blaikie noted the process by which a culture of rule breaking develops within the corporation:

There are all kinds of situations that I'm aware of, in the railway and everywhere else, where there are all kinds of rules that everyone's supposed to follow, but there's an expectation on the part of management that you will not follow those rules if there's a train they want to get out or if there's some deadline they want to meet. You're in trouble if you don't break the rule. If you break the rule and everything's fine, then everything's fine. But if you break the rule and something happens, well, then, it's your fault as the employee rather than the company, when in fact there's a culture of expectation that the rules will only be observed when it suits efficiency, so to speak. (Justice Committee, 2 May 2002, 10:15)

Although MPs from other parties did not expressly support the corporate culture approach, they nevertheless offered comments in recognition of the external factors that shape workplace safety. As Conservative MP Peter MacKay noted to a witness during the Justice Committee's hearings,

we take very seriously this task before us. You've acknowledged, and I think you've seen through some of the questions, the complexities of all of this. But you and I both know, back in Pictou County, the reason a lot of people went into that mine was economic circumstances. I dare say – and I say this with the greatest respect – if a mine opened up tomorrow, there'd be people lined up across the bridge to get jobs there. That's the reality we have to take into consideration too, that there are these external forces that come into play and sometimes contribute to these disasters. But your testimony is a very solemn reminder that for every action and reaction there's got to be some sense of responsibility for what people do and what decisions they take. (Justice Committee, 7 May 2002, 10:25)

Throughout the Justice Committee hearings, there was strong support for the corporate culture model within the private members' bill. A representative from the Ottawa and District Injured Workers Group argued that introducing legislation based on such an approach would help to ensure that safety concerns extended beyond line managers to directors and officers (Doug Perrault, Justice Committee, 2 May 2002, 11:25). Other witnesses were more overt in lobbying for a corporate culture approach to corporate criminal liability, as evidenced by the statement of one witness, who argued: "It's crucial that our *Criminal Code* acknowledge [that is, criminalize] that some corporate cultures are criminogenic, that they tend to produce, or at the very least encourage, the breach of law" (Susan Dodd, Sociologist, Justice Committee, 22 May 2002, 15:45). A witness from a community-based organization offered a similar observation in her assessment of the corporate form:

Corporations are institutions created by law. Laws spell out the rights, powers, and responsibilities of the corporation, and these in turn inspire the goals, rules, and purpose that form the basis of any corporate culture. Therefore, the corporate culture this bill rightfully addresses is necessarily a function of the corporate structure as it exists in law, and unless that structure is addressed, the type of corporate culture that overlooks employee safety will always be an issue. (Clare Mocherie, Aurora Institute, Justice Committee, 28 May 2002, 11:10)

The written submission of the Shareholder Association for Research and Education to the Justice Committee also supported the concept of corporate culture contained in the private members' bill, arguing: "It is necessary that legal regimes be able to transcend the legal fiction of corporate personhood in order to ascribe liability to corporations and corporate personnel for harm caused to individuals and the environment through wilful acts or negligence" (Shareholder Association for Research and Education 2002, 1).

Finally, a legal academic argued before the Justice Committee that it was problematic to conceptualize workplace death as "accidents" and, hence, important to include reference to corporate culture in workplace safety legislation:

When somebody dies at the hands of another person, we usually call it murder; when this happens in war, we call it a casualty; and when this happens at work, it's an accident. I'll say right now that I'm in favour of the adoption of a bill like the one that is proposed, because this culture has to change. (Anne-Marie Boisvert, Justice Committee, 23 May 2002, 9:40)

The witness encouraged MPs to consider the Australian model as a source of innovation in responding to workplace injury and death and as a way of balancing the traditional common law (individuals are still culpable under a corporate culture model) with the idea of a "deficient" corporate culture: "Why not try it, even if it later needs some adjusting? I would say that we have nothing to lose" (Anne-Marie Boisvert, Justice Committee, 23 May 2002, 9:50).

Overall, there was strong support for the NDP's approach to corporate criminal liability – a recognition of the association between corporate culture and corporate malfeasance. However, as the next section illustrates, in juxtaposition to this support were various legal concerns that downplayed the corporate culture model as a viable reform option. Although these concerns were not expressed in opposition to the idea of making workplaces safer, they nevertheless imposed limits upon establishing corporate criminal liability.

Concerns with the Corporate Culture Model

From the outset of the Justice Committee's work, it was clear that reference to corporate culture in the private members' bill was a problematic concept for many MPs and witnesses in terms of the need to establish *mens rea* and maintain established principles under the *Canadian Charter of Rights and Freedoms*.[11] Of particular concern was the fact that assigning responsibility based on the concept of corporate culture strayed too far from the established legal parameters of individual guilt. For instance, in responding to a question from an MP about whether the government ensures the constitutionality of legislation as part of its drafting process, a Department of Justice representative raised the spectre of a *Charter* challenge to the corporate culture bill:

> One would expect a challenge to a corporate culture model as one model, based on whether you were attributing culpability to the corporation as a person, as the accused, in an inappropriate way. It's an accumulation of factors in some ways. It sets a standard ... for encouraging conduct, etc. So there may be issues of the *mens rea*, and the actual intent and culpability of the corporation may be challenged under the charter. I have to say we have not done a full-scale analysis on this. (Dave Whellams, Justice Committee, 2 May 2002, 10:35)

In response to a question from another MP about whether the introduction of federal criminal legislation raised the possibility of double jeopardy if enforced in parallel with provincial regulatory offences, the departmental representative responded affirmatively, once again citing particular concerns with the corporate culture model:

> Yes. I think you're going to see double jeopardy arguments in most cases, especially if you go the corporate culture way. There's a lot more analysis to be done. It's legalistic but important. For example, with corporate culture, you have to transcend some of the classic problems of *mens rea, actus rea,* etc. Professor Healy, in one of his articles – it's excellent on the subject – goes to great length in describing the intersect or non-intersect between what he calls regulatory offences and *mens rea* offences. The question, without my answering it, is that with a corporate culture concept, in a way, you do find ways to transcend the problems of a traditional *mens rea* and *actus rea* analysis. It is not a question of forming the specific intent in the classic criminal law sense. The corporate culture showed an intention, through the

accumulation of evidence, about conduct, standards, rules, edicts, etc. You have a problem clarifying the nature of the offence. Are you simply not worrying that regulatory offences are one thing and *mens rea* offences are another? I know it's not a full answer ... It is going to arise because there has been, first of all, a lack of testing in jurisprudence of corporate culture, if you go for that model. As to what it does to offences that are not *mens rea,* or, conversely, *mens rea* offences, you're going to have exactly that defence on double jeopardy. (Dave Whellams, Justice Committee, 2 May 2002, 10:55)

From this perspective, the concept of corporate culture was judged by the strictures of existing criminal law and the threat of a constitutional challenge. Established legal frameworks became the benchmark to which all other perspectives were to conform in order to receive serious consideration.

Other members and witnesses also raised questions about notions of corporate culture in corporate criminal liability law. Liberal MP John McKay suggested to a witness that the corporate culture model undermined the notion of *mens rea,* potentially holding certain people within the corporation to account for things they were not aware of:

Your essential thesis is that the Australian culture model is one we should explore and adopt, moving away from, if you will, our *mens rea* thesis, which is somewhat more precise: you have to be able, as a crown counsel, to demonstrate some intention, some recklessness, or some knowledge of what people were doing. If you move to the Australian idea, presumably, the directors could set out this directive, which may or may not be followed. Then it would be down to management to possibly also send out directives, which may or may not be followed. Then that would go to junior management, and may or may not be followed, and down to the employees, and may or may not be followed. Those are quite a number of degrees of separation between directives and actual action. This leads to a certain level of imprecision and vagueness, which generally heretofore our criminal law has not contemplated ... I wonder whether adopting that model might also result in some pretty bizarre exercises in corporate liability, where someone way down the feeding chain was doing something of which the people up the feeding chain had no real active knowledge. (John McKay, Justice Committee, 7 May 2002, 11:55)

Some witnesses identified the corporate culture approach as being vague, lacking the legal precision necessary for criminal matters. As a representative from the CBA observed, "there are concerns with respect to vagueness and over-breadth; some of the words associated with corporate culture do not have precise legal meaning" (Greg DelBiggio, CBA, Justice Committee, 23 May 2002, 11:02). This witness urged the committee to consider whether a corporate culture model unnecessarily complicated attempts to hold corporations to legal account:

> Sometimes, complicated law – law that is fraught with terms that are vague or terms that are overly broad – will result in a prosecution that goes sideways. That is certainly not in the public interest, nor would terms that are vague or overly broad comply with constitutional standards. In Bill C-284 [the NDP's private member's bill], I would ask you to consider phrases like "tolerate or condone practices" and "allow the development of common attitude." These are phrases of uncertain meaning, and I would suggest that these terms should be very carefully scrutinized. (Justice Committee, 23 May 2002, 11:05)

Echoing the concerns of this witness was the CBA's written submission that accompanied his testimony:

> Are we to have criminal liability and criminal sanctions because a board of directors failed to meet and therefore "tolerated" a situation or practice of which it was actually aware? Is an outside director who follows the dictates of an overbearing and secretive management nevertheless to be found guilty of having "allowed the development of a culture" or having "condoned" things which, in hindsight only, ought to have been brought to the light of day? (CBA, Justice Committee, 22 May 2002, 3)

The comments of two witnesses, who testified together, provide further indications of the general concerns with the corporate culture approach. The Justice Committee MPs accorded special status to the testimony of Patrick Healy and William Trudell, with their legal "expertise" and authorized voices, providing the backdrop to their presentations and subsequent exchanges with members. Both witnesses argued adamantly against the notion of corporate culture, employing the language of legal precision in their defence. For example, Healy argued that the concept of corporate culture was incongruent with notions of individual liability:

> There's a reference in the [private members'] bill to the notion of corporate culture. This leads me to make a couple of observations. One is that there is

nothing in this bill that would deal with the specific evidentiary problems raised by corporate criminal liability. If Parliament were to rely on a notion of corporate culture as a basis for the liability of corporations, it seems to me it would be impossible to do it without specific evidentiary mechanisms that would allow for the compulsory production of information that would allow for proof of what that corporate culture actually is. And if that is the case, it's going to be extremely difficult, in my view, for the provisions on corporate criminal liability to coexist with the liability for directors and other officers. (Justice Committee, 28 November 2003, 11:05)

At another juncture, Healy provided a blunt assessment of the corporate culture model:

As for the corporate culture point, I don't mean to be flippant about it, but the idea is, was it in the air that this kind of activity would be tolerated on behalf of the corporation? That obviously is a much more nebulous notion, a wider notion, and one that raises, in my respectful opinion, severe evidentiary problems, since, at the end of the day, criminal liability requires proof beyond a reasonable doubt. (Justice Committee, 28 May 2002, 12:05)

William Trudell, from the Canadian Association of Criminal Defence Lawyers, shared Healy's concern with the lack of precision associated with the corporate culture approach: "As far as I'm concerned, the Australian definition of corporate culture – which is in the discussion paper from the Department of Justice – creates problems. It is defined as 'an attitude, policy, rule, course of conduct or practice.' It's vague" (Justice Committee, 28 May 2002, 12:25).[12]

The corporate culture model was judged as vague and imprecise throughout the Justice Committee's examination of corporate criminal liability. Regardless of the desire to hold corporations to legal account for their harmful actions, there were certain legal rules and traditions that had to be adhered to for the reform process to succeed. These concerns outweighed any desires to push the legal envelope – better to take the conservative root and stick with the familiar than upset the legal status quo in the face of unique problems that lie outside of traditional criminal law concerns with (street) crime.

Legal Precision and Corporate Culture

When asked about the differences between the NDP's private members' bill and the government's legislation, some research participants also referred to issues of legal precision as it relates to the concept of a corporate culture. As a government official noted, the private members' bill sought to attribute criminal liability "when you couldn't establish what you would normally consider *mens rea,* just on the basis of the position you occupy and imposing very heavy penalties upon people ... and that's not the way Canadian criminal law operates" (Government official, Interview 3). One corporate lawyer offered his opinion as to why the notion of corporate culture was a problematic concept in law:

> Corporate culture isn't sufficiently articulated, I don't think, for people to really know what that means. The problem is ... there is fundamental principle in criminal law, as opposed to other areas of law, but it is specific to criminal law, that you must know, with some level of precision, the law that you must obey, because the sanctions of non-compliance are so serious. So there is a level of precision required in criminal law, and I think the fear was, if you enact the law that there could be a *Charter* issue, if you enact a law that really nobody knows what it means, it is going to be challenged as being too vague and unconstitutional. (Corporate lawyer, Interview 7)

A legal academic concurred with this assessment, noting that corporate culture lacks the precision necessary for someone to understand what they are being charged with and that it would be extremely difficult to train police and crown attorneys about what to look for when investigating offences (Legal academic, Interview 8).

In general, the concept of corporate culture provided the conduit for various MPs and some witnesses to voice their concerns about the introduction of corporate criminal liability legislation. As one politician noted when discussing the concerns in relation to the private members' bill, "absolutely there was some resistance ... I think there always is amongst some individuals the fear that you are giving workers maybe too many rights and corporations too many regulations, and I think that was an underlying factor" (Politician, Interview 11).

The Culture of Political Reality

The dominance of legal discourse does not suggest that these principles were all encompassing and that there was no resistance to these perspectives. In addition to the overall support for the NDP's proposed legislation, some individuals took umbrage with comments that downplayed the significance of addressing the issue of corporate culture. A union representative argued that the anti-corporate culture sentiments were politically expedient for the ruling Liberal Party, which allowed them to avoid its reference in the Westray bill, therein claiming that they were being proactive by introducing new legislation while, at the same time, reassuring their corporate base that the law would not be overly intrusive (Union representative, Interview 6).

In addition, there were counter-arguments to the suggestions that certain legal parameters had to be respected throughout the reform process. For example, in responding to dominant notions of the guilty mind, or *mens rea,* a union representative argued:

> The guilty mind of what? The guilty mind that knowing it's your responsibility to make sure that health and safety is being looked at properly given the nature of the corporation, the nature of the organization, which is what we thought the test was suppose to be, or is it you're not suppose[d] to pull the gun that actually killed someone. Well we already knew that one! (Union representative, Interview 9)

In her testimony to the Justice Committee, Poonam Puri challenged the committee to look beyond issues of *mens rea* to consider the potential benefits of corporate criminal liability legislation:

> The criminal law is a policy tool that we have available to us to regulate undesirable conduct. The criminal law is a social tool. It's a means to an end, not an end in itself, so I don't think we should get hung up over questions about how a corporation can have a guilty mind. I think we need to keep in mind that what we label as criminal activity is a policy choice. Criminal activities are the worst sorts of behaviour that members of societies can engage in. If corporations commit some of the worst sorts of activities, then we should be entitled to label them as criminal. In terms of some of the questions like how a corporation can have a guilty mind, I think reasonably intelligent people such as us should be able to modify criminal law principles that are aimed generally at individuals in order that they fit the corporate context. (Poonam Puri, Justice Committee, 23 May 2002, 9:40)

However, regardless of these dissenting voices, the predominant concern was staying within established legal boundaries, respecting law's capital "T" truth status. Even those advocating for reform were restricted by law's parameters and understood the limits of the corporate culture approach. As a union representative noted, "the argument against the Australian [model] was that culture was just not clear enough, it was new language ... we don't know what it means and from a criminal defence perspective it was too vague" (Union representative, Interview 9).

The demise of the NDP's private members' bill does not mean that it represented (or represents) the most appropriate model of corporate criminal liability. For one thing, the Australian Capital Territory, Australia's smallest jurisdiction with the fewest annual workplace fatalities, is the only jurisdiction thus far to adopt the country's model corporate culture law, and this law has yet to be used in any criminal cases (Haines and Hall 2004; Keith 2011b, 48). What is more, Harry Glasbeek (2005) argues that adhering to a corporate culture approach risks further obscuring the criminal responsibility of individual corporate executives, board members, and major shareholders – the "beneficiaries of anti-social behaviour," as Glasbeek notes (54). In essence, if the law's focus is the organization's culture, then the very individuals targeted by the Westray inquiry's recommendations to amend the *Criminal Code* could potentially remain hidden behind the corporate veil.

However, the focus here is not the effectiveness of the corporate culture model but, instead, how a commitment to traditional notions of individual liability limited the reform options that were accorded serious consideration by legislators. A narrow legal frame helped to prioritize the status quo (or to at least stay as close to it as possible), effectively reinforcing legal principles consistent with the *Criminal Code,* therein limiting debate about the structural causes of serious injury and death in the workplace. As a union representative noted to the Justice Committee, "the Code has a long history, there are certain ways things have been done in the Code over the years, and we want to stay consistent" (Andrew King, Steelworkers, Justice Committee, 8 May 2002, 16:15). In this respect, the "effectiveness" of the corporate culture model to hold corporations and their senior executives to account was never at stake – just the belief that it failed to cohere with existing legal standards. Backed up by dominant notions of individual liability (the legal status quo), the corporate culture model therefore provided a significant conceptual stumbling block for everyone contemplating the introduction of corporate criminal liability legislation.

In many ways, a sense of political realism characterized discussion and debate about the NDP's private members' bill, particularly in that its proponents did not want their commitment to the corporate culture model to detract from the enactment of some form of corporate criminal liability legislation. As one politician suggested,

I would have preferred, as I think a good number of people would have, that [the legislation] had continued from the perspective of a corporate [culture] type criminal offence. What came out of the discussions over time was that it would have been tougher, if not impossible with the government of the day, to get that model. (Politician, Interview 11)

In response to my question of whether the corporate culture model was that much of a stumbling block for moving corporate criminal liability legislation forward, the politician noted: "Well I think it can be made to be that way, because it is not the easiest thing to prove, but in some cases it's so blatant that it is not hard to prove either" (Politician, Interview 11).

The various concerns expressed with the private members' bill illustrate that certain concessions had to be made for corporate criminal liability legislation to become reality. One politician spoke of a desire to avoid yet another situation where the bill would die on the order table, citing the importance of ensuring the enactment of some form of legislation (Politician, Interview 11). In this context, compromise was the only way to ensure that the government introduced new law. This goal meant setting aside certain commitments to ensure that the reform process continued to move forward: "You get a lot more just by trying to work with people and [identify] where their main concerns might be ... Sometimes you've got to do it because ... [getting a law enacted] ... is a step in the right direction" (Politician, Interview 11). In this respect, compromise was born from an adherence to legal precision and a persistent fear that the law might never come to fruition.

Law's Privilege

Overall, various legal discourses converged and coalesced around discussion and debate regarding corporate criminal liability to narrow the horizons and limit the reform options. In the process, the concept of corporate culture was abandoned as an option for corporate criminal liability law reform because it was seen as vague and imprecise. It could not, dominant voices said, be stipulated in precise legal language, through acceptable legal methods, according to historic principles of *mens rea*. This narrow technical frame ruled out any consideration of the structural causes of workplace death, any examination of the roots of corporate power, or any use of the privileged legal status and extensive rights conferred by limited liability (Glasbeek 2002; Tombs and Whyte 2007). The overwhelming moral, political, economic, and social capital of the corporation was thus judged irrelevant from the get-go. It also meant that those in positions of power – the individual executives and directors who make the decisions and reap the financial rewards – remain largely hidden behind the corporate veil. The Westray bill means that some corporations will be held to account for their harmful acts, although individual responsibility within the *Criminal Code* remains unchanged. Adherence to traditional notions of individual responsibility rendered it difficult for legislators to conceptualize criminal responsibility at the higher end of the corporate ladder. While the fixation with individual responsibility means that traditional street offenders are readily held to account for breaking the law, it conversely means that those in positions of power can obscure their responsibility through legal reasoning. This line of reasoning helps to reinforce the dominant belief that guilt can only be established by identifying the individual who removed the safety mechanism, the person who dumped the toxic chemicals, or the manager who directed the worker to climb the building without a safety harness. Clearly, law's discourse continues to work to the advantage of the privileged few.

5

Visions of Economic Grandeur: The Influence of Corporate Capitalism

> I dreamt I came here [to Parliament] and the [Westray] bill had already been passed, and I was running to a phone to call all the persons I know who are directors of corporations to tell them to resign immediately before I was reported to the law society.
>
> – William Trudell, Canadian Council of Defence Lawyers (Hansard, 28 May 2002, 11:20)

The Importance of Corporate Capitalism

In early 2002, the New Democratic Party (NDP) withdrew its private members' bill from the order paper after the government agreed to send the issue of corporate criminal liability to a parliamentary committee for further study and review. The Standing Committee on Justice and Human Rights (Justice Committee) was an obvious choice for this task, particularly since it had already considered the issue in the context of the Progressive Conservative (PC) Party's private members' motion, which asked the government to act on the recommendation of the Westray inquiry's report by introducing *Criminal Code* measures to hold senior executives and board members to account for workplace safety.[1] Instead, the government pondered sending the issue to the Standing Committee on Industry, Science and Technology (Industry Committee). Although they ultimately decided otherwise – a decision made after the NDP negotiated for it to be sent to the Justice Committee – according to one politician, its mere consideration reflects a general trepidation with introducing measures to hold corporate actors to legal account (Politician, Interview 11). Was the intent to send the issue to the Industry Committee to evaluate it from a corporate perspective? Was it to examine the impact of corporate criminal liability law on the very people that it was meant to hold to account? As one politician noted when commenting on the possibility of sending the issue to the Industry Committee, "the focus was totally going to be that we [were] going to side with industry instead of what [was] necessary for justice for workers who are killed because of a corporate culture" (Politician, Interview 11).

As the previous chapter has illustrated, despite general support for the introduction of corporate criminal liability legislation, various legal discourses dominated, and set limits to, the reform options. However, legal discourses do not exist in a vacuum and, instead, draw their moral authority from, and are constitutive of, the broader social context within which they emerge (Hunt and Wickham 1994; Smart 1989; Woodiwiss 1990). As Frank Pearce and Steve Tombs (1998, 99) suggest, law is "both an effect of and affects other fundamental social relations." In this respect, there are extra-legal considerations when examining the constitution of corporate criminal liability law – discourses that occupy the political-economic-ideological space that shape, but do not determine, corporate crime and corporate criminal liability. In contemporary Canadian society, this examination includes dominant notions of the economy, particularly as it relates to corporate capitalism and its hegemonic status as society's primary wealth-generating mechanism.

This chapter examines the economic discourses that characterized the reform process of the Bill C-45, *An Act to Amend the Criminal Code (Criminal Liability of Organizations)* (Westray bill), including how this language provided a dominant frame to evaluate, and speak about, corporate crime and corporate criminal liability.[2] These discourses emerged in two distinct, yet related, ways: first, through frequent reference to the importance of corporate capitalism for Canadian society and through the understanding that any attempts to hold corporations and corporate actors (particularly executives and board members) to legal account for their harmful acts should not be too stringent – after all, we should avoid measures that potentially impede a corporation's ability to produce and accumulate. Second, a general commitment to pro-capital and neo-liberal ideals characterized discussion and debate of who is responsible for workplace safety. Can corporate actors be asked to bear the bulk of the responsibility for workplace safety? dominant voices asked, somewhat incredulously. What about workers and unions? they wondered. Should they, too, not be culpable? Is that not the fair thing to do, to ask everyone "responsible" to accept blame for workplace injury and death?

What is particularly revealing about the Westray bill reform process is that dominant economic perspectives flourished in the absence of any direct involvement by representatives from the corporate world. Unlike past examples of corporate crime law reform where corporate actors openly and actively displayed their distaste for, and resistance to, government interventions (Snider 1993), the "captains of industry" were publicly silent when it came to discussion and debate regarding the merits of corporate criminal liability law (Glasbeek 2002). However, as we shall see, there was little need for corporations and corporate actors to stake their claim in relation to the proposed legislation. The (hegemonic) common sense of corporate capitalism was alive and well throughout the reform process, given voice by legislators and backed by "credible" experts.

The World According to Neo-Liberalism

In Chapter 3, we saw that a dominant and defining feature of the Canadian social formation over the past thirty years is the "tectonic shift" in public policy toward privatization (Fudge and Cossman 2002, 3). Concomitant with this neo-liberal commitment to the free market economy, corporate actors successfully argued that laws governing the economic realm are unnecessary, even redundant, given that the marketplace is the best way to separate out the bad apples. No need to worry, they suggested, as those who act inappropriately will suffer accordingly when they cannot find anyone to work for them because they operate in an unsafe manner, when nobody will purchase their products because they are tainted by malfeasance, or when they are outperformed economically by corporations who operate as good corporate citizens. According to dominant corporate voices, law simply interferes with the effective functioning of the market, making the introduction of new laws a dangerous proposition (Williams 2008).

Beginning in the 1980s, deregulation of the economic realm became the prominent mantra within neo-liberal circles, underscoring the belief that government regulation produced economic inefficiencies (Snider 2002, 218). Fuelled by visions of bureaucratic "red tape" and "regulatory burden," governments in most Western nations began to ditch many forms of regulation deemed to be in the way of (corporate) economic "progress," including "safeguards governing some forms of anti-social business activity, perhaps most notably worker safety" (Tombs and Whyte 2007, 158). According to Laureen Snider

Visions of Economic Grandeur

(2001, 112; 2000), it was during this time that corporate crime disappeared as both a concept and in law, washed away by knowledge claims that were "compatible with hegemonic interests" (Snider 2000, 181). Judy Fudge and Brenda Cossman (2002, 19-20) refer to this regulatory shift as a process of re-regulation, not full deregulation. It is not that the state got completely out of the regulation business but, rather, that it reconfigured its regulatory responsibilities in pro-business and pro-market ways. In particular, while the state preoccupied itself with befriending corporate capitalism, it was at the same time busy sharpening its regulatory teeth when it came to traditional street crimes (Fudge and Cossman 2002, 20; Tombs and Whyte 2007, 158).

Corporate culture, the so-called lynchpin of the free market system, therefore became something to be celebrated, even lionized, for its contributions to society. The neo-liberal message was (and is) that corporations are an unequivocal good, a mechanism that will contribute to society's overall well-being – profitable corporations are in everyone's best interests (Glasbeek 2002; Pearce and Snider 1995). This message, however, stands in stark contrast to the resistance that emerges when it is suggested that this same culture is responsible for untold harm and unlawful behaviour, per the comments in opposition to the NDP's proposed corporate culture approach to corporate criminal liability. In this respect, it is permissible to speak of the benefits of the free market culture and the essential role of the corporation therein but inappropriate to suggest that this same culture has a dark, harmful downside, especially for those injured or killed working on the corporation's behalf.

The ascendancy of neo-liberalism also reinforced the belief that an individual is free to choose how he or she wants to participate in the market (Fudge and Cossman 2002). From this perspective, workers submit freely to the conditions within which they work, and they are compensated accordingly for enduring unsafe conditions in the workplace (Tombs and Whyte 2007). Part of this neo-liberal mindset is that the market will self-regulate when it comes to unsafe workplaces, including the idea that companies will have a difficult time getting workers if things are too risky or dangerous. However, as one participant for this research suggested, this theory ignores the contradictory and unequal choices that many individuals face when trying to earn a living:

> Historically, you know, there's danger pay, there's the discourse ... in the law and economy ... about why bother regulating asbestos exposure because the economy will take care of it, workers won't want to work with it ... and that is still being, to some extent, there's some people that still believe that; that workers have sold their right to a healthy workplace because they are getting

good money. Well first of all they are not getting good money, and secondly, the idea that you can sell the right to a healthy environment is a morally difficult, difficult thing to accept. (Legal academic, Interview 19)

The common sense of neo-liberalism has provided a dominant political and economic frame for more than two decades. As Steve Tombs and Dave Whyte (2003a, 262-63) suggest, as the dominant "conventional wisdom," neo-liberal ideology contributes to the prevailing notion that "there is no alternative." Although questions about the free market economy abound following recent and ongoing examples of massive corporate fraud in both Canada and the United States (Laufer 2006; Resnick and Wolff 2010; Snider 2009), the commitment to neo-liberal political and economic ideals was alive and well in Canada's Parliament during discussion and debate of the Westray bill. It may be necessary in some circumstances to introduce new laws to regulate and govern the corporate form, dominant voices submitted, just as long as it does not interfere with the natural flow and function of the market economy and the essential role of the corporation therein.

Where Are the Captains of Industry?

As we examined in Chapter 2, the history of corporate crime law reform reveals a pattern of resistance by those from the corporate world to most new laws aimed at governing and controlling the corporate form (Carson 1970, 1980). Corporations have consistently and at times forcefully, if not blindly, voiced their concerns when confronted with the prospects of new laws perceived to be against the corporation's interests (Goff and Reasons 1978; Noble 1995; Snider 1978). The trend continues today in Canada and the United States with recent laws introduced in response to cases of massive corporate fraud, whereby corporate actors warn against the perils of government (legal) overreach, downplay the significance of legal measures to deal with corporate wrongdoing, and lobby for reduced enforcement levels (Lauter 2006; Snider 2009).

Contrary to historical examples of corporate actors openly voicing their concerns about the nature and scope of particular laws, representatives from corporate Canada were noticeably absent from the Westray bill reform process. While some participants suggested that many in the corporate world were simply unaware that Parliament was contemplating corporate criminal liability legislation (Criminal lawyer, Interview 5; Corporate lawyer, Interview 18), many others explained this absence in terms of how difficult it was for corporate actors to publicly state their opposition to workplace safety measures – that

Visions of Economic Grandeur

it was too great of a risk for such declarations given the negligence associated with the Westray disaster (Government official, Interview 1). As a government official suggested in discussing why corporate Canada did not appear before the Justice Committee: "I'm not sure I would want to go in there when talking about the Westray disaster, and all that stuff, and start talking about our directors ought not be liable, director chill, or words to that effect" (Government official, Interview 3). Several other participants also suggested that the business community was in a difficult position to lobby against the proposed law:

They were in a tricky situation ... I mean they couldn't ignore the fact that this was a serious consequence of negligence, corporate negligence ... So they had to be careful, I think, how they were lobbying the government. They couldn't say to the government, "we don't need anything," but I think they were trying to mitigate what the government put in place. (Union representative, Interview 12)

It was kind of a tricky issue, if I can be frank for a moment. It was tricky in one sense, because I think, especially for ... [organizations] ... that represent such a broad array of businesses ... So on the one hand one always ... wants to appear progressive and recognize what is going on, but can't be totally insensitive to issues and concerns of other members who may not be there, so I think that most business groups, and the reason most didn't write a lot of letters to the Minister of Justice and do other things, is I think most businesses thought this was a reasonable balance. I don't think frankly that anyone thought they could argue against it, effectively. I mean that would have been very difficult to put a credible position forward. Again, if some of the worst ideas from the Private Members' bill had found their way into this, then you would have seen more of a reaction. (Private sector representative, Interview 14)

Well, I don't know why it is [that the private sector did not appear before the Justice Committee], so it would only be speculation, and I want to make that point, but we [politicians] all speculated at the time that nobody wanted to be seen to be on the side of not taking responsibility for things that people should be held responsible for. Nobody with an obvious interest in the outcome – that is, some president of some company or some member of a board of directors of a company that could conceivably see themselves affected by this bill, nobody wanted to be on the public record saying, "I don't think that I should be responsible for this," and those sort of things. (Politician, Interview 15)

A union representative suggested that the absence of corporations from the reform process indicated their unwillingness to stand up to corporate wrongdoing. As he stated,

> unfortunately [it] reflects the unwillingness these days for corporations to take any responsibility for how other corporations behave ... By any standard what Westray did was utterly unacceptable in any other mining company, at least to the major players, some of the smaller places I'm not so sure. But it was a real opportunity for the industry to come out and say, "this kind of bottom feeding is not acceptable. We believe in complying with the law, we believe in health and safety, and we practice it." Not a single one spoke out. So, you know, they failed to show up. What does that mean? Is it arrogance, ignorance? Could be; it's sad though. (Union representative, Interview 9)

To underscore his point, he noted that the owners of the Westray mine, Curragh Resources, received the John T. Ryan award for coal mining safety just prior to the deadly explosion and that the sponsoring agency only rescinded it after receiving considerable pressure to do so from the unions.[3]

In many respects, the visible absence of corporate actors from the reform process speaks volumes to an inherent contradiction within corporate capitalism. Contrary to dominant claims of the corporate form's universal benefits, the fact that workers (not directors) are injured and killed in the workplace suggests otherwise (Glasbeek 2002). In addition to sounding cold and arrogant, standing up in public to argue against legal protections for workers would risk exposing the reality of this contradiction, drawing undue attention to the fact that workers suffer life and limb while the privileged few enjoy the fruits of their surplus labour.

Corporations Entered through the Back Entrance

Despite the absence of corporate actors from the formal reform process (particularly the Justice Committee hearings), there was some belief that they found alternative, less public ways to express their opinions about corporate criminal liability legislation to government. For some research participants, it seemed implausible that the corporate world remained completely silent about such a prominent issue. As one non-governmental organization (NGO) representative suggested,

> I think if you could see the true picture of what went on, the lobbying, they [corporate representatives] would have said look, this is the [NDP's]

Australian approach ... don't go down this road, make it more limited, because it is going to increase our costs if we have to change our corporate culture ... and they would have said things like we are going to get trouble getting directors. (NGO representative, Interview 2)

A union representative noted that corporations typically are not shy about sharing their opinions and postulated that they found other ways to share their thoughts with the government (Union representative, Interview 6). Another union representative agreed and argued that it was conceivable that at least some corporations found a way to express their concerns, even if they thought that the legislation was inevitable:

I'm sure [corporations lobbied]. I mean I wasn't there with them, but they were talking to the politicians of the day, as we were ... I don't think that corporations were trying to prevent the legislation. I think they were trying to mitigate the legislation, so it would have the least impact as possible. Let's put it this way, they didn't want it to have as much teeth as we wanted. And I don't think they wanted it to have as much teeth as it has, because what it does to them, it not only puts them in a situation where they know they can be held liable, corporations have the view that they totally want to be self-regulated, to the greatest fault possible. And they don't want any interference in what they do, and any regulation or legislation, even this being under the *Criminal Code,* puts a spoke in the wheel, I guess, in progress, because they always have to be doing more than what they would normally, and what they had traditionally done around some of these issues. (Union representative, Interview 12)

In responding to a question about whether corporations had an opportunity to express their views outside the Justice Committee's process, a politician responded: "Absolutely ... I believe there was, and I believe that's why some [members of parliament] were really cautious in how they approached [the private members' bill]" (Politician, Interview 11). She continued: "I think ... industry decided that it didn't want to get into the fray of the discussion at the [Justice] Committee, and let's just say that I knew there were meetings happening on the side" (Politician, Interview 11).

Another politician noted that private sector interests are always heard behind closed doors on just about any issue that makes its way through the political process – a matter of fact in the political world that all members of parliament (MPs) accept and work with, or around:

We watched what happens when the corporate forces get, you know, into the back rooms and get to influence things, and I think what you saw was pretty predictable – that every attempt would be made to either kill it or water it down. But it didn't succeed because it was too compelling for nothing to happen at all ... it just wasn't going to be allowed to happen for nothing, would have been horrible. In fact, we knew there were going to be compromises. If anything was going to succeed at all, it wasn't going to be as strong as it needed to be. You know, and that's sort of the art of the possible, to some extent in the political arena. There's no victories for holding out for the perfect piece of legislation and saying, you know, those bastards wouldn't allow it to happen if there is a possibility of making some headway through some compromises that will get you something. (Politician, Interview 20)

During one exchange in the House of Commons, NDP MP Alexa McDonough asked Canadian Alliance MP Jim Abbott about his concerns with the possibility that the legislation might die on the order paper if Parliament prorogued for an election and that the Liberal leader (then Paul Martin) was too pro-business to reintroduce the bill should his party be re-elected. While Abbott expressed concern with the potential for the legislation to fall by the wayside, he also stated that he was familiar with the pressures coming from the business world, referring to the fact that he was "approached by some people in businesses identical to Westray who were expressing a deep concern about this" and that he was "very much aware of the pressure that there is from corporate Canada" (Hansard, 15 September 2003, 17:25).

Although no representatives from the corporate world appeared before the Justice Committee, the Department of Justice Canada did organize consultations with representatives from corporations and umbrella organizations that represented different corporate sectors as part of their examination and drafting of the law (Government official, Interview 3). A private sector representative spoke of his involvement in this consultation process, at which he learned about the nature and scope of the proposed legislation and the rationale behind its introduction. He recalled being reassured by the message of legal restraint from government officials:

To be fair, I think, you know, the lawyers at justice tended to approach it from a fairly legalistic viewpoint, which [the new law] was to deal with these particular circumstances, these particular situations, there is a high burden of proof, you have to prove all of these elements in order to get a criminal conviction, you know presumably any crown is not going to be interested in

Visions of Economic Grandeur

launching a prosecution with a low likelihood of success because they're likely to be very costly prosecutions and it is not as though many crowns in many jurisdictions have a lot of experience in dealing with those issues. They'd have to delve into the inner workings of the corporations and codes of practice and employees, who's responsible for what and those sorts of things can become a fairly complex case. And presumably they are not going to launch a lot of those unless they feel they have a pretty strong case. (Private sector representative, Interview 14)

This individual also suggested that, based on his experience from the consultation process, the introduction of the Westray bill was not as much of a watershed moment for the corporate world as many observers suggested. As he noted, "I didn't get the sense that there were a lot of people out there [in the corporate world] that were worried that this was adding a huge new field of liability to the corporation" (Private sector representative, Interview 14). In this respect, there was a general understanding in the business community that there were some (limited) situations for which the existing criminal law was inappropriate and that certain reforms were necessary.

Corporations Are Always on My Mind

Regardless of whether there was any direct lobbying by corporations, concern for corporate interests – corporate common sense – permeated the reform process and shaped the nature and scope of the government's legislative approach. Several examples illustrate the fact that legislators had their corporate thinking caps on when it came to contemplating the proposed reforms. One politician suggested that the perspectives of the business world were always at the back of his mind:

I think you can just read a bill and know what the concerns [of corporations] would be. I don't remember anybody; in fact I can pretty much say that nobody ever called me ... specifically, as a business person, to say here is the problem with this bill. But there was a sort of an understanding that there were concerns, whether there were concerns maybe, and I don't remember, but maybe they were expressed publicly, but not at committee, by commentators or business people or whatever, but I think on my part I just knew in reading it that here's where they are going to have a problem. (Politician, Interview 15)

124   Chapter 5

Another politician admitted that her belief that corporate representatives lobbied other MPs influenced how she approached the reform process, particularly in terms of ensuring there was sufficient support to pass the new law:

> And knowing that [corporations were lobbying], I ... didn't stand as firm in some of the areas where I would have liked to have seen stronger legislation, because I wanted to have at least something [passed] and then we could work on that in the future. (Politician, Interview 11)

During question period, the minister of justice and attorney general of Canada thought it was "unfortunate" that the Justice Committee had not heard from the corporate community or from labour during its consideration of the private members' motion (Anne McLellan, Minister of Justice and Attorney General of Canada, Hansard, 9 May 2001, 14:40). Another MP admitted during question period that he used a corporate lens to examine the government's legislation: "Before getting into the pith and substance of the legislation, I would like to say that I examined this bill as my party's industry critic to see what impact it would have on the industry sector, while recognizing the fundamental merit of plugging a loophole in the *Criminal Code* that absolutely had to be plugged" (Paul Crête, Bloc Québécois, Hansard, 15 September 2003, 17:50).

Protecting Capital's Interests: Avoiding Director Chill

In addition to questions about "what would corporations think," there was ample articulation throughout the reform process of the common sense of corporate capitalism. In particular, concern with the impact of the law on corporations, or the notion that there would be strong resistance if the legislation "went too far," helped frame the reform process. Even if corporations were not present physically (at least publicly), they were most definitely present in spirit. Questions regarding the potential chilling effect of the NDP's private members' bill and whether overly stringent laws would drive corporations out of the country (or even out of business) were two ways in which the perspectives of corporations were well represented. Harry Glasbeek (2002, 13) refers to arguments against recent calls to hold corporate directors and officers to legal account as being groundless and "touched by arrogance." As Glasbeek argues,

there is unconcealed anger that law-makers are seeking to make directors
and officers of corporations, that is, corporate actors, answerable as if they
were ordinary mortals like you and me. There are vehement (unsupported)
claims that the best and brightest will no longer make themselves available
to serve corporations. Then we – the rest of us – would truly be sorry.
(Glasbeek 2002, 13)

In the case of the Westray bill, this anger and arrogance flowed through those
individuals with the responsibility for legislating against corporate illegality.

Consider, for example, the comments of two MPs, both of whom expressed
concern with the impact of corporate criminal liability law for the brightest
lights of the corporate world:

People become directors for a lot of reasons. Some of the reasons are very
good reasons and some of the reasons are not particularly good reasons.
You've [a witness at the Justice Committee] frequently used the phrase
"sending a message." I would suggest to you that by engaging in legislation,
we are sending a message. The message may not be heard in the same way by
all people at all times, particularly by directors who may well have to reconsider their positions as directors. (John McKay, Liberal, Justice Committee,
Hansard, 23 May 2002, 10:30)

We do not want to create the situation where we dissuade competent people
from being the directing minds of corporations. We want to encourage competent people who exercise sound skill and judgment to continue working
through the vehicle of corporations to ensure that jobs are preserved and
created in Canada. (Vic Toews, Canadian Alliance, Hansard, 20 September
2001, 18:05)

Some of the witnesses who testified before the Justice Committee expressed
similar sentiments. A criminal defence lawyer argued: "Whether it's a big
company or a small company, corporations are important. Some are offensive,
but corporations are important. You will not have people who want to be directors and officers. Then we're in a different state" (William Trudell, Justice
Committee, 28 May 2002, 11:55). A representative from the Canadian Bar
Association (CBA), a powerful and influential voice for lawyers in Canada with
a membership that includes lawyers from the corporate ranks, suggested that
the criminal law offers legislators the opportunity to send a clear message that
particular behaviours are unacceptable, but that this possibility creates certain

challenges when attempting to send such a message to corporations and corporate actors:

> Here are my remarks with respect to the possible chilling effect – it is of course the case that corporations must be competitive. Competitive corporations are essential to the vitality of the Canadian economy. Corporations must operate competitively within the domestic and international markets, and that requires dedicated and talented directors and employees. There's a concern that by casting too broad a net of liability, this could have a chilling effect. It could deter the participation of the people you would otherwise want to have acting in the capacity of director or officer, and that could result in less competitive corporations. This is an issue to consider, and it is a concern expressed particularly by the representatives of the CBA's business section. (Greg DelBiggio, CBA, Justice Committee, 23 May 2002, 11:05)

Shortly thereafter, the CBA witness once again raised the issue of director chill in response to a question from a Justice Committee MP:

> With respect to the question of director chill and whether or not good directors will stay, the CBA puts this forward as a consideration: it's a difficult issue. In fact, it is a question for which there might be empirical data, but there's no doubt that, in the face of increased risk, at least some people will be deterred. The extent of the weight of that which would be attached to that particular consideration is for you to decide. We, however, are of the view that there is little doubt that, in the face of increased risk, it will have a deterrent effect. It's not the case that good people will stay regardless of the risk. If there is an unfair risk, even good people will leave.[4] (Greg DelBiggio, CBA, Justice Committee, 23 May 2002, 11:05)

Another witness characterized the issue of director chill to the Justice Committee in dramatic terms: "I dreamt I came here and the bill had already been passed, and I was running to a phone to call all the persons I know who are directors of corporations to tell them to resign immediately before I was reported to the law society" (William Trudell, Canadian Council of Defence Lawyers, Justice Committee, 28 May 2002, 11:20). A committee MP seized the opportunity to agree with this comment, arguing that there would be "mass resignation of directors from corporations" the day after the new law was introduced: "I probably would agree with you [Mr. Trudell]. It would immensely, over time, have an adverse impact on the workers we're actually trying to protect" (John Maloney, Liberal, Justice Committee, 28 May 2002, 12:30).

The fear of offending corporate stalwarts was thus front and centre in the minds of many of those individuals participating in the reform process. Unfair targeting of corporate actors would negatively affect the Canadian economy, dominant voices suggested, and workers would be left jobless when corporations relocated or folded because they lacked the talent to compete in today's much celebrated global economy. The unfounded basis of this argument is evident from the fact that, despite examples of manslaughter convictions for corporate directors in the United Kingdom and the United States, many individuals continued to seek corporate directorships (Slapper and Tombs 1999, 22). Glasbeek (2002, 173-77) makes a similar point in examining the increased statutory responsibilities of directors and managers in recent years (for example, through new environmental and occupational health and safety regulations) – a trend that corporate directors see as raising their level of risks and responsibility. And yet, as Glasbeek notes, "famous and supposedly intelligent people are continuing to fall over themselves to become directors of large publicly traded corporations," and there is little evidence to suggest "any accelerated loss of directors due to resignations brought on by the increases in risk [related to any statutory responsibilities]" (176). A union representative noted the arrogance and inanity of the director chill argument when recalling his appearance before the Justice Committee:

> One of the Liberals raised the kind of director chill argument. A stupid argument, right ... I always had the notion ... the vision of this guy [who] goes down to the labour exchange. They are looking for corporate directors for ten thousand bucks a meeting, plus expenses, stock options, and he says, "I'm kind of worried about this potential criminal liability stuff. No, I'm going to hold out for that eight buck an hour job." (Union representative, Interview 6)

A stupid argument? Yes. Inconceivable? Apparently not.

In the end, the government's decision to jettison the corporate culture model in favour of an approach that holds all organizations to legal account – with provisions to punish individual executives and board members – assuaged any fears of a director chill. As a representative from the private sector stated, with some relief, when asked about the potential chilling effect of the NDP's legislation, corporations can be held liable, and that's my understanding about what's different with the law now, is that the corporation as an entity can be criminally responsible, but I don't believe that individual board members can be held criminally responsible. Unless there really is some, I assume unless there really is some proof that individual "A" on the board actually was involved in day-to-day operations, knew what was going on and either told the people to do the irresponsible thing or wilfully ignored what they must have known was going on. I'm not sure that that situation is likely to arise, but I guess potentially they could be held responsible. Yeah, that was my sense of one of the problems with at least one of the [NDP's] Private Members' bills ... because that's an obvious concern for corporations because how do you get people to serve on your board? (Private sector representative, Interview 14)

A corporate lawyer noted that the director chill argument is essentially void in the Westray bill given that it does not increase the personal liability of directors. From his perspective, the only way that people might be discouraged from becoming directors is if there were a number of convictions based on the actions of directors and senior officers, which he suggested might have a cumulative chilling effect:

In terms of director chill, I don't see it, because it hasn't increased individual liability of directors ... I suppose the only impact could be this, if there was a range of C-45 charges, let's hypothesize that in the next ten years there is a bunch of C-45 charges and the basis of the convictions is the actions of directors or senior officers. Although they are not personally liable, it is not really a career-maker to have brought down the corporation because of your actions. That might I suppose create some chill. (Corporate lawyer, Interview 7)

However, he quickly added that it seemed highly improbable that this will ever happen, particularly given the apparent lack of impetus to enforce the new law (an issue that is discussed further in Chapter 6).

Corporations Will Leave If We Are Not Careful

A related expression of concern for corporate capitalism surfaced through suggestions that corporations would leave the country in the face of overly stringent laws, a decision with potentially devastating effects for the economy,

Visions of Economic Grandeur   **129**

or so we are told. Corporations will threaten to relocate when confronted with new rules or laws that they perceived to be overly stringent or that will reduce profitability, or they will leverage favourable government policy decisions, such as reduced taxes or low interest loans. However, these threats are more apparent than real, with few corporations possessing the ability, or actual desire, to pack up and leave a particular country on a moment's notice. In addition to requiring access to a skilled workforce, something that is not always available in countries with cheap labour, many corporations face geographical constraints from the markets they need access to for purchasing materials and selling their products (Hirst and Thompson 1996, 198; Pearce and Tombs 1998). The primary resource industry is a good example, where a corporation's existence hinges on access to a country's natural resources, such as in mining, forestry, and oil production. In addition, corporations consider the "social, economic and political stability" of a country before deciding to set up shop (Pearce and Tombs 1998, 54).

In the context of the Westray bill, the sell job worked. Several MPs expressed their worries over legislation they perceived to be too stringent for those in the corporate world, and they feared that some corporations might leave Canada as a result. For example, Canadian Alliance MP Vic Toews argued that the NDP's bill would adversely affect "economic growth and jobs," investment, and add to the costs of production, although he acknowledged that safety should come before profit (Hansard, 20 September 2001, 18:00 and 18:05). Similarly, Reform MP Gary Lunn argued that the law would have "a serious impact on investment and would add dramatically to operating costs and consequently the profits and the motivation to expand. Employment levels in corporations would no doubt be reduced" (Hansard, 18 February 2000, 14:00). While recognizing the limits of the relocation argument, another MP suggested that

> you have to be very careful, if you believe all these Canadian corporations and companies are just going to stay around if we put in something that's a little too tough on them. I'm not suggesting that's what you've been proposing here. But I can tell you, there are many companies right now who look at our tax laws and other laws and are on the verge of heading somewhere else. Obviously, our resource-rich country means that a lot of them have to stay here, because this is where the resources are. (Kevin Sorenson, Canadian Alliance, Justice Committee, 2 May 2002, 12:20)

Concern for corporations also emerged in terms of the negative impact that criminal sanctions would have for a convicted corporation. As one MP responded to a witness who argued that there may be occasion when a suitable penalty would be to shut down a corporation, "one of the sanctions you suggest could be corporate capital punishment. I wonder how you justify that to the 50, 100, or 500 other employees of that firm" (John Maloney, Liberal, Justice Committee, 22 May 2002, 16:50). The MP added that holding directors criminally liable would reduce the corporation's competitive advantage, which would not be in anyone's interests, employees and employers alike. As the MP quipped, "why would anybody in their right mind want to be a director? How would this affect the competitive advantage of corporations and the economic seas companies have to negotiate these days, to the benefit of all, employees, shareholders, officers, and directors?" (John Maloney, Liberal, Justice Committee, 22 May 2002, 16:50). Another MP argued that holding corporations to legal account would disrupt the economy: "The economics of Westray were such that had someone gone out and said, this has to be shut down, and they were going to be fined appropriately, as an alternative method of punishment, it would have also put them out of business and would have collapsed the economic process" (Paul Harold Macklin, Liberal, Justice Committee, 8 May 2002, 16:20).

Corporations are the most effective and efficient means of generating wealth, according to these dominant voices. This is particularly so in neo-liberal times when the state enthusiastically embraces the role of ensuring the smooth flow of capital and wherein the government relies on corporations to carry the bulk of the country's economic load (Pearce and Tombs 1998). As such, governments are in a difficult position when it comes to disciplining the very mechanism that they helped catapult to such prominence.

Hesitant Resistance

> Well, look, if you cannot run a safe workplace, then go. The only possible response to that is if the only way you can run this place is unsafe, that you are going to be vulnerable to criminal charges because it is that unsafe, it's not worth killing people for. It really doesn't hold up. I have never seen any place that shuts down, they shut down for all kinds of reasons: the dollar going up, labour costs, yeah, and a variety of other things. But I've never seen anybody present the notion on the ground ... [that] it's the health and safety environment that is putting us in trouble. (Union representative, Interview 6)

The dominance of pro-capitalist discourse does not mean that there was a wholesale purchase of the suggestion that corporations need to be protected from undue legislative intrusion. Various MPs, union representatives, and some academics offered counter-hegemonic perspectives throughout the reform process. Take, for example, the following comments from different NDP MPs:

It is not a justifiable excuse for CEOs to say their work is in the office, that they have never set foot in the plant or that it is only one of many enterprises they have under their direction and control. That is no excuse. The buck should not stop at the frontline manager who works in the plant where the offence might have taken place. The buck stops at the CEO's desk. If CEOs do not know what is happening in their plants they have an obligation to know. (Pat Martin, NDP, Hansard, 8 November 2001, 18:20)

It's interesting to me that a lot of our economic freedom is based on this equivalency between corporations and persons when it comes to freedom, but when it comes to responsibility, all of a sudden there's a big difference and they can't be held responsible in the same way. (Bill Blaikie, NDP, Justice Committee, 2 May 2002, 10:05)

I'm a little disturbed that I'm actually hearing around this table that somehow, by wanting to improve a system where corporations, directors, and managers should be held accountable if they are found to have neglected the lives or the well-being of employees or others, that's moving backward ... From the earliest of times we have had this economic argument that corporations and industries can't survive if they have to meet what I think many of us have seen as progressive changes, decreasing the hours of work, putting in place safety standards, putting in place employment equity standards, making sure certain safe practices were put into the workplace. Somehow these are seen as always too much of a cost for industry, yet most corporations and industries survived just fine with these rules, and they don't have to neglect the rules. (Bev Desjarlais, NDP, Justice Committee, 7 May 2002, 12:25)

Similar counter-hegemonic perspectives came from some of the witnesses appearing before the Justice Committee, particularly those supporting the NDP's corporate culture model. As one witness argued during her presentation,

we need to recognize organizational culture as something people make and remake on a daily basis, and that deaths like those in the Westray mine are not the inevitable outcomes of things left undone. It's not a matter of neglect, but of the consequences of positive acts, of choices made in pursuit of profit, and these days, of increasingly deregulated workplaces. Often the authors of those choices are hidden within the black box of the corporate hierarchy, and this black box is a culture within which corporate decision-makers decide on the priorities of the organization. If this government wants people to believe there is justice in this country, it will need to draw on the rich literature on corporate criminology and develop ways to either shed light on the contents of such black boxes or to compensate for this lack of transparency by finding means to discipline the corporation as if it were an agent in its own right. (Susan Dodd, Sociologist, Justice Committee, 22 May 2002, 15:45)

Regardless of this resistance, there was general recognition of the inevitability of corporate capitalism and that this dominant frame, or common sense, limited the reform options. This perspective was most obvious in comments from those struggling over balancing the goal of enacting new legislation with the need to protect corporate interests. For example, the sponsor of the private members' motion, Peter MacKay, recognized that any legislative measures must consider the potential financial impact for corporations, particularly during competitive economic times (Peter MacKay, Justice Committee, 6 June 2000, 10:45). Likewise, a non-governmental organization (NGO) representative, who criticized the lack of corporate accountability, suggested that increased regulation would undoubtedly produce extra compliance costs for corporations and therefore discourage economic growth:

They [politicians] don't want to be truthful and say ... "We are in a dilemma. We have a trading economy and we have signed on to a bunch of free trade deals, and it means that we can't regulate our corporations." And you don't even see the NDP or the Greens speak about this reality, and this reality is a big problem. We know in these big areas there are hundreds and thousands of Canadians that have jobs, and we as a government do not want to threaten those jobs. But at the same time, everyone else should realize, and the workers should realize too, we can't even regulate the health and safety of those workers, really. *So we are in a really difficult position here.* (NGO representative, Interview 2 [emphasis added])

A NDP MP also noted the difficult position of legislators in trying to hold corporations to account without upsetting the economy:

One thing to keep in mind is that there is a fine line to be walked between accountability and the public interest. For example, sometimes it would not

make sense to indict a corporate director or other people in corporate management and impose massive criminal fines if those fines meant having to
wind up a company which employs 500 people to meet those liabilities. It is
important to note that in a situation where a corporation is only competitive
because of its low operating costs which were achieved only at the expense of
worker safety, for example, a sweatshop, it may be in the best interests of the
public to completely liquidate the company. (Lorne Nystrom, NDP, Hansard,
15 September 2003, 16:25)

The common sense of corporate capitalism was thus firmly rooted in the sensibilities and mentalities of many of those involved in the reform process. While
not denying that there may be cause to hold some corporations to account,
the prevailing belief that corporations are essential for the proper functioning
of Canadian society meant that any reform options that were given serious
consideration needed to be carefully crafted so as to not upset the corporate
status quo.

Responsibilizing Workplace Safety

Neo-liberal and corporate interests also dominated discussions of responsibility
for workplace safety. Along with the prominence of neo-liberal political ideals
comes the triumph of individualism – the notion that we are all economic
beings who are equally equipped to make rational and prudent choices (Barry,
Osborne, and Rose 1996; Fudge and Cossman 2002; Pearce and Snider 1995).
From this perspective, an individual can choose freely whether to participate
in the market, including the choice of entering into contractual relationships
for work (Fudge and Cossman, 1996, 21-22). Workers are equal market participants who are free to work for whomever they want, under whatever conditions they choose, and they receive appropriate remuneration based on the
skills needed to complete the work and the risks involved in the job (Pearce
and Tombs 1998, 16). However, this dominant rhetoric ignores the premise of
capitalist arrangements in which those who own the means of production aim
to extract maximum surplus labour from the production process – to essentially
squeeze as much free labour as possible from workers to maximize profits.
What is more, today's global economy amplifies this dynamic in that control
of the workplace rests primarily in the hands of the privileged few and workers
confront increasingly precarious and decreasingly unionized working conditions over which they have little control (Pearce and Tombs 1998, 23-24; see
also Cranford et al. 2005).

In addition to the fact that most workers are not paid all that well for what they do, particularly within a context of stagnated wages for workers compared to the handsome salaries of corporate directors, or for the risks that they take (and one has to ask why it is acceptable for someone to be paid for the potential to be injured or killed), control of the workplace directly relates to one's ability to mediate risks (Resnick and Wolff 2010). Even in instances where employers and employees co-operate to address workplace safety issues, such as through joint health and safety committees, these arrangements are often dysfunctional and change little in terms of the ability of employees to ultimately control their work environment (Tucker 1995a, 2007). In addition, as the Westray example clearly highlights, workers die when they are so desperate to find and keep employment that they believe they have little choice but to continue working in overwhelmingly unacceptable conditions (Jobb 1994; Richard 1997).

There has been much written in recent years about the impact of neo-liberalism on traditional forms of crime and its control (Garland 1999, 2001; Shearing 2001). According to David Garland (2001, 124-26), neo-liberal crime control strategies divest responsibility for crime from the state to the individual, a process that he refers to as responsibilization. Obscuring the broader structural factors of crime, including the socially constructed notion of what constitutes crime, responsibilization strategies abstract the individual from his or her social circumstances and challenge them to act in a "prudent" manner (Hannah-Moffat 2001, 522; Rose 2000, 327). However, contrary to official claims that everyone has an equal opportunity to enjoy economic success, the growing disparity between the rich and poor over the past two decades suggests otherwise (Fudge and Cossman 2002). In the Canadian context, the asymmetry of these opportunities means that the affluent enjoy unparalleled (economic) freedom and opportunity, while marginalized populations – for example, lower-class, racialized, and Aboriginal peoples – are subject to increasing surveillance and control (Boyd, Chunn, and Menzies 2001).

Within the context of occupational health and safety, neo-liberal responsibilization strategies play out in a similar manner in that they reduce the burden of responsibility for workplace safety for those in positions of power (particularly those who own and control the means of production) and spread it across the entire workplace, emphasizing the role of the individual worker in preventing his or her own injury or death. Garry Gray (2006, 2009) observes that the workplace is going through a process of responsibilization in that workers are increasingly the subject of regulatory health and safety enforcement. Gray (2009, 330) examines Ontario's health and safety ticketing program, which provides for the ticketing of both workers and employers (which Gray likens to a parking fine) for health and safety violations. In particular, he finds that the ticketing patterns of labour inspectors reveals that "health and safety ticketing falls more heavily on frontline workers than high-risk employers" (336). In effect, responsibility is pushed down the corporate ladder, rendering the worker responsible for guarding against his or her own victimization.

Tombs and Whyte (2007, 74-80) refer to the dominant discourse of the "accident prone worker" as a subtle, yet insidious, form of victim blaming. As an entrenched part of the occupational health and safety lexicon, the notion that workers are prone to accidents – whether through "incompetence, carelessness, apathy, recklessness and so on" – results in the individualization of safety crimes, putting the onus on the individual worker to address his or her victimization (75). In the process, the authors note, the structural causes of workplace safety, including the relationship between workplace accidents and the pressures of profitability, remain untouched. Instead of addressing the root causes of workplace injury and death, individual workers face increased surveillance and regulation.

Shared Responsibility for Workplace Safety

Throughout the Justice Committee hearings, there was frequent reference to the importance of shared responsibility – the idea that if people wanted responsibility for workplace safety, then responsibility they would get, as long as everyone – workers, unions, and employers – accepted this expectation equally. Comments from different MPs illustrate the perception that workplace safety is a shared responsibility, not just the bailiwick of those who own and control the means of production. Of particular concern was the idea that workers and unions accept their share of responsibility.

In discussing his private members' motion, PC MP Peter MacKay suggested that corporations needed to consider the input and knowledge of workers when it comes to workplace safety. At the same time, however, he argued that workers must share "culpability and responsibility," although he recognized it was not a "politically popular thing to say" (Hansard, 23 April 1999, 12:30). Another MP similarly argued that, although not "politically popular," it was important to understand that workers share "culpability and responsibility" and that any legislative reform should "ensure that accountability and responsibility are held by all" (Inky Mark, PC, Hansard, 15 September 2003, 16:20). During the Justice Committee's hearings over the private members' motion, another MP suggested that negligence applies to everyone equally and also that workers must bear responsibility for workplace safety:

There's no question in my mind that Westray must never happen again. It's just that I'm trying to say that although we can quote statistics of how many people die a day, it would be difficult to say if a person died of their own negligence or because of someone else's negligence. Most important here is to come up with a resolution in law that is well done, well researched, and appropriate. (Aileen Carroll, Liberal, Justice Committee, 6 June 2000, 11:05)

The interventions of one Justice Committee MP underscore the suggestion that workers bear responsibility for ensuring their own safety. In responding to a witness who suggested that employers should ensure that workers receive adequate training, Conservative Alliance MP Kevin Sorenson argued that workers should simply refuse to work in unsafe conditions:

So there's no responsibility on that worker to say, listen, I haven't been adequately trained here? I realize that at Westray it was totally different, but you're saying that never is there any responsibility on the worker to say, I'm not picking up this equipment, because I have not been trained on it. (Justice Committee, 22 May 2002, 16:25)

At another juncture, Sorenson questioned a former Westray worker about shared responsibility. Vern Theriault had just finished sharing his experiences at the Westray mine with the Justice Committee, explaining how management had bullied employees and undermined workplace safety. It was an emotional presentation that affected all of the MPs on the committee. Towards the end of the session, Sorenson asked Theriault about the Murphy switch on mining machines, a mechanism that detects methane gas levels in the mine and automatically turns the machine off when it senses dangerous levels. Theriault noted how it was common practice to disconnect the Murphy switch to ensure uninterrupted production, something that was condoned by management. The following exchange ensued:

Kevin Sorenson: My concern is this. The legislation we see here mentions directors, those involved. It mentions management, it mentions directors of the company, and any of those individuals way down the chain. What happens if all of a sudden, included with this, they were to include you?
Vern Theriault: To include me for blame?
Kevin Sorenson: Well, yes, because –

Visions of Economic Grandeur

Vern Theriault: Actually, they themselves tried to blame the miners. I've been blamed too, in a way, but if everybody else down the line is going to take the charge for it, I'll get the blame too.

Kevin Sorenson: But was it management that unhooked the Murphy switch, or could it have been a worker who just went over and said, "I'm getting tired of this" and unhooked. (Justice Committee, 2 May 2002, 12:25)

From this exchange, it is clear that an "ideology of individual responsibility" animated the discussion and debate about assigning responsibility for workplace safety (Walters et al. 1995, 285).

Notions of shared responsibility also surfaced in reference to union culpability for workplace safety.[5] Pearce and Tombs (1998, 58) note that "continuous antagonisms between capital and labour" characterizes capitalist relations. To ensure maximum profits, corporations attempt to control the production process to the greatest extent possible. As a result, relations between corporations and labour often are strained as corporations attempt to extract maximum surplus labour (and, hence, profit) from workers. With the dominance of neoliberal political and economic reasoning, the balance of power between capital and labour has tilted in capital's favour. In particular, it means that corporations have self-regulated (and self-controlled) the workplace, becoming the most logical and effective mechanism for undertaking this task (150).

With the push and pull between capital and labour as the backdrop, it was problematic (even antagonistic) for unions to argue for legislation with the potential to alter the workplace in favour of workers' rights and in a manner that is beyond the control of those who own the means of production. For those individuals espousing pro-corporate ideals, it was a difficult pill to swallow for labour to dictate the nature of the production process, particularly in suggesting that directors are ultimately responsible for ensuring workplace safety. In response, many legislators argued that unions must also accept their share of responsibility for workplace safety. For example, Canadian Alliance MP Vic Toews expressed concern with the possibility that unions would not be held to the same level of accountability as corporations:

I have concerns with some of the comments I heard, and hopefully, matters will be clarified, either in your comments here today or in the documentation. Let's start on the first point. Unions participate in management decisions; there is joint management of certain areas. If unions are aware of certain oversights of the law, should they be held to the same standard you're proposing corporations be held to? They, in many respects, are very similar to a corporate entity, with the same kinds of problems about the entity and the individuals under it. I'd specifically like to hear from you on that, because I think we want to ensure that our workplaces are safe. Should all of those involved have that level of responsibility you're seeking to impose as corporate responsibility? (Justice Committee, 7 May 2002, 11:25)

In answering Toews' question, the presenter noted that anyone involved in the management's structure would be responsible for workplace safety. Toews pressed further: "So some of the recommendations on corporate liability you made may well be applicable to unions in regard to the standards of mental intent required?" The presenter had little choice but to agree with this line of inquiry (exchange between Vic Toews and Duff Conacher, Corporate Responsibility Coalition, Justice Committee, 7 May 2002, 11:25-11:30).

A similar concern about union responsibility emerged shortly thereafter, when a representative from the Ottawa and District Labour Council noted the ineffective and dysfunctional nature of joint health committees, which would make it difficult and inappropriate to try and hold unions to account. An MP from the Bloc Québécois replied:

It is obvious that we must look at the criminal responsibility of corporate entities, but we must not forget that unions are also corporate entities. I am a little surprised to hear you say that it should be applied to one but not to the other. I think we should have laws that will apply to all corporate entities and take care in the drafting and implementation of those laws. (Robert Lanctôt, Bloc Québécois, Justice Committee, 7 May 2002, 11:30)

Shared responsibility also emerged during the testimony of representatives from the United Steelworkers of America (Steelworkers), in which an MP asked the following question:

So if there were evidence that even if the recommendation wasn't followed, the union simply went along with it, didn't go [to] the workplace safety and health officer in the province to file a complaint, were just silent and moved along, should the union or union officials not be liable? (Vic Toews, Justice Committee, 8 May 2002, 15:55)

The union representative answered "no" to the question, arguing that unions are not part of the decision-making process of corporate executives or boards. The MP replied:

Visions of Economic Grandeur

I understand that, but should they be considered part of the management process? Unions, and rightly so, hold a very important role in the workplace. The power of a union official to make a recommendation and then to bring in government officials is a necessary power, an important power.[6] (Vic Toews, Justice Committee, 8 May 2002, 15:55)

Although politically right-leaning MPs most commonly raised the spectre of union responsibility, other MPs also cited this issue. As a Liberal MP stated to a witness,

I'm a little disappointed in your not wanting unions to take any responsibility in this. Before I became smart enough to run my own company, I worked for a very large company where health and safety were the primary concern. They said it paid in the end. That was their philosophy, but I know of companies where, if a worker feels he's doing something that's unsafe, he goes to his union steward, and the steward passes it on. He should pass it on, but if he doesn't and nothing happens, if the employee's told to go back to his work, that union steward would have no responsibility, even though it was in the agreement that it was his duty to report that. I think he has an equal responsibility with the plant management or even the director of the company. (Ivan Grose, Liberal, Justice Committee, 8 May 2002, 16:40)

At times, debates about shared responsibility focused on who controls the production process. In one exchange, a Justice Committee MP pressed a union representative with the idea that unions share responsibility for workplace safety. Although the representative agreed with the notion that, in certain circumstances, a union member might be responsible for workplace accidents, he underscored the fact that shop stewards have little power to control the work environment (that is, to stop production for safety concerns). The MP disagreed, suggesting that shop stewards oftentimes have more power than plant managers: "I don't think you've ever seen a CAW shop steward in action. Believe me, some days the plant manager doesn't have much influence" (Ivan Grose, Liberal, Justice Committee, 8 May 2002, 16:40-16:45). Immediately following this exchange was a statement by another MP regarding union responsibility:

Continuing on, because I'd like to come full circle on this, I understand very clearly most of what you said. However, if the board of directors follows a union recommendation that proves to be unsound, or if the union fails to make a wise recommendation, then you're telling me that the union cannot be prosecuted as a body corporate. The union, which operates in close proximity to its members, may do nothing or make a poor recommendation that the board of directors implements. Why not include every eventuality at this time? When will we come back to a bill such as this? In my opinion, we have a duty to protect all workers. If, as you said, it's possible to shut down a mine or a plant before a worker dies, then why not consider all of these possibilities now? It's not that we absolutely want unions to be held accountable, not by any means, but if we tell the corporate managers and directors who testify before our committee that unions are to be fully excluded, we'll certainly hear both sides of the story. However, if we propose some compromises and arrive with a suggestion like this – and there are certainly others – it would demonstrate your good faith without putting you in a difficult position. Your job is to protect your workers. (Robert Lanctôt, Bloc Québécois, Justice Committee, 8 May 2002, 16:45 [translation from the Justice Committee's transcript])

As these comments suggest, antagonisms between labour and capital over who controls the workplace informed the debate over responsibility for workplace safety. Confronted with the prospects of having the balance of power altered, by introducing criminal legislation that would potentially threaten the dynamic of corporate self-regulation, the dominant reaction was to argue that everyone needed to accept responsibility for ensuring workplace safety – to spread responsibility across the entire workplace to ensure that it did not fall solely to those at the higher end of the corporate ladder.

Objections to Shared Responsibility

Despite the dominance of neo-liberal notions of shared responsibility, some legislators (particularly left-wing politicians) took umbrage with the suggestion that workers and unions share the blame for workplace injury and death. For example, NDP MP Wendy Lill argued:

It is difficult for me to understand why some are opposing the bill. After all it does have a noble and practical objective ... I would hate to think that anyone in this place would believe that a corporation or a boss should be above the law simply because of status. I hope that all members would condemn that notion. I have heard from some who oppose the legislation. They believe workers in Canada are protected from dangerous workplaces and predatory actions from bosses because they can always refuse to work. That argument is basically that it is the victim's fault. That argument is not only immoral and offensive, it is also inaccurate. (Hansard, 8 November 2001, 17:35)

Similarly, NDP MP Bill Blaikie referred to suggestions that workers and unions should share responsibility for workplace safety equally with corporate executives and board members as "spurious and vaguely malicious" (Justice Committee, 9 May 2002, 10:20). As Blaikie commented,

I think it would be regrettable if somehow we got off on this path of discussion of what the liability of unions is with respect to accidents in the workplace. I'm sure people in the trade union movement would be glad to accept responsibility once they were granted the same amount of power over the workplace as management, but that's clearly not the case in the law or in the way corporations are run. I think this is something of a blind alley we're going up. (Justice Committee, 8 May 2002, 16:10)

I do urge the [Justice] committee not to forget what we have been charged with, the subject matter of the private member's bill, a bill intended to address the situation that was reported on with recommendations by Justice Richard following the Westray mine disaster. I don't recall there being any dimension of this that had to do with the culpability of workers or unions or any esoteric points that can somehow turn this into a discussion about how people who don't have any power over the workplace, who don't own it, who don't manage it and don't run it can somehow be made the object of this committee's work. (Justice Committee, 9 May 2002, 10:20)

Unfortunately, however, these dissenting voices paled in comparison to the dominant perspective that workplace safety was the responsibility of everyone, not just those with decision-making powers. The comments by a Conservative Alliance MP encapsulate this prevailing ideal:

One of the things we need to be sure of is that there is a sense of fair play in the bill and that it addresses both sides of the equation. It's an issue that has been raised at this committee a number of times. It basically deals with union culpability and the culpability of union officials. For example, if a union official fails to observe his or her legal obligations – and I'm talking about legal obligations that we see in places like the Workplace Safety and Health Act, and of course, you're familiar with the Manitoba act – should that disregard, where there is the appropriate degree of criminal intent, carry a similar criminal intent? That's the question I think many of us are going to be asked about in this bill. (Vic Toews, Justice Committee, 9 May 2002, 10:05)

Overall, notions of responsibilization place the onus on the individual to take control of his or her environment, to make the prudent decision to behave appropriately and in accordance with certain rules and normative standards. However, since we are not all "equally located structurally," these decisions have different applications depending on one's social location (Morrison 1995, 213). And with the growing precariousness of work in contemporary society, along with the declining number of unionized workplaces, it is increasingly difficult for workers to control decisions in the workplace (Cranford et al. 2005; Tucker 1995a, 253). In addition, given the very different structural location of employers and employees, responsibility in the corporate context means that individual workers bear the greatest burden for ensuring workplace safety, while the corporation and its senior executives remain hidden behind the corporate veil, making all of the decisions and reaping the greatest rewards while taking the fewest risks (at least in terms of life and limb) (Gray 2006, 2009; Tombs and Whyte 2007). Despite claims of equality embedded within notions of shared responsibility (who can argue against the idea of everyone ensuring workplace safety), the reality is that this sharing is anything but symmetrical, favouring those in positions of power who have the capacity to avoid the law's reach.

The Definition of Organization

Following from dominant notions of shared responsibility, the government's legislation differed from the NDP's private members' bill in that it abandoned reference to corporation in favour of organization. While the NDP's proposed bill explicitly refers to "offences by corporations, directors and officers," the government's legislation employs the much broader notion of "public body, body corporate, society, company, firm, partnership, trade union or municipality." Although the definition of organization applies to the entire *Criminal Code* – that is, it is used for purposes beyond the Westray bill – some research participants argued that this difference was a legal sleight of hand with particular effects, both ideologically and ontologically, for workers and unions. As Todd Archibald, Kenneth Jull, and Kent Roach (2004, 375) state, "the explicit reference to [organizations] in this legislation sends a green light to policing bodies and private complainants that they may now become potential targets."

One union representative expressed concern with the potential impact of the definition of organization for unions and employees, wondering if there is now a risk that they will be held criminally culpable for workplace injury and death (Union representative, Interview 16). Another union representative expressed concern that unions will be responsible for workplace accidents, noting that unions and employees have little decision-making control over the organization:

> Basically we wanted the legislation to go after corporate bosses, basically, because they're the ones that make the decisions. At the end of the day any decision that's made on anything to do with the business comes about as a result of management's decision. It doesn't come about because of a union decision. We wish, but it doesn't. They have the ultimate authority to manage, and that authority is only restricted by terms of a collective agreement, and in very few cases, maybe in terms of regulations or legislation. So we were hoping that it would focus more on criminal liability for those that have the power to make decisions. But in reality what it does is that it will hold anybody accountable if the investigation shows there was any part played in any particular incident by anybody from the janitor right up to the CEO. Now some people will argue, why not? Well normally, in my experience in almost forty years, is that any decision made by the janitor is usually something that is usually handed down from above, right. And there are very few cases where you could actually cite where somebody at that level had any type of malicious intent to do anything to cause harm. (Union representative, Interview 12)

Despite this concern, most union representatives supported the Westray bill given that it addressed issues of corporate liability. As one union representative noted,

> if there was something beyond corporations it would be worth addressing, but it's not. The corporation is the problem, but they [government] expanded the coverage beyond the corporate identity to include those who do not have an individual identity. So a non-profit, any kind of organization could potentially get scooped-up in [the new law], which we think is both a mistake and will be a source of problems for the legislation going forward. But since it did have clearly corporate responsibility in it as well, then it's okay ... because the notion that a charity, a hospital, or even a union has somehow got the

same kind of issues and responsibilities as a corporation is odd, to say the least. (Union representative, Interview 9)

Another union representative similarly suggested that the expanded definition of organization was worth the risk to ensure the legislation's enactment:

> Most of the time, the union is not in the position to stop it [an accident] happening anyway. We don't direct the workplace. The employer directs the workplace. By benefit of some case of legislation, certainly on the health and safety side ... we can put certain limits on what the employer does, but very, very rarely can we actually force the employer to do anything that isn't sort of a statutory requirement. The employer organizes the workplace. I guess you are always concerned that they are going to find the scapegoat. They will find the supervisor, if they can get to be the co-worker doing the unsafe things, they [the corporation] will do it. So there is always that possibility. (Union representative, Interview 16)

Although this individual believed the legislation was a step forward in terms of corporate criminal liability, he also expressed trepidation with the historic reality that the law works to the advantage of powerful corporations, leaving workers to assume responsibility and pay the price for unsafe work conditions.

Economic Discourses at Work

Intertwined with the legal discourses that we examined in Chapter 4, dominant notions of the economy limited the reform options that were given serious consideration. Although there was general support for the introduction of corporate criminal liability legislation, concerns with the potential impact for the economic well-being of corporations tempered any enthusiasm for this law. The dominant voices argued that we need to be careful when attempting to hold corporate actors and corporations to legal account. We must ensure that any law that we introduce is not too strict or overly intrusive to the point that it impedes corporate capital's wealth-generating capacity, or so we were told. We will all be sorry, they argued, if the best and the brightest no longer want to serve as corporate directors because of the legal risks involved or if corporations pack up and leave when confronted with overly stringent laws.

Despite the absence of corporate Canada from the reform process (at least in terms of a visible presence), pro-corporate legislators and some witnesses appearing before the Justice Committee represented the interests of corporations. Similar to the framing of the debate through legal discourse, these voices were not part of any concerted or organized effort to resist corporate criminal liability legislation – even if the claims of backdoor politics involving corporations were vaguely instrumentalist in their implications. The (re)production of capitalist relations of power is not so omnipotent or automatic; otherwise the Westray bill would never have come to fruition. On the contrary, it was a commitment to neo-liberal common sense that informed perspectives regarding the importance of the corporation as society's vital wealth-generating mechanism (Glasbeek 2002). The ascendancy of neo-liberal ideals, along with the power of corporate capital, over the past three decades has contributed to the prevailing assumption that corporations are the most "efficient way of organizing production" (Pearce and Tombs 1998, 5), leading to the dominant belief that there are few (if any) alternatives to "the global expansion of neo-liberal capitalism" (Tombs and Whyte 2003c, 262-63). And while some of this corporate cheerleading is more subdued today in the wake of serious and ongoing cases of corporate fraud in Canada and the United States, pro-corporate ideals were most definitely present and accounted for in the Westray bill context.

The hegemony of pro-capital ideals provided a powerful reference for shaping the state's corporate crime law reform process. Hegemony, according to Antonio Gramsci (1971, 244; as quoted in Pearce and Tombs 1989, 36) is the "entire complex of practical and theoretical activities within which the ruling class not only justifies and maintains its dominance, but manages to win the active consent of those over whom it rules." The capitalist class maintains and (re)produces its hegemonic position in society through the formation of historical blocks, which occurs when those with the ability to extract surplus from the economy convince others "to accept its moral and political leadership and to both accept and contribute to its mode of governance. This block must be constituted, to some extent, in and through the state" (Tombs and Whyte 2003c, 10). This is what happened in the case of the Westray bill, and it explains how, and why, dominant voices supported particular legislative perspectives. In essence, the political sensibilities of corporate capitalism formed an essential component of the reform agenda, acting as the dominant ideology from which to evaluate options for corporate criminal liability law (10).

In addition to these economic ideals, dominant voices repeatedly characterized workplace safety as the responsibility of workers, labour, and unions as much as (or more than) management and executives. In particular, workplace accidents were seen as a result of defective low-level employees – not bad corporate management, malign corporate culture, or profit-maximizing strategies. There are no structural flaws in corporate capitalism. As Glasbeek (2002) has said, they looked for the rotten apples in the barrel, not at whether the barrel itself was rotten.

Focusing on individual responsibility coheres with neo-liberal beliefs that individuals are free to choose the conditions within which they work, thereby obscuring the broader context within which decisions about workplace safety are made (Pearce and Tombs 1989, 133). An ideology of individual responsibility directs legislative attention down the hierarchy, not up, ignoring the power gap between workers, unions, and bosses and the structural/legal realities that give executives and management the right to set production targets, shut down the plant, and hire, lay off, and fire workers. Senior management reaps the lion's share of the benefits of not fixing the unsafe workplace; employees take the lion's share of the risks. Corporate harm and wrongdoing become a shared problem, not an artifact of corporate culture and most definitely not "the natural by-product of the pursuit of the corporate capitalist agenda" (Glasbeek 2002, 4).

At its heart, discussion and debate regarding shared responsibility is about which parties, interests, and agendas control the workplace. While corporations hold themselves up in official discourse as having everyone's best interests in mind – including workers, unions, and the general public – in actuality it is the privileged few who enjoy the bulk of the corporation's financial rewards (Glasbeek 2002; Pearce and Tombs 1998; Snider 2008). Putting forward the mirage of shared responsibility as a basis of corporate criminal liability therefore ensures that this myth is (re)produced, effectively downplaying attempts to pierce the corporate veil to expose the inherent contradictions of the modern corporate form.

6

Obscuring Corporate Crime and the Corporate Criminal

Between crimes that are characteristically committed by poor people (street crimes) and those characteristically committed by the well-off (white-collar and corporate crimes), the system treats the former much more harshly than the latter, even when the crimes of the well-off take more money from the public or cause more death and injury than the crimes of the poor.

– Jeffery Reiman (2004, 146 [emphasis in original])

Everyone grows up "knowing" what crime is. From a very early age children develop social constructions of robbers and other criminal characters who inhabit our social world. But in reality there is nothing intrinsic to any particular event or incident which permits it to be defined as a crime. Crimes and criminals are fictive events and characters in the sense that they have to be constructed before they can exist.

– Paddy Hillyard and Steve Tombs (2004, 11)

They're Not Really Criminals, Are They?

The previous two chapters explored how various legal and economic discourses constituted corporate criminal liability and, with it, corporate crime. Overlapping and "mutually reinforcing," these discourses limited the reform options to which legislators gave serious consideration and, in the process, raised questions about the culpability of workplace injury and death (Tombs and Whyte 2007). Dominant voices claimed that criminal law is an ill-fitted and misplaced tool to deal with corporate wrongdoing and decried that corporations and corporate actors are too important to be treated harshly or subject to overly stringent laws. Corporations are a vital wealth-generating mechanism, or so we were told, so handle with care.

This chapter further interrogates the constitution of corporate criminal liability by considering the ways in which dominant and culturally embedded notions of crime animated the development and enforcement of Bill C-45, *An Act to Amend the Criminal Code (Criminal Liability of Organizations)* (Westray bill) – discourses that provided the space for constituting the meaning of corporate criminal liability.[1] In contemporary Western capitalist society, it is an anathema to label corporations as criminal (Glasbeek 2002; Snider 2008). Although recent and ongoing cases of massive corporate fraud raise questions about corporate accountability (and some high profile cases have resulted in significant prison sentences) (Rosoff, Pontell, and Tillman 2005; Snider 2009), corporate harm and wrongdoing continue to be primarily beyond the criminal justice system's gaze (Reiman 2004).

As we shall see, ideologically based notions of crime provided an important backdrop to the Westray bill. These are not "real" crimes, dominant perspectives suggested, but unfortunate accidents – the regrettable, but mostly unavoidable, incidents that happen along capital's road to success. Although there was general agreement in the House of Commons over the need for new legislation to hold some corporations to legal account for workplace safety, it was deemed necessary only for the Westrays of the world – the so-called rogue corporations that represent the exception to the rule, definitely are not criminals, and certainly are not the result of a problematic corporate culture or the structural realities of corporate capitalism (Glasbeek 2002).

The first section of the chapter considers how particular cultural scripts of crime and disorder informed the Westray bill, exploring how these perspectives acted as conceptual barriers to contemplating workplace injury and death as crime and influenced the law's enforcement. The mere fact that there have been few charges and convictions since the law came into effect in 2004 is itself a reflection of the priority accorded to safety crimes. Many participants offered their opinions about the law's poor enforcement, reasons that speak to dominant discourses of crime and the structure and focus of the criminal justice system.

The second section examines the Westray bill's capacity to address issues of workplace safety, a topic that many participants have contemplated, given the lack of charges and convictions. A particular focus is the law's symbolic impact, whether its mere introduction encouraged or forced some corporations to improve their safety measures. In many respects, there is a symbolic import to the new legislation that deals with corporate criminal liability – it signals official approbation of corporate harm and wrongdoing. At the same time, however, what is the value of this message if the law is not enforced? Is it merely "symbolic but ineffectual law" (Smandych 1991, 47)? Although it is beyond the scope of this study to empirically evaluate the extent of the Westray bill's impact on workplace safety practices in corporations, it is possible to examine the discourses that underpin some of the measures undertaken within the corporate world thus far in response to this legislation.

As we shall see, the most significant development following the Westray bill's enactment is not its enforcement but, rather, the emergence of a cadre of legal experts and consultants poised to provide for-fee services to corporations about how to avoid getting caught in this newly spun crime control web. Although these initiatives will encourage some corporations to change their approach to workplace safety, their nature and scope suggests that they are more about profit-making ventures to help corporations avoid criminal responsibility than about embracing the value of workplace safety. In true entrepreneurial form, the Westray bill produced what is referred to herein as a crime *(un)control* industry, one that reinforces dominant beliefs that corporations cannot be criminals. As such, many of the cultural assumptions about corporate crime and the fact that it is somehow different than traditional street crimes continue to hold sway beyond the development and introduction of Canada's corporate criminal liability legislation.

What Is a (Corporate) Criminal?

In contemporary society, crime is a social and political obsession. It is almost impossible today to escape the constant messages about the perils of crime and disorder, warnings about dangerous individuals who lurk behind every street corner waiting for their next victim (Boyd, Chunn, and Menzies, 2001; Christie 2004). On a daily basis, we are reminded about the so-called "crime problem," whether it be through sensationalized media coverage of interpersonal violence, stories of cops and robbers on television or in movies, or the constant political chatter about the need to "crack-down" on crime and criminals (Menzies,

Chunn, and Boyd 2001, 11). In reality, however, there is little evidence to support these claims and concerns, with, for example, official statistics demonstrating a steady decline of crime rates for a number of years (Silverman, Teevan, and Sacco 2000). As Robert Menzies, Dorothy Chunn, and Susan Boyd (2001, 12) argue, "by every account, the 'average' Canadian today is less likely to be victimized criminally by another individual than at any time since the 1970s." And yet "conventional wisdoms" about crime continue unabated.

From an early age, we are all taught what is a crime (Hillyard and Tombs 2004, 11). What these "common sense" lessons do not acknowledge, however, is that crime and its control are ideologically based, social constructions (Henry and Lanier 2004). There is nothing inherent about any particular act that gives it a criminal quality; it only becomes a crime when it is officially labelled as such (Christie 2004; Hillyard and Tombs 2004). As Nils Christie (2004, 3) argues, "crime does not exist. Only acts exist, acts often given different meaning within various social frameworks." Witchcraft was once considered to be criminal, so were most forms of gambling, at least until governments saw the revenue-generating opportunity of state-run casinos and lotteries. And slavery was once deemed acceptable under the US Constitution (Glasbeek 2002). Crime is therefore historically and socially specific, its constitution contested, its definitions never complete.

What is important for the current discussion is that, for the most part, corporate wrongdoing is absent from dominant considerations of crime. As Harry Glasbeek (2002, 118) reminds us, "when corporate actors commit crimes they are rarely charged; if charged, they are rarely convicted; and if convicted, they are rarely punished severely." The exclusion of corporate wrongdoing from crime's lexicon is puzzling when one considers that corporations cause exponentially more harm than "all the street thugs, youth gangs, home invaders, illegal (im)migrants, pot growers and squeegee kids that our society can produce" (Menzies, Chunn, and Boyd, 2001, 13). Although political rhetoric creates fears around violent street crime, the truth is that most people have a much better chance of being victimized on the job than on the street (Tombs and Whyte 2007). And regardless of the growing concern with the abuse of corporate power – fuelled by cases of corporate fraud and high profile workplace disasters, including Westray – the notion of corporate crime has a long way to go before it can be accused of being part of mainstream "law and order" agendas.

Steve Tombs and Dave Whyte (2007, 67) suggest that a key reason why safety crimes (and corporate crime more generally) remain beyond discussions of crime control is the overwhelming political priority given to crime committed by the "usual suspects." Throughout the 1980s and 1990s, during the rise of neo-liberal political and economic reasoning, the idea that corporations and corporate actors were criminals became increasingly problematic, even unthinkable (Slapper and Tombs 1999; Tombs and Whyte 2007). During this time, the temperature of the state's crime control policy making shifted from cool to hot, expressing a "collective anger and a righteous demand for retribution rather than a commitment to a just, socially engineered solution" (Garland 2001, 10-11). However, these demands for justice varied considerably depending on the crime and offender. While penalties and punishments for traditional street crimes became considerably more punitive (Boyd, Chunn, and Menzies 2001; Garland 2001), corporate wrongdoing enjoyed a period of unprecedented deregulation, effectively becoming "*exempt* from legal control" (Snider 2008). As Laureen Snider (2008, 3) notes, "the urge to criminalize ... stopped at the door of the executive suite; jail sentence and criminal fines, ideal for the poor and powerless, somehow became ineffective and inappropriate responses to business assault, homicide and fraud." Deemed to be the economic lifeblood of the country, corporations could do no wrong. Corporate crime was therefore irrelevant, defined away as of little concern or consequence, despite overwhelming evidence to the contrary.

These dominant, socially based conceptualizations of crime, which largely exclude corporate wrongdoing, also have structural roots. That is, they do not emerge in a vacuum, drawing their moral and cultural authority from different discursive formations. For example, as the previous chapters illustrate, legal and economic discourses shaped and limited the nature and scope of corporate criminal liability legislation, therein downplaying the seriousness of corporate crime. Cultural scripts of crime and disorder therefore represent another "mutually reinforcing" discourse that shaped and animated the Westray bill (Tombs and Whyte 2007, 69). Mainstream notions of crime ensured the differentiation of safety crime, and through it corporate crime, from "dominant definitions of 'crime, law and order'" (Tombs and Whyte 2007, 66).

Illegal, Yes, but Not Criminal

Throughout the Westray bill reform process, there was reference to historically rooted, culturally based beliefs that corporations and corporate actors are not criminals.[2] While not expressed in absolute terms – nobody argued that corporations cannot commit crimes – dominant voices suggested that only a minority of corporations are guilty of such sins and that most corporate crime cannot be considered "true" crime. Corporate crime is the exception to the rule, not something that constitutes too much cause for concern.

The hesitancy to equate corporate wrongdoing with crime first emerged during discussion and debate of the types of corporations that should be subject to the New Democratic Party's (NDP) proposed legislation. The prevailing sentiment was that it should apply only to the handful of corporations that deviate too far from acceptable standards and norms. For example, NDP member of parliament (MP), Bev Desjarlais, sponsor of the private members' bill, offered the following observations during the hearings of the Standing Committee on Justice and Human Rights (Justice Committee):

> Quite frankly ... I don't believe this legislation will ever deal with probably 99% of the corporations and industries in our country. What it will deal with is the 1% or 2% that do carry on this kind of action. They're the ones we want to deal with. (Hansard, 9 May 2002, 10:20)

Similarly, Desjarlais also suggested:

> If we have such an absolute objection from industry in different sectors to a bill such as this ... methinks they protest too much. What are they worried about? You would have to be so blatantly negligent to fall into this category that you shouldn't even be able to stand up and look anyone in the face. That's what we're dealing with. We're not dealing with corporations or individuals who are honest and caring, which I believe the majority of our companies and corporations in this country are. I wouldn't expect that they would ever fall into this legislation. (Justice Committee, 7 May 2002, 10:55)

The problem, however, is that corporations of all shapes and sizes have been guilty of serious occupational health and safety offences (Pearce and Tombs 1990, 426) – "corporate crime is not an aberration," as Glasbeek (2002, 133) argues. In addition, suggesting that only rogue corporations are guilty of wrongdoing obscures the organizational and socio-economic factors associated with corporate crime. This does not mean that individuals are without fault but, simply, that structural factors ("pressures of profitability") influence actions (McMullan 1992, 45).

A general reluctance to define corporate wrongdoing as criminal also emerged in reference to "true" crimes versus regulatory offences. For instance, in response to a question from a Justice Committee member about the challenges of drafting corporate criminal liability legislation, a witness argued for the need to differentiate between types of offences:

> First of all, there has to be some attention given to the differences between true crimes as we know them and offences that are more of a regulatory nature. In current Canadian criminal law, this is one of the most intractable, difficult problems. We do not have, in current law, a workable distinction between regulatory liability and criminal liability, and it's absolutely central to the problem of corporate liability. (Patrick Healy, Justice Committee, 28 May 2002, 11:50)

What this fails to consider, however, is the socially constructed basis of the distinctions between "true" crime and regulatory offences (Pearce 1992, 319). It reinforces the dominant belief that corporate (regulatory) offences are somehow objectively distinguishable from traditional street crimes (Tombs and Whyte 2007).

Justice Committee members provided a telling instance of the generosity of spirit accorded to corporate wrongdoers when they interrupted hearings on the Westray bill to discuss a motion relating to legislation on violent crime by individuals. In an abrupt change of tune, one committee MP wanted to summon the commissioner of corrections to answer questions concerning an individual on statutory release who committed a homicide (Peter MacKay, Progressive Conservative (PC), Justice Committee, 7 May 2002, 10:34). Conservative MP Peter MacKay asked why this individual was given parole and why it was not revoked – ignoring the fact that no law justified his continued detention. Others used this example of individual violence to criticize how "criminals" are dealt with post-incarceration (Chuck Cadman, Canadian Alliance, Justice Committee, 7 May 2002, 10:45). What is particularly revealing is the shift in discourse: precise legal language and maximum legal protection is required for corporations and corporate officials involved in corporate violence, but these can be ignored when dealing with individuals involved in interpersonal violence. Such issues become mere legal niceties. Take, for example, comments from Conservative Alliance MP Vic Toews:

> I don't think it serves this committee well to say we don't know whether this is conditional or statutory release. Who really cares? Let's not get into that kind of thing; I think that brings discredit to this entire committee. I don't really care what the difference is, and I don't think it's particularly relevant.

There are certain rules that govern those releases. I think the prior witness, Mr. Martin [a former Westray mine worker who testified before the committee], would just be shaking his head if we hinged our decision on that kind of thing. (Justice Committee, 7 May 2002, 10:45)

Likewise, another member expressed little concern with the difference between statutory release and parole, preferring instead to talk about the gravity of the offence:

To me, somebody breaching a condition of parole is a slap in the face of society. We've told that person we're going to give them a chance, they breach the conditions they've been given that chance on, and parole is not revoked. That concerns me, and I think it goes to the heart of this. (Chuck Cadman, Canadian Alliance, Justice Committee, 7 May 2002, 10:45)

Finally, as MacKay argued in response to concerns by some MPs that there is a difference between statutory release and parole,

as to ... [the] ... point about whether it was statutory or conditional release, my information is that it was statutory release, but I think such things are minutiae. What happened here is that this man breached conditions of his parole and may have been picked up if there were proper mechanisms in place that would have prevented Mr. Hearn [the victim] being beaten with a claw-hammer in his own home. (Peter MacKay, PC, Justice Committee, 7 May 2002, 10:50)

In general, this example underscores the vastly different discourses used to characterize interpersonal violence (traditional crime) compared to corporate violence. Gone were concerns with legal precision and the need to do things in accordance with certain legal principles – ideals that were obvious during the discussion of corporate criminal liability – replaced instead by concerns with the "proper" administration of justice and the need to get to the bottom of the issue, and fast. No more commitments to justice and fairness, just the criminal justice hammer waiting to swing into action at a moment's notice.

Making Corporate Crime Saleable
In many respects, this differentiating, or "othering," of corporate offences from traditional crimes was an artifact of the lobbying for the Westray bill's

introduction. To make the legislation saleable, a key message was that it would deal with only the most egregious cases of corporate malfeasance. A private sector representative understood from consultations with the Department of Justice that the legislation was not meant to open up a new level of prosecutions but, rather, to deal with cases of extreme negligence (Private sector representative, Interview 14). Likewise, a criminal lawyer noted that corporations are reassured of the law's restricted application by the lack of charges:

> You know what I think? It's gone back to where we were before. You don't have to worry about it. It's for those other guys. It's the bad, greedy few, not us. We run a good company, we're careful. There's a certain sense of complacency. (Criminal lawyer, Interview 5)

References to reasonableness and fairness therefore assuaged fears that the law would go too far in holding corporations to legal account. By attributing corporate wrongdoing to organizational and individual bad apples (therein ignoring the role of the corporate form or the nature of capitalist production in workplace injury and death), dominant perspectives ensured that the Westray bill did not upset the corporate apple cart. In this respect, it was as if the premise of the entire reform process was to maintain the status quo (Haines 2003).

The Westray Bill in Action

Dominant assumptions of crime and its control also animated the Westray bill beyond its enactment. There are valuable insights to be gleaned from examining the differences between "law-as-legislation" and "law-in-practice," namely that what the law promises on paper is oftentimes substantially different than what is achieved through enforcement (for example, see Chunn and Lacombe 2000; Smart 1989). An important consideration herein is that law plays an integral role in reproducing a "repressive social order" (Chunn and Lacombe 2000, 11), whether it is in terms of recreating a "gendering practice" (16), a racialized space (Razack 2002), or a capitalist ideology (Woodiwiss 1997).

For some respondents, particularly those from the labour movement, *R c Transpavé inc* (the only conviction at the time of the interviews) did not bode well for the potential of holding corporations and corporate actors to legal account for workplace safety.[3] As one union representative noted, the *Transpavé* case involved a small company where there was little difficulty tracing the chain of responsibility throughout the organization (Union representative, Interview 9) – hardly the sort of complex matter that critics had in mind when arguing for changes to the identification doctrine. Another union representative raised similar concerns, suggesting that the only reason the *Transpavé* case made it to court was because the Quebec Federation of Labour (QFL) aggressively lobbied the Crown to proceed with charges. According to the union representative, the QFL believed that the accident report of the Commission de la santé et de la sécurité du travail, the province's occupational health and safety authority, underscored the criminal negligence of the case in finding that the machine's safety mechanism was purposely disabled (Union representative, Interview 16). Compounding the negligence was the fact that most everyone in the company knew this except the victim, who was not properly trained to operate the machine. Adding to the union representative's frustration was the perception that the safety mechanism was deactivated to save time and money:

> Some people told us ... the only reason it [the safety mechanism] was deactivated was to save about $600 per production day ... it would speed up the fix when there is a jam in the production. Because to reactivate the [machine] you've got to get out of the area [and] press the button, and there's a two-minute delay before it starts over again. (Union representative, Interview 16)

In addition to these concerns, a number of participants offered insights regarding problems with the law's enforcement. Three main factors emerged from these discussions. First, provincial occupational health and safety regulations provide built-in disincentives for enforcing the Westray bill – that is, the new law operates within the context of a "bifurcated model of criminal process," in which attempts to "assimilate" corporate wrongdoing into the criminal law operate alongside a robust regulatory frame that involves a separate, non-criminal sphere for dealing with occupational health and safety offences (Tombs and Whyte 2007, 110). Second, there is a lack of education regarding the legislation among police and crown prosecutors. A related point is the traditional focus of criminal justice actors on "real" crimes, the sensational stuff of guns and gangs. Finally, corporate crime, and more specifically safety crime, is not an important societal priority – it occupies a marginal position on law and order agendas. Collectively, these factors are constitutive of dominant and culturally based notions of crime and its control, socially constructed beliefs that, for the most part, exclude corporate crime.

Enforcement in Context: The Regulatory Frame
An important factor animating the Westray bill is the regulatory environment

that dominates the state's response to occupational health and safety offences. Within Canada's constitutional framework, the federal government has the power to enact criminal law, while responsibility for the administration of justice falls to the provinces, primarily through the provision of a system of police, courts, and corrections.[4] However, despite the fact that criminal legislation is within the federal government's bailiwick, the provinces can enact provincial laws and regulations, some of which include provisions for fines and imprisonment that resemble federal measures. This division is particularly relevant for discussions of workplace safety in that the provinces are responsible for establishing and enforcing occupational health and safety regulatory regimes. While there is no constitutional division of power that stipulates that occupational health and safety are exclusively federal or provincial matters, it is the provinces that assume this responsibility in a majority of cases (Keith 2004, 97-98).[5]

It is within this context that the Westray bill came into effect. Corporate criminal liability legislation was set against a backdrop of a well-established set of provincial (non-criminal) regulations meant to address issues of workplace safety. In this respect, there was a pre-existing non-criminal structure and process – albeit characterized by weak and underfunded government enforcement strategies – that the Westray bill had, and has, to compete against, both practically from an enforcement viewpoint and ideologically in terms of which mechanism constituted the most appropriate and accepted method for responding to corporate harm and wrongdoing (Barnetson 2010; Storey and Tucker 2005; Tucker 1995a).

Even before the enactment of the Westray bill, this dominant regulatory frame helped raise questions about the appropriateness of the law's development. The perception that occupational health and safety is the bailiwick of the provinces meant that the idea of adding criminal law to the mix represented an uneasy proposition for some legislators. For instance, a Liberal MP expressed concern that corporate criminal liability legislation was "far reaching" in its implications and required further study given that its potential to infringe on the "constitutional" right of the provinces to deal with occupational health and safety (Marlene Jennings, Hansard, 23 April 1999, 12:35-12:40; see also Monique Guay, Bloc Québécois, Justice Committee, 6 June 2000, 10:40).

Similarly, a Liberal MP cited the difficulties of "extending the federal model to include workers outside the federal jurisdiction," given that it is a "provincial concern." The MP cautioned that any initiative at the federal level that treads on provincial jurisdiction may not "be viewed positively by those other levels of government" (Brent St. Denis, Hansard, 18 February 2000, 14:20). Finally, a Bloc Québécois MP raised the spectre of infringing on provincial jurisdiction in response to a union representative's suggestion that it might be necessary for the federal government to assume responsibility for workplace safety regulations to adequately protect workers (Robert Lanctôt, Justice Committee, 9 May 2002, 12:25). A Liberal MP quickly added:

> We're wandering off here. We've talked in the last hour mainly about something that concerns us not at all, provincial jurisdiction ... Health and safety is not our jurisdiction, it's not our problem. We don't want to get into it, as far as I'm concerned. We want to get this thing done, I want it to happen. All we're being asked to do is provide a hammer to hold over them, and someone else is going to have to provide the nail. That's the way our federation is made up. (Ivan Grose, Justice Committee, 9 May 2002, 12:30)

A politician interviewed for this research acknowledged that federal politicians are aware of the federal-provincial split when developing criminal law but that in most cases they cannot do much about it. His comments are revealing about the complexities of federal-provincial relations, as well as the different priorities accorded traditional street crimes and corporate offences:

> We're [federally] stuck between a rock and a hard place. If we're too prescriptive around what provinces might do, then the charge is that we are interfering. If we don't even mention it, then we are grandstanding. So ultimately I think the balance generally is we recognize that we're imposing some burden on the provinces to take actions, and we *hope* they will. And in some cases ... there's accompanying financial resources, and I'm thinking of the *Youth Criminal Justice Act*. I don't think there were any resources attached to this [the Westray bill] ... and I don't think frankly that you would see it as being of the volume, and history has demonstrated that, *the volume* [of offences and charges] *is not comparable to the volume around the Youth Criminal Justice Act.* (Politician, Interview 15 [emphasis added])

The dominant regulatory context also animated the Westray bill after its introduction, which many respondents believed to be a prominent factor in the law's virtual disuse. For example, one respondent suggested that the criminal law was used as a tool for securing convictions for provincial occupational health and safety offences:

What I found with the people I deal with, the issue of labour, and other people, is that it is more of a tool that is being used to, if you are a corporation that has had a fatality or lethal injury, they go in and say, "here's your choice. You can either have a charge under C-45, or we you can take the charge under the provincial offences act, and no criminal record." I don't know if it is a tool to get them to accept the provincial, but that seems to be the way that it is, at least in Ontario. (Non-profit representative, Interview 10)

A corporate lawyer noted that it was the policy of Ontario's crown attorney to first consider if it is more effective to use provincial regulations than criminal charges when dealing with corporate offences – a regulation first policy (Corporate lawyer, Interview 18). Others spoke more generally of how labour inspectors are more familiar with provincial regulations, therein providing an incentive to rely on these rules as opposed to incorporating new criminal laws into their daily routines. As a private sector representative suggested,

you know, the thing that struck me at the time and I think is probably still the case is that clearly there is health and safety legislation in every province and that would be the natural thing that people would look to ... To go the *Criminal Code* route you'd have a much higher burden of proof to actually try to determine, which is not impossible in some of these cases, you have to determine what practices were in place, what was the likelihood of harm that anyone did it – did they totally ignore it or was it a matter of having some policies, but they weren't adequate. (Private sector representative, Interview 14)

Provincial regulation is therefore the default starting point for investigating safety crimes (this despite the ineffectiveness of this approach, as noted earlier). In this respect, the federal-provincial split is a significant discursive formation that limits the application of the Westray bill and ensures that it does not unduly infringe upon provincial matters. In the process, it helps reinforce the dominant belief that corporate offences are *mala prohibita* (wrong because prohibited), not *mala in se* (inherently evil and wrong).

Lack of Legal Education and Interest
Another factor that respondents noted when contemplating the lack of Westray bill charges and convictions was the poor knowledge of, and disinterest in, this legislation among police and crown prosecutors. As Glasbeek (2002, 149) notes,

an ideological bias against criminalizing corporations and corporate actors "saturates the efforts of the police forces, prosecutorial offices, and policy-making institutions." A union official described the law's status as having "our feet planted firmly in mid-air," which he argued is a familiar position for occupational health and safety law:

> It's like all legislation that you get. I mean we have some great health and
> safety legislation on the books in Canada, both at the federal level and the
> provincial level ... but our biggest thing is ... that there is lack of enforcement
> out there. And I think it's the same thing with this particular legislation, you
> know that part that was put in the *Criminal Code*. It's not being used, frankly.
> (Union official, Interview 12)

The union official found it puzzling that government officials had done very little to ensure the proper enforcement of such important legislation:

> And what bothers me about [the lack of enforcement] is ... it had such a high
> profile introduction into the *Criminal Code*. I would have thought that there
> would have been an effort with the solicitors general and attorneys general of
> the provinces to get together and say, "this is important stuff, we want to make
> sure that this is not going to be just put on the shelf ... and never see the light
> of day." That never happened; it never happened. In fact there was more in-
> formation and education among corporate managers than there was around
> those with those who have to actually enforce that legislation. (Union repre-
> sentative, Interview 12)

Frustration with this lack of enforcement surfaced in the context of the United Steelworkers of America's (Steelworkers) unsuccessful private prosecution, which alleged the criminal negligence of the sawmill company Weyerhaeuser in the death of one of its workers. Union officials condemned the Crown's decision not to proceed with the case, questioning why provincial authorities seemed reluctant to prosecute negligent corporations and why "governments and [the] justice system continue to disregard the deaths of so many workers" (United Steelworkers of American 2011).

A corporate lawyer cited the lack of education and training for police and prosecutors as the "biggest single impediment to the enforcement of this law" (Corporate lawyer, Interview 7). He argued that prosecuting corporations criminally requires "pretty sophisticated" knowledge of corporate law and of

Obscuring Corporate Crime and the Corporate Criminal   **161** the ways in which corporations are structured (Corporate lawyer, Interview 7). Unfortunately, he noted, Crown prosecutors do not have the time, expertise, or requisite training to undertake such work, particularly in comparison to the legion of well-paid corporate lawyers that stand waiting to defend against criminal charges. Another corporate lawyer concurred with this argument, adding that it was puzzling given the number of annual workplace fatalities in Canada:

> Lack of awareness and education on the part of the police – clear problem. Some of our clients have probably benefited from the ignorance of police, but I am not saying that is really the way the enforcement of law should be. I'd rather argue that the law is a bad law and you shouldn't pass it, or you should amend it, rather than pass it and pretend it's not there, because that is essentially what is going on, a fact that many corporations have probably benefited from ... There are approximately 1,000 workplace fatalities every year in Canada according to the National Association of Worker's Compensation Boards, and I am hard pressed to believe that some of those aren't pretty serious in terms of potential criminal negligence. (Corporate lawyer, Interview 7)

Some participants attributed the lack of enforcement to the traditional focus of criminal justice actors. For example, one union representative argued that police tend to conceptualize violence from a narrow, stereotypical perspective:

> Another part of the problem is that the police, when they end up where there's been a death, work related, their only concern ... is to make sure that it is not a murder that has been camouflaged by a work accident, that it is really an accident. That is their concern. It seems that their approach, the way they are looking at work accidents, hasn't changed. (Union representative, Interview 16)

Similar concerns appeared in reference to crown prosecutors, who generally do not consider occupational health and safety offences to be an important part of their work. A legal academic suggested that those who become crown prosecutors are more focused on, and interested in, prosecuting traditional street crimes than they are corporate offences: "I just don't know that most criminal prosecutors think about this realm of criminal law when they are thinking about being a prosecutor in law school, or even before law school" (Legal academic, Interview 8).

Not on Society's Radar

Some research participants suggested that part of the reason for the Westray bill's lack of enforcement is that safety crimes are not an important societal priority. Although there is not a one-to-one relationship between the (non)-enforcement of corporate crime and societal priorities (for example, some research suggests that, when asked, many people identify corporate crimes as being as serious, if not more so, than many traditional crimes), there is a prevailing belief that society is more interested in issues of cops and robbers than corporate criminals (the exception being cases of massive corporate fraud, à la Bernie Madoff in the United States or Earl Jones in Canada).[6] As one criminal lawyer suggested, a majority of people in society do not pay much attention to occupational health and safety issues until such crimes affect them personally:

> If it touches you and I, like the Maple Leaf food case [the listeriosis case of 2008] [then people pay attention] ... but not, you know, the door that collapses on a worker at a construction site, or the worker that falls seventeen stories to their death. No, it's got to be, it's got to touch everybody. That's like criminal justice; it's a microcosm of criminal justice. If it doesn't touch you, it's for those other people, those bad people, those guns and gangs people, until it's your kid. But workplace safety is not sexy. (Criminal lawyer, Interview 5)

A legal academic similarly noted that societal attitudes undervalue workers' safety and overvalue the economy, a process that downplays the importance of corporate criminal liability. Case in point is her reference to a presentation she attended where a medical doctor argued that doctors hurt the economy when they sign a sick note for a worker:

> I saw a professor of medicine giving a training course to doctors ... it was one of these all day training sessions ... and he said, every time you write a doctor's note for a person saying that they should be off work because they are ill, you are jeopardizing the economy and you are jeopardizing the livelihood of hundreds of workers, and he said that just like that. And there were 300 doctors in the room and they were taking their notes, and they all probably didn't agree with that, but the fact ... [is that] ... this is the very senior doctor ... the one who's running the show. (Legal academic, Interview 19)

For other respondents, the lack of enforcement reflects an overall inability to equate workplace injury and death with violence and murder. A union representative argued that society does not think of death in the workplace as killing, whereas he saw it as being no different than killing someone by driving drunk (Union representative, Interview 9). To support his argument, he compared the response to the death of a police horse on the same day that an employee was killed at a large industrial workplace:

> It's now a few years old, but a worker … [at an industrial plant]… was killed on the job. There was nothing in the newspapers, nobody shows up at his funeral except his family and the union members, etc. On the same day, you want to know what was on the front page of the Toronto Star? The death of a police horse. It warranted an honour guard, the mayor showed up, I think McGuinty [Ontario's premier] was there. (Union representative, Interview 9)

Another union representative expressed similar frustration when discussing the workplace death of the Transpavé worker, Steve L'Ecuyer:

> There's 97 people who died on the job in Afghanistan over a five-year period [at the time of the interview]. Every Canadian knows about it. Ask any Canadian how many people die on the job other than those [military workers] … when a fireman dies on the job, national funeral. When a policeman dies on the job, national funeral. Why is it different for Steve L'Ecuyer? And there's a lot more Steve L'Ecuyers who die in a year than there [are] policemen or firemen. (Union representative, Interview 16)

Once again, dominant, culturally based notions of what constitutes crime permeated the Westray bill reform process and helped characterize its enforcement.

Law's Symbolic Value: They've Changed, Honestly

Despite the lack of Westray bill charges and convictions, many participants in this study suggested that the law's enactment has persuaded many corporations to improve their occupational health and safety practices. The potential of the law's productive contributions was underscored by a politician who suggested that it would encourage corporations to practise their due diligence, ensure that employees know about the law, and protect workers from risky and unsafe conditions (Politician, Interview 15). As NDP MP Pat Martin argued during debate in the House of Commons, introducing corporate criminal liability law into the *Criminal Code* would force corporate actors to "make a point of knowing" about their company's safety policies and practices.[7] Martin continued:

> People would not accept directorships on boards without first asking solid questions about the enterprises that would be under their control. They would ask if reasonable steps were being taken to ensure the workplace was safe so that there would be no problem ... If [the legislation] were in effect executives would take an instant interest in the workplaces under their control. They would ensure that basic, reasonable steps in workplace safety and health were taken. Smart managers and CEOs know that a clean, healthy and safe workplace is more profitable and that safety is not a cost factor. (Hansard, 8 November 2001, 18:25)

From this perspective, the Westray bill contained a general deterrence message – it established a moral benchmark to which all corporations were expected to aspire. Respondents offered a variety of opinions as to whether the law had achieved, or could achieve, this lofty goal.

Some respondents suggested that the Westray bill immediately impacted corporate activities, with corporate representatives determining what they needed to do to comply with the new law. One corporate lawyer suggested that more "sophisticated" corporations responded by introducing policy changes, while many "unsophisticated" ones made no changes at all (Corporate lawyer, Interview 7). Similarly, a union representative agreed that some corporations responded positively to the Westray bill but added that this only applied to those who already understood the importance of workplace safety:

> I would say ... the large company that was already training their officers, supervisors, whatever you want to call them, their management team, on health and safety, and are doing the things right, mostly, are the same ones where they give the training for their people on ... [the Westray bill] ... because they were already concerned with health and safety, and now it's just another incentive, of being concerned, but it's the same ones. It's the ones who are organized, and quite often there are unions present to keep knocking on the door saying, "if this doesn't work people are going to get injured." And with time you realize that it's an investment to work on prevention. (Union representative, Interview 16)

As the following quotes illustrate, other respondents were even more convinced that the Westray bill encouraged corporations to improve their occupational health and safety practices:

> I attended a conference not all that long after the legislation was put into force, and different workers around the country got up and said right after this was done there were meetings in the workplace to start dealing with some of the issues that they had not been dealing with. So it had some immediate impact. I think that if even in one instance an employer improves a situation and we save lives, it's been beneficial. I would much rather have a situation where they make the preventative changes and we never, ever have to charge anyone under this legislation. But it's like anything, having the legislation makes a difference. (Politician, Interview 11)

> I think the message being sent was that we've taken notice of this practice in the industry and that we're not, we're kind of giving the heads-up now that we're not going to let this continue. And I guess we are waiting to see what kind of an impact it has out there to determine if there is a need to go past that ... I think it's more symbolic than practical right now, especially since the past has shown that. I think it has had the desired effect that they [government] wanted to wake up the industry and say, "okay times have changed." (Non-profit representative, Interview 10)

A private sector representative argued that senior officials in his organization took notice after the Westray bill's introduction: "When the can was tied to senior leadership, and they were made aware of it [the Westray bill], they opened their eyes to ensure that the accountability mechanisms that were being passed down throughout the company were being followed." He suggested that the law provides health and safety experts with a strong mandate to give more and frequent updates to senior executives and management regarding potential criminal liabilities within an organization. From his perspective, it provides the checks and balances that are necessary to ensure the implementation of appropriate safety programs and that employees have the proper skills and training for their jobs (Private sector representative, Interview 23).

In many respects, there is symbolic import to the introduction of the Westray bill. If we understand law as a site of struggle where meanings are contested and various knowledge claims take root to shape law's development, then the Westray bill represents a challenge to corporate dominance – a form

166   Chapter 6

of resistance to the corporate status quo (Chunn and Lacombe 2000; Comack 2006). At the very least, its mere introduction shifts the boundaries of what constitutes acceptable corporate decision making when it comes to workplace safety. At the same time, however, as the next section explores, there are certain limits to this resistance in a capitalist society.

Symbolic of What?

Not everyone was convinced of the Westray bill's ability to encourage changes in a corporation's occupational health and safety practices. For example, a government respondent argued that, at most, the law raised awareness of the issue and helped police and prosecutors deal with serious cases of workplace injury and death (Government official, Interview 1). Similarly, another government official suggested that the law is an after-the-fact response and, therefore, lacks a preventative element (Government official, Interview 3). For some respondents, the introduction of the Westray bill allowed the government to claim that it was taking the issue of corporate criminal liability seriously, without fundamentally changing things. As a non-governmental organization (NGO) representative argued,

> where politicians stop when regulating the corporate sector, across the world, is they stand at the podium and say, "we have passed this law and it is now illegal." Well, illegal does not mean that there are words on paper. Illegal means that if you do it, that there is a very high chance of getting caught and the penalty you face will stop you from doing it again ... the penalty is much higher than could be absorbed by doing it, paying the penalty and just writing it off as the cost of doing business. (NGO representative, Interview 2)

A legal academic suggested that the Westray bill was a typical government response to a high profile disaster:

> For me when [the Westray bill] was enacted it was a typical case. We have a problem, let's enact a new crime. We've resolved it. If you know somebody in criminal law who for one minute believes this would change anything, please tell me ... And what I remember is that after, or around the enactment of this, I got a few phone calls. The business community was very worried, and what's going to happen to us, are we going to be prosecuted, what does it change? And I remember saying, I don't know, it doesn't change much. (Legal academic, Interview 17)

Some respondents argued that the law is irrelevant in situations where corporations act as amoral calculators. One union representative suggested that, although corporations do not always make decisions in economic terms, they will ultimately, and if necessary, calculate workplace safety as the cost of doing business:

> There is this tendency to kind of impute this absolute fiscal rationality in management behaviour and corporate behaviour and say, "well they all do this very fine cost benefit analysis." I mean I don't think that's true. But still, it is ultimately a matter of, "okay, it happens, we pay the fine, and we go on." [Corporations] try to avoid your worker's comp fees, and that's it. (Union representative, Interview 6)

A non-profit representative echoed a similar sentiment, noting that another Westray is out there waiting to happen and that some companies still believe that workplace injury and death is "just the price of doing business" (Non-profit representative, Interview 10). A union representative argued that another high-profile disaster was imminent, underscoring that unsafe practices remain a concern despite the introduction of corporate criminal liability legislation:

> There's still another Westray out there waiting to happen, I know there is. And unfortunately, I know there is. And the next Westray actually could be in the tar sands in the Alberta north, to be honest about it. I'm just waiting for a catastrophe to happen out there because they have a large proportion of foreign workers that they bring in, because they're saying they don't have enough skilled trades, and everything. The foreign workers are not being trained properly, they're not being informed of their rights, there are all kinds of barriers involved, language barriers, cultural barriers, all kinds of things, that these workers, I believe, are in jeopardy, because they're not, I don't think they're being trained properly in a lot of cases. In some cases they are, I don't want to put one big broad brush on it, but I know and I've heard examples ... and this is just a disaster waiting to happen out there. And that could be the next, probably worse than Westray. (Union representative, Interview 12)

Although he acknowledged that the law probably encouraged some corporations to reconsider their occupational health and safety standards, he suggested that the lack of enforcement undermined the law's ability to promote change:

I think that because there hasn't been any high profile charges [against] CEOs or corporations [under] the *Criminal Code* that that has been leading to, how should I put it. I think it's leading to almost ignorance of the legislation that's there, or a lack of seriousness of the legislation that's there, not taking it seriously. Because even though in the back of their minds they know it's there, they're seeing that in every major incident that's happen[ed] so far ... everything is being charged under the occupational health and safety act of the province. And they know under that particular legislation, even though there could be some serious fines, they could be fined up to a couple of million bucks, but you're not going to jail under the acts of the provinces. And that's sort of my fear, is that it's one of those things were you have good legislation ... but in this case the legislation, that basically becomes almost abstract to people. And that doesn't help the cause, and I can see down the road that things are going to deteriorate again. I mean they're not the best because Canada still injures and kills more workers than ... most of the G-8 countries. (Union representative, Interview 12)

A regulator suggested that some corporations may not be taking the legislation all that seriously, although he was unsure to what extent (Regulator, Interview 15). In his mind, part of the problem was that regulatory overload or fatigue means that many corporations only focus on what they have to do to comply with a particular rule, as opposed to seriously and thoroughly reflecting on what it takes to operate safely:

There became a sense that has evolved with so much regulation that says "as long as I'm in the regulation, okay, I'm following all the rules." And these people are not breaking any rules; they are following everything, meeting all of the conditions, and following all the rules. They've lacked the judgement to say, the rules are not enough, there is more to it than just the rules. (Regulator, Interview 15)

In this regard, some of the potential changes that corporations have made in response to the Westray bill are akin to what Garry Gray (2006) refers to as Potemkin villages, the idea that some corporations will make it appear to regulators that they are complying with occupational health and safety standards, even though the company's day-to-day practices are anything but safe and compliant.

Against the backdrop of the capitalist social formation, we can begin to understand the limits of the Westray bill's symbolic effect. Even if the new law

Obscuring Corporate Crime and the Corporate Criminal

challenges corporate hegemonic interests, it does so in a manner that leaves the capitalist class process – the production of surplus value – fundamentally intact (Resnick and Wolff 2010; Soederberg 2010; Wolff 2010a). As we shall see in the next section, these limits are further evident in the educational and training tactics developed in response to the law's implementation.

The New Crime (Un)control Industry?

When broaching the issue of the Westray bill's symbolic import, a legal academic warned that it is difficult to determine the law's impact without a thorough empirical analysis and that it would be erroneous to conclude that the law's enforcement (or lack thereof) is the sole benchmark of success:

> Well, in other contexts ... we have this new harassment legislation ... [for example] ... and it's very clear to me that the measure of the impact is not the measure of the outcome of the cases that have been brought. I mean that's part of it, but it's a very, very, very minor part of what types of changes were implemented and why there were implemented. So that in measuring efficacy of legislation the number of cases and the size of the fines is really not how you measure that. (Legal academic, Interview 19)

Although it is beyond this study to evaluate the relationship between the Westray bill and improvements to occupational health and safety practices (particularly given that the law was still in its infancy at the time the study was completed), we can interrogate the nature and scope of some of the education and training offered to corporations since the law's introduction. That is, we can examine the discourses that underpin this work, including how they make sense of the law and the perceived steps that corporations need to take in response to its introduction.

As we shall see, the signs are not encouraging in terms of holding corporations to legal account for safety crimes. In fact, the most significant development since the Westray bill's introduction is the emergence of for-fee services offered to corporations on the measures needed to avoid criminal responsibility. In addition to various newsletters and advertisements from law firms and occupational health and safety consultants, this body of work includes various training courses, seminars, and books, all of which detail the law's parameters, how to avoid getting caught, and what to do in the event of serious injury or death in the workplace.[8] As one respondent noted when discussing the measures that have popped up in the wake of the Westray bill, go on the Internet and look for training for C-45, many of the legal firms, that's one of the courses that they push for right now is compliance with C-45, or understanding C-45. And they're making a ton of money by going out and doing these presentations to companies. (Non-profit representative, Interview 10)

Another respondent similarly suggested that the various for-fee courses and training on the Westray bill appear to advise corporations about how to avoid criminal responsibility:

Even before the legislation was declared there were consultants that already had their whole, you know, presentations and educational materials on this legislation in place, and were going after the corporations. I mean you could go on the web and you had god knows how many different consultants who were going to go and tell corporate leaders what the dos and don'ts were that would impact them as a result of this legislation, and they are still doing it today. They're making a lot of money basically going out there, and some of this stuff I've read is that they're almost advising people how to get around the legislation, right. It's more subtle than really blatant, but I've dealt with these guys for a long time, so you've got to read between the lines, and I get pretty good at reading between the lines of the stuff they say. (Union representative, Interview 12)

Yet another respondent noted that many law firms are more than happy to help corporations set up programs to help ensure compliance with the law – for a fee, of course:

The interesting thing is that some of the sensational coverage of this bill, particularly those that were saying, boy oh boy you better have a good workplace safety program in place, and you better have it well understood by your employees, and because of the attribution, you better have or managed to have a way to monitor it and report back to the company. Oh, and by the way we'd be happy to set that up for you. (Private sector representative, Interview 22)

Of particular note is how the available training and information on the Westray bill emanates from law firms and occupational health and safety consultants that are, at their core, profit-making enterprises. Although these organizations have legitimate interests in helping improve workplace safety, they nevertheless occupy a contradictory position in that they are making money by informing corporations on how to avoid being punished criminally in the event that they are accused of a safety crime. In this regard, they help (re)produce workplace injury and death as non-criminal, ensuring that corporations and corporate actors remain largely beyond the criminal justice system's reach. Several examples help illustrate how these profit-making endeavours are part of what is referred to herein as a crime (un)control industry.

The first example is the various newsletters that provide information about the new law. On the surface, this material is for information purposes – to keep interested parties informed of the law. At the same time, however, given that law firms and consultants who specialize in labour law and occupational health and safety matters provide a majority of these items, one cannot overlook that it is for the consumption of both clients and potential clients. At its core, this information emanates from organizations with an underlying profit-making mentality, underscored by the fact that most newsletters end by encouraging readers to contact the firm if they have any questions or need advice setting up an "effective" health and safety program. For example, one newsletter from a large law firm lists the contact information of its occupational health and safety specialists beside an information item on the Westray bill (Gowlings 2004). Another invites readers to contact its employee and labour relations staff to seek more information about the new law (McMillan Binch 2004). One item even provides a disclaimer, as required by the provincial law society, which states that the information constitutes "advertising material" and "commercial solicitation" (MacPherson, Leslie and Tyerman 2005).

Similar profit-making endeavours surface through the various for-fee courses and training sessions offered on the Westray bill. Not unlike the traditional crime control industry, much of this information plays on people's fear of crime, the difference being that the traditional industry exploits fear of victimization (Christie 2004; Garland 2001), while the (un)control industry exploits the fear of being charged as an offender.[9] Instead of frightening people into purchasing home alarm systems or personal safety devices (doesn't everyone need a cell phone to protect themselves?), the Westray material warns corporations that they could be charged with a criminal offence if they do not purchase the relevant information to ensure that they understand the law and can defend themselves "in the event that a workplace accident occurs."[10]

The products of one major law firm aptly reflect this burgeoning crime (un)control industry, particularly the relationship between the Westray bill, profit-making opportunities, and keeping corporations out of the criminal justice system. In addition to various newsletters and updates on the law, this firm has hosted a series of Westray bill-inspired seminars across the country.

The first, "From Boardrooms to Courtrooms: Bill C-45 and the New Health and Safety Crime," was a half-day session ($369.15, including tax, continental breakfast, coffee breaks, and seminar materials) that outlined the law and what corporations need to do to protect themselves from criminal liability. Advertisement for the session read: "Join us for a *half-day (morning) seminar* to learn about the Bill C-45 *Criminal Code changes* that could put corporate decision-makers in jail. Neglecting workplace health and safety has become a crime ... punishable up to *life imprisonment*."[11] The second, "Bill C-45 Five Years Later: Understanding the New OHS Crime, the Cases, and How to Prevent Liability" ($275 per person, plus GST, and including continental breakfast, coffee breaks, and seminar materials), covered similar topics and provided analysis of existing case law (two charges and one conviction). In addition, a prominent lawyer with the firm has written two editions of a book relating to the Westray bill (Keith 2004, 2009). Finally, the firm offers a trademarked legal auditing service that will review an organization's health and safety program to "help reduce potential risk for legal liability under OHS law and Bill C-45" (Gowlings 2004, 3).

Various occupational health and safety consulting companies also create profit-making ventures that prey on fears associated with the Westray bill. "An ill-equipped and ill-prepared employer is more likely to suffer severe consequences than one which is properly prepared," exclaims one firm that sells online training on the Westray bill. "Due diligence is the primary defence for corporations charged with an offence under health and safety legislation," the company reminds the reader: "Are you ready?" For only $799.50, reduced from the original price of $1,595.00, corporations can ensure that up to ten of its employees receive training to identify "foreseeable" workplace risks and practice appropriate due diligence to avoid criminal responsibility.[12] (It is difficult to know whether the price reduction reflects the lack of interest in, and concern with, the Westray bill or is an enticement for would-be consumers to "act now," which leaves one wondering if the training includes a free set of steak knives.) For $150.00, Occupational Health and Safety (OHS) Canada, an occupational health and safety magazine, offers an online course that provides information on the new law, as well as details on how corporations can "mitigate risk and losses within the organization, and provide due diligence for corporate executives."[13]

The Sundown Interactive Communication Corporation warns companies of the risk of criminal liability. The company offers online training, referred to as the WebWSIT Training Program, which provides important health and safety information as well as "saves all the information in a database." That way, if a company is ever asked for its training records (for example, following an accident), the employer simply has to "click" on the "inspector's report" and press print. "Don't get caught," the company warns, "get WSIT!"[14] Similarly, the Excellence in Manufacturing Consortium offers due diligence training ($250.00 for a one-day session, $295.00 for non-consortium members), the goal of which is to reduce, if not eliminate, a "company's liability from potential charges." The consortium decries: "This is a must attend seminar for lead hands, supervisors and managers [apparently executives do not need disciplining] to enable them to reduce the company [sic] and personal liabilities."[15]

Another advertisement warns school principals and vice-principals (not exactly the upper-echelon of the corporate world) that they could be subject to criminal charges if they fail to take the necessary precautions to protect their students. The document includes an ominous description of a school fundraising event where a young student with peanut allergies eats cookie mix before she checks the ingredients for peanuts. As the author warns, "while the above could best be described as a series of unfortunate events, if a school principal failed to take reasonable measures to protect any child with an identified life threatening condition, he or she perhaps could face criminal charges under Bill C-45." The hypothetical horror ends with information on "professional legal expense insurance for principals and vice-principals" and by encouraging the reader to contact their nearest insurance broker (Elston 2005). Yet another company, Canadian Onsite Medical, warns employers that the Westray bill highlights the importance of establishing due diligence within the organization, an ideal that they suggest is linked with developing systems to "prevent the commission of an offence." This system includes purchasing safety programs and site evaluations as well as medical and safety equipment (for example, first aid kits, defibrillators, fire protection gear, and equipment), all of which the company happens to sell.[16]

Finally, a private security firm, Group 4 Securicor, raises the spectre of criminal charges under the Westray bill as a reason why corporations should purchase its security services. "Did you know that as an employer, you may be held criminally liable if one of your employees gets injured in the workplace?" the security company asks. A description follows that plays on a corporation's fear of being both a victim of street crime and a safety crime offender:

> If your worker is harmed while taking your deposit to the bank, your company can now be charged under the *Criminal Code*. The risk of robbery and harm to you or your staff is a very real and viable threat no matter the value of the deposit that you are transporting. Any risk is a real risk. If your

employee is injured in a robbery attempt – your company may be exposing itself to criminal charges.

And what does the security firm believe is the solution? Let them transport your cash deposits safely and securely, of course: "It not only exonerates you from being criminally liable (Bill C-45), but also protects your employees' safety while meeting your fiscal needs."[17]

What is revealing about these various profit-making ventures is how they are dominated by the language of due diligence. Due diligence offers corporations an opportunity to defend themselves against a criminal charge by illustrating that they took all "reasonable" steps to prevent bodily harm. Law firms and consultants capitalize on this by encouraging corporations to implement new safety programs to illustrate their achievement of this standard. "To avoid becoming the subject of a *Criminal Code* prosecution," suggests one law firm, corporations must implement appropriate safety practices, ensure that senior managers are aware of any health and safety concerns, and "document all preventative policies, procedures and preventative actions" (Stewart McKelvey Stirling Scales 2005). Another firm suggests that establishing due diligence is necessary to avoid "triggering" any "major legal issues" and to "becoming the subject of a potentially precedent-setting action" (McMillan Binch 2004). "Employers can limit their liability and reduce the chances of being charged under the provisions of the Criminal Code by implementing an effective workplace health and safety program," notes the Canadian Centre for Occupational Health and Safety, a federal government agency with the mandate to support "the vision of eliminating all Canadian work-related illnesses and injuries."[18] Other due diligence warnings employ similar language:

- It will take some time for the real impact of Bill C-45 to be felt by those it governs. In the meantime, attached is a checklist that provides some guidance on how to avoid liability under Bill C-45 (Erickson and Partners 2009).
- Poorly considered language in financing and other agreements could now expose unwitting organizations and supervisory employees to criminal liability for health and safety, environmental and other accidents. Fortunately, it's relatively easy to develop appropriate language to mitigate that risk (Kirby and Perrin 2004).
- Although a comprehensive compliance program will not provide a complete defence to criminal offences, it will demonstrate a measure of due diligence and may be considered as a mitigating factors by a court when considering liability and assessing the appropriate penalty (Standryk 2009).

One law firm spells out a number of considerations that corporations must address in the wake of the Westray bill. In particular, they suggest that senior management should issue policy directives to illustrate that they exercise reasonable care to ensure workplace safety. The firm also highlights the need for "immediate accident response" that allows corporate actors to co-operate with authorities without incriminating the organization. As the firm states,

> obtaining immediate advice in the event of a tragic workplace accident at a construction project often means the difference between an imprudent, crisis-driven approach that reveals unnecessary incriminating information, and a legally compliant but thoroughly managed approach to incident reporting, preserving details and evidence, obtaining expert analysis and privileged expert reports, and protecting the rights of organizations and individuals. (Edwards and Thibault 2009)

Note, however, that due diligence is about risk management and not about eliminating risk as is common in the traditional crime control realm.[19] Instead of eliminating bodily harm, the goal is to reduce it to the greatest extent possible and defend against criminal charges in the event that such harms do occur. The overriding message is to avoid criminal responsibility, not to implement an ethic of safety or ensure that nobody is killed at work, no matter what the circumstance – safety as a means to an end, not an end in and of itself.

All of this should not deny that some good could come from companies that make changes to their safety practices as a result of purchasing risk management advice and programs. At the same time, however, the point here is to identify the limits to the (profit-making) measures that have emerged to encourage corporations to comply with the law. As Eric Tucker (2006, 303 [emphasis in original]) observes in noting the "professional risk managers" that have sprung up in response to the Westray bill, while some companies may improve their safety practices as a result of this training, "they may also adopt legal strategies, such as invoking their right to counsel and their right to remain silent in the aftermath of a workplace death or serious injury, that do nothing to reduce *worker* risk exposure." In this respect, as Courtney Davis (2004, 60) suggests, risk assessments easily become "paper exercises" that are more about insulating an organization from legal responsibility than seriously improving workplace safety.

One union representative suggested that this due diligence "speak" bordered on instructing corporations on how to commit a crime without being held responsible. While he noted that this was not the explicit goal of such advice – particularly that it would be unethical and illegal for lawyers to do so – he nevertheless found it puzzling that defending against criminal charges was the primary message of these initiatives – serious injury and death was inevitable, so just prepare for it the best you can (Union representative, Interview 12)! It is hard to imagine similar reasoning being applied to traditional street crimes. Would legislators tolerate young offenders receiving advice from lawyers on how to avoid criminal responsibility in the event that they found themselves committing an offence? "Try to avoid breaking into houses," the advice would suggest, "and to help with this you should implement (even purchase, if young offenders were in a position to afford such luxuries) measures in your daily life to avoid committing such crimes." The advice would continue: "However, we know that there will be occasions when breaking and entering will be unavoidable, so that's why we suggest that you practice due diligence so that you can launch an effective defence when you do get caught breaking the law."

What Is the Westray Bill's (Symbolic) Value?

Overall, the Westray bill on the books and in action illustrates the very contradictory market of crime control in contemporary society. While traditional street crime is bound up with an industry that depends on continuous criminalization to realize profits, the crime (un)control industry makes money by securing the non-criminal status of corporations and senior executives – zero tolerance for some crime, acceptable tolerance for others (see, for example, Christie 1993, 2004; Garland 2001). It would therefore appear that Jeffrey Reiman's (1979) observation "the rich get richer and the poor get prison" remains as cogent today as when he first made it thirty years ago.

If corporations were confident about the occupational health and safety measures that they adopted (if any) in the wake of the Westray bill, then why are they not advertising so? After all, the captains of industry are quick to applaud themselves for their efforts at good corporate responsibility and citizenship, wearing them as a badge of honour and as indicators of their contributions to society and the economy (which is in everyone's best interests, after all).[20] While it is still too early to fully understand the nature and extent of any changes made by corporations since the introduction of this legislation (even though the law came into effect in 2004), if the experience of this research is any indication, then they are likely to remain hidden behind the corporate veil, treated as proprietary information.

For instance, it was difficult to get anyone from the corporate world to talk about the Westray bill for this study. Even individuals from umbrella organizations who represent different corporate sectors were hesitant to speak about the law, although many were only vaguely familiar with it. And once I eventually found someone from the private sector who was willing to participate, he changed his mind just before the interview took place, informing me that his company's senior management had discouraged him from participating. Feeling badly about the situation, he introduced me to someone who worked in the private sector as the head of an occupational health and safety program. Several days after interviewing this individual, he contacted me to say that he was having second thoughts and was considering withdrawing his participation from the study. After informing him that the decision to do so was within his rights as a participant, I asked him if there was a problem with the interview or with any of the questions that I had asked. He responded no but that he had spoken with some of his colleagues after the interview who expressed concern that his participation might bring undue attention to the industry in which he worked. They were particularly worried that the information he provided might reveal the industry's safety standards and practices and that authorities might unfairly target the industry for investigation and inspection if they believed that safety was not being taken seriously. He eventually agreed to remain in the study after I reassured him that the research would not identify the company he worked for or the industry that he worked in.

Another example of the corporate world's reticence to speak about the Westray bill came during an interview with a lawyer who represents corporations on occupational health and safety matters. I asked this individual why I might be having difficulty getting people from the corporate world to speak about the new law. Her response was telling: corporations are hesitant to share any information about their occupational health and safety strategies and regimes, not only from a fear of revealing what they might not be doing but also from a fear of of revealing themselves to regulators and competitors. She also added that, if asked, she would advise her clients against participating in any research on the Westray bill for these very reasons (Corporate lawyer, Interview 18).

Conclusion: Is There Not Still Reason for Optimism?

For some respondents, regardless of any problems with the law, the mere introduction of the Westray bill represented an important victory. A politician argued that the law's enactment was in and of itself an important accomplishment given that it was not the most pressing piece of legislation in the House of Commons:

> There's probably some [MPs] that thought it would never ever happen [that the law would be introduced], certainly those who had some uneasiness about supporting it in the first place ... I know there were Liberal members who weren't totally happy with it, and there were Conservative members who weren't totally happy with it. I'm not aware of any Bloc members, and certainly the NDP totally supported it. But it was that uneasiness, so, again I saw that as a plus in a sense that they did follow it through because it was the government that made the commitment to doing that, and their members followed through. (Politician, Interview 11)

For those in the labour movement, the enactment of the Westray bill came at a time when workers' rights were increasingly jeopardized by neo-liberal policies and decisions:

> The introduction of the legislation was sort of a bit of a victory, I guess. Well, quite a victory considering how long from the time that Westray took place until the bill actually became law. It was several years of quite hard lobbying by the Steelworkers to make it happen. And everybody was quite happy at the time because, even though it wasn't perfect and wasn't necessarily what we would have written ourselves, [what] the Steelworkers would have written. It did go a long way to hold corporations liable for negligence in the workplace causing serious injury and death. Overall, the initial reaction of most folks within labour was quite positive. (Union representative, Interview 12)

Similarly, another union representative noted:

> I think from their [the Steelworkers] point of view ... it was a big victory, they looked at it as a victory ... it was a very small step ... recognition that some people should be held accountable, at least the possibility in very egregious cases. (Union representative, Interview 6)

Once again, it would be overly dismissive and deterministic to suggest that the Westray bill presents no challenge to the hegemony of corporate capitalism. The fact is that corporate criminal liability legislation is now part of the

Criminal Code, and corporations that ignore it in its totality do so (potentially) at their legal peril. At the same time, thus far any achievements associated with the Westray bill appear limited to moral victories. A union representative admitted that the Westray bill was not worth much if under-enforced, but that it did provide some hope, a starting point from which to address future incidences of workplace injury and death. His argument is worth quoting at length to illustrate the complexities and contradictions of engaging the process of law reform in the hopes of promoting change:

> Question: What is the law's symbolic value? Response: On its own, virtually none. If you look at it as a step saying that we have brought in legislation, you can maybe make it stronger. You say this is the first step to get it on the books. It's there, it's in the *Criminal Code,* at least it's a possibility, and then you can build. That would be the argument that you would get. I guess it is a step. You say, okay, it is a step. If this is all it is going to be ever. Again, you sort of say, well, *there is so few victories.* I mean it's funny we go through all sorts of stuff in terms of the anti-scab bill that didn't pass in the last Parliament. A lot of what we do in trying to sell it is say it is not going to be bad ... it's not going to have a huge impact, don't worry, that sort of stuff. Still you got to do it. And still, in terms of your activists and everybody else you've got to say we are doing this and it is a good thing to do and it's a step. Again, you have to have victories. You are telling people why it is important to be involved in political action, why is it important to all this sort of stuff. You got to have some sort of positive stuff there. If it is simply just banging your head against a wall, people will lose interest ... if you want to be cynical about it, it's a way to get a victory, even if it is more symbolic than anything else, and look upon it as a step, but a very, very small step, but it's a step, which can be depressing ... how many decades before we get the next step? (Union representative, Interview 6 [emphasis added])

In some respects, there was recognition of the limits of what the Westray bill could achieve in terms of holding corporations to legal account for workplace safety. As one politician noted,

> I would very much have liked corporations to have a lot stronger penalties and corporate directors to have stronger penalties in some areas, but this was a step in the right direction. And it was important to have something on the record in terms of legislation. (Politician, Interview 11)

Similarly, another politician offered a sobering account of her expectations for this legislation:

> I don't think we [those lobbying for reform] ever had any illusions, because the legislation wasn't as tight as it would need to be, for there to be a lot of convictions. I don't think that was ever the greatest value by far, not that I'm saying that wouldn't even be better if the legislation was tougher and tighter and so on, but the biggest factor was always going to be, in my mind, the deterrent factor, the threat of finding yourself on the wrong side of the law, the threat of the financial liability, the criminal culpability was always going to be the biggest value in the legislation ... It's not as strong as it should be, but it's as strong as it was going to be if we were going to get it. We knew that, you know, we knew that. Well, I'm partisan, some people would say jaded and cynical enough to think as long as the country is governed by people who were, you know, at the behest of the corporate boardroom, we weren't going to get something stronger than that. And it was a take it or leave it thing, really, at that point. We were either going to get something, it's also the point at which, I know I'm in over my head legally ... I don't have the research and legal resources with which to launch a bigger, more successful campaign to win a tougher piece of legislation, you know. A lot of things compete for your scarce resources ... [and] you can't pretend to be an expert on something like that while you're trying to cover off on huge numbers of things. I guess I would say, not to either apologize or not, it was kind of the best thing we could get at the time given the political realities. (Politician, Interview 20)

In the end, although many participants believed the Westray bill was symbolically important, their expectations were low as to what it could achieve in practice. Limited by dominant discourses that claimed corporations were not really criminals, Canada's corporate criminal liability law has been largely ineffectual, reduced to the hope that some corporations have changed their safety regimes as a result of its enactment.

Throughout the Westray bill's development, and following its enactment, dominant voices maintained that even if some corporations occasionally do bad things they cannot be painted with the same brush as "common" criminals. From this perspective, crime and its control is about the street level violence that strikes fear in everyone, not about corporations who, but for the rogue few, have everyone's best interests in mind. However, even if corporations provide a social benefit (at least theoretically) that street criminals do not, this should not deny that distinctions between these offences are arbitrarily and socially constructed, rooted in a dominant ideology that downplays the seriousness of corporate harm and wrongdoing in favour of punishing the most marginalized and disadvantaged members of society (Pearce and Tombs 1990).

All of this should not deny the importance of the Westray bill's introduction, even if the lack of charges and convictions limits its accomplishments to a largely symbolic development. Its introduction means that corporate power is not absolute and that some corporations will be held to legal account for serious injury and death in the workplace. At the same time, however, this and previous chapters demonstrate that corporate criminal liability is a highly contested term that is constituted by different, yet "mutually reinforcing," discourses (Tombs and Whyte 2007, 69). Although these discourses did not, and do not, determine the Westray bill's fate, they nevertheless significantly shaped its nature and scope, downplaying the need for its introduction and minimizing the seriousness and extent of safety crimes.

7

Disciplining Capital: More of the Same or Hope for the Future?

Whatever happened to the Westray bill? Why are we *still* dying for a living?

– United Steelworkers of America (2006 [emphasis in original])

If there is only the "iron hand of necessity shaking the dice-box of chance" then under the "constructed unity of things" there is only disparity, dispersion, difference, and the play of dominations.

– Frank Pearce (1988, 264)

Visions of Law and Order

Crime stories on television and in movies are prominent sources of mainstream entertainment. The typical plotline revolves around a gruesome, if not sensationalistic, murder or assault. In most cases, the response is swift, certain, and, to everyone's satisfaction, severe. Viewers listen to political figures make public pronouncements about the importance of solving crime and making the streets safe once again. Meanwhile, police and prosecutors waste little time leaping into action, spending considerable resources investigating the crime, catching the perpetrator, and prosecuting the offence. Although they do not always "get their man," justice most often prevails, with everyone in the case working together to ensure that someone is punished – the ultimate message being, "do the crime, do the time." And while these are contrived visions of "reality," they nevertheless represent contemporary society's dominant crime control image.

The introduction of Canada's corporate criminal liability legislation does not make dramatic storytelling. Despite official rhetoric in support of cracking down on corporate criminals – and holding corporations and corporate executives to legal account for safety crimes – the manner in which the law was developed and introduced, along with the lack of charges and convictions, runs counter to dominant crime control narratives. It is hard to fathom a politician proclaiming crime-fighting success in taking more than ten years to introduce a new law in response to the mass killing of twenty-six Canadians. It is equally implausible to imagine legislators taking great care to ensure that the laws they developed were not unnecessarily stringent or overly punitive. Nor does it seem likely that criminal justice officials would boast about securing a handful of charges and a couple of convictions seven years after the introduction of a new law. In reality, there is little crime control drama to Bill C-45, *An Act to Amend the Criminal Code (Criminal Liability of Organizations)* (Westray bill) – no declarations of justice served and no law-and-order rhetoric for politicians to hang their fortunes on; just the "pretence and rhetoric of a benign big gun" (Laufer 2006, 198).[1]

As an example of corporate crime law reform, the Westray bill paints an all too familiar picture. A much publicized disaster prompted legislators to contemplate changes to the law, to react incredulously to the fact that a corporation and its actors went unpunished for such a tragic and preventable disaster (Braithwaite 2005, 61; Snider 1993, 89-113; Tucker 2006). The contradictions were too great to ignore. Although politicians frequently valorize the corporation for its wealth-generating capacities, the liberal democratic ideal of protecting life and liberty meant that a program of reform was necessary, perhaps unavoidable (Glasbeek 2002). After considerable political discussion and debate, and amid much fanfare, the state introduced new legislation, bringing with it the potential for a new era of corporate criminal liability (Archibald, Jull, and Roach 2004). The problem, however, is the law quickly faded into the background, overshadowed by the priorities of a criminal justice system more accustomed to dealing with guns and gangs than corporate miscreants. As a legal academic who participated in this research quipped when summarizing the Westray bill's effects, "something is done, nothing is fixed."

This final chapter outlines some of the key empirical and theoretical observations regarding the development and implementation of the Westray bill. First, a series of relatively autonomous, yet "mutually reinforcing," discourses animated the introduction of Canada's corporate criminal liability legislation

(Tombs and Whyte 2007, 69). Although these discourses were not part of a consciously orchestrated campaign against the introduction of corporate criminal liability legislation, they nevertheless converged to downplay the seriousness of safety crimes and limit the reform options that were seriously considered. This production of corporate crime and corporate criminal liability raises questions about the potential of holding corporations to criminal account for workplace injury and death. Second, this ensemble of discourses contributed to the (re)enforcement and (re)production of the capitalist social formation. The Westray bill's constrained development and poor enforcement has prevented any undue legal intrusions into the day-to-day functioning of the corporation. As such, the corporation remains a capitalist site in which those who own and control the workplace make all of the decisions and receive the economic rewards, while workers continue to face stagnated wages and take all of the health and safety "risks" (Pearce and Tombs 1998; Resnick and Wolff 2010; Tombs and Whyte 2007). Third, the Westray bill's reform process reminds us that the state plays an important role in "the operation and exercise of power in society" (Comack 1999, 67). Although the state does not automatically or necessarily (re)produce capitalist interests (otherwise corporate criminal liability law would never have come to fruition), it nevertheless provides the space within which powerful discourses coalesce to inform important legal and policy decisions. Finally, although the current status of the Westray bill does not leave much room for optimism, we should not (must not?) lose sight of the import of corporate criminal liability's inclusion in Canada's *Criminal Code*.[2]

The Making of Corporate Crime and the Corporate Criminal

Still Dying for a Living critically interrogated the dominant discourses that informed conceptualizations of corporate crime and corporate criminal liability as well as how these discourses corresponded to the broader social-political-economic context. Michel Foucault's ([1972] 2001) insights helped to identify the dominant knowledge claims that animated the Westray bill's development. Neo-Marxist notions of class antagonisms at the political, economic, and ideological levels helped reveal the extra-discursive factors that informed the selection and retention of particular discourses of corporate crime and corporate criminal liability as well as how these discourses helped stabilize, reproduce, and transform the class-based capitalist social formation (Althusser [1968] 1997, [1971] 2001; Hindiss and Hirst 1975; Resnick and Wolff 1987, 2006).[3] In carrying out this task, I took Cohen's observation seriously that "a major part of criminology [and socio-legal studies] is supposed to be the study of law-making – criminalization – but we pay little attention to the driving forces behind so many new laws: the demand for protection from abuses of 'power'" (Cohen 1996, 492, as cited in South 1998, 444).

Building from the findings and recommendations of the Westray inquiry's report, federal legislators acknowledged the seriousness of the Westray mine disaster and the need for legal reforms to ensure adequate protections for workers (Richard 1997). At the same time, however, this goal was not always compatible with various legal, social, and political considerations. We agree with the need to bring forth new legislation, dominant voices submitted, but in doing so, we need to respect certain values and principles. These contradictory messages were mediated through legal, economic, and cultural discourses that constituted the reform process and resulting legislation. Although each set of discourses had its own unique genesis and particular influence, together they contained a "mutually reinforcing" character that downplayed the seriousness of workplace injury and death, effectively isolating "these crimes from 'crime, law and order' agendas" (Tombs and Whyte 2007, 69).

Fuelled by a commitment to legal precision and established legal principles that favour individualized guilt – not exactly conducive to investigating complex chains of responsibility within the modern corporate form – dominant legal discourses narrowed the horizons and limited the reform options that were deemed "reasonable." Legal discourses downplayed support for a corporate culture approach to corporate criminal liability, defining it away as vague, imprecise, and constitutionally unsound. This narrow technical frame ruled out any consideration of the structural causes of safety crimes, any examination of the roots of corporate power, or the privileged legal status and extensive rights conferred by limited liability (Glasbeek 2002; Tombs and Whyte 2007). This line of inquiry marginalized discussion and debate of the moral, political, and economic capital of the corporation, helping ensure that individual executives and directors of corporations who make all of the decisions and reap the lion's share of the economic rewards remain obscured behind the corporate veil (Glasbeek 2002).

There also was an overriding concern with the economic well-being of the corporate form. Despite the physical absence of Canada's captains of industry from the reform process (at least in terms of a visible presence), the interests of corporations were thoroughly articulated by pro-corporate legislators and some witnesses appearing before the Standing Committee on Justice and Human Rights (Justice Committee). A commitment to neo-liberal common sense – that corporations are necessary for the economy and the most "efficient means of organizing production" (Pearce and Tombs 1998, 262-63) – provided the dominant ideology from which to evaluate corporate criminal liability law (Tombs and Whyte 2003a, 10). Alignment with neo-liberal ideals also meant that workplace safety was conceptualized as the responsibility of workers, labour, and unions as much as (or more than) management and executives (Gray 2006, 2009; Tombs and Whyte 2007). The prevailing myth was that workplace accidents result from the actions of defective low-level employees, not bad corporate management, malign corporate culture, or profit-maximizing strategies. These voices meshed well with historic beliefs that individuals are free to choose the conditions within which they work – beliefs that mask the reality of hierarchical decision making within the workplace (Pearce and Tombs 1998, 133).

Dominant ideas that corporate wrongdoing is not a crime also characterized the Westray bill's development and enforcement. Informed by cultural notions that crime is an act committed by individual street offenders, legislators found it conceptually difficult to contemplate corporations and corporate executives and board members as criminals. Even if some corporations commit crimes, they argued, surely these are the exceptions to the rule, and they most certainly do not present the same threat as "common" criminals. A similar mentality permeates the Westray bill's enforcement, wherein it occupies a marginal position within mainstream law-and-order agendas. In fact, the most significant development since the law's enactment is not its enforcement but, rather, the emergence of a cadre of legal experts and consultants ready and willing to provide for-fee services for corporations to learn how to avoid getting caught and punished. From this perspective, the Westray bill in action has produced a crime (un)control industry that is more about making money to keep corporations and corporate actors from becoming entangled in the crime control web than about embracing the value and ethic of workplace safety.

As a recipe for law reform, the making of Canada's corporate criminal liability brought together a number of key ingredients. To begin, it required a healthy portion of established legal principles, with more than a pinch of respect for the legal doctrine of *mens rea*. It then called for (neo)liberal concern for the economic prosperity of the corporation. Be careful, the recipe warned, you need to ensure that the law you make is not so repulsive that corporate board members will not buy it or that corporations will move elsewhere to avoid its acrid taste. The next ingredient suggested folding in skepticism about what constitutes crime. After all, those subject to the finished product are really not

Disciplining Capital

that bad. They may overindulge from time to time, causing "unanticipated" injury and death, but they do not mean any harm; they are simply doing what is in society's best (economic) interest. It is "real" criminals that you need to worry about, but that is for another recipe. As a final tip, the recipe suggested taking time putting all of the ingredients together to ensure that expectations did not get overheated and that unnecessary ingredients did not make it into the mix. In the end, legislators got credit for trying something new but avoided criticism for being too outlandish or over-cooking the law.

The Westray Bill's Class Relevance

The concoction of discourses that animated the Westray bill has important relevance in terms of (re)enforcing and (re)producing the capitalist social formation. This does not suggest that law can single-handedly transform the corporate form and the broader social conditions within which it thrives. However, as Frank Pearce and Steve Tombs (1998, 286) note, the law's constitution is an important site of "struggle for safer workplaces." It provides the space within which discourse becomes "implicated in and constitutive of power," a process that recreates the conditions necessary for valorizing the capitalist economy (Gibson-Graham, Resnick, and Wolff 2001, 20; Jessop 2002, 31). Two points drawn from this study illustrate the class relevance of the Westray bill.

First, corporate criminal liability law has constituted an object of struggle over the nature and scope of workplace safety and, hence, about who owns and controls the means of production. The mere suggestion of introducing this legislation has necessitated the reproduction of the ideologically dominant position of the class-based capitalist social formation (Hindess and Hirst 1975). This struggle was given life through the convergence of relatively autonomous discourses that, despite their differences, shaped and set limits to the reform process. In essence, a legal duty of care to provide a safe and safer working environment has the potential to alter the relationship between workers and employers as well as add costs for the corporation that must spend money to change its safety practices or pay a fine if found guilty of an offence.

However, in the struggle over the meaning of corporate crime and corporate criminal liability, the final product has favoured, and hence (re)enforced, dominant corporate interests. In particular, the law was sufficiently constrained so as to prevent any undue intrusions into the day-to-day functioning of corporations (deemed to be private property). The entire process leading to the law's enactment ignored the fact that the capitalist arrangement is premised on the ability of those who own the means of production to extract maximum surplus labour from the production process, to essentially squeeze as much free labour as possible from workers to maximize profits (Hindess and Hirst 1975; Resnick and Wolff 1987, 2006). The corporation thus remains a capitalist site in which the exploitation of workers continues unabated.

This constraint to corporate crime law reform is particularly relevant in today's vaunted global economy where power and wealth is monopolized in the hands of the privileged few and where workers face increasingly precarious and decreasingly unionized work environments of which they have little control (Cranford et al. 2005; Pearce and Tombs 1998, 23-24; Resnick and Wolff 2010). This is the culture within which the corporate form operates, the very basis that creates the conditions where concerns for safety take a backseat to the pressures of profitability. In this respect, while corporate criminal liability legislation gives the illusion of change, the corporation can, for the most part, continue to produce in ways that are deemed to be in its best (economic) interests – interests that are often incongruent with ensuring workers' safety (Glasbeek 2002; Tombs and Whyte 2007; Tucker 2006).

A second and related way in which the Westray bill contains class relevance is the politics of engaging the process of law reform. Although the reform process provided the opportunity for a variety of perspectives, the main impetus for the legislation came from unions (most notably the United Steelworkers of America) and pro-labour politicians. It was union and labour that pushed for the Westray inquiry's report to recommend that the federal government introduce corporate criminal liability legislation, and these same groups subsequently and aggressively lobbied the federal government to enact new legislation. The evidence of this commitment also surfaced during the interviews for this research in that union and labour representatives were the most familiar with the legislation, providing intimate details about the reform process and the law's enforcement (or lack thereof).

However, the act of engaging the law is fraught with political difficulties and pitfalls.[4] Law impacts class processes through the provision of certain powers to unions and managers "permitting them to establish and enforce rules necessary for the extraction of surplus labor" (Resnick and Wolff 1987, 21-22). However, while these rules may empower some workers to have greater controls over their workplace (such as the right to refuse unsafe work or the reminder to managers of the need to protect against corporate criminal liability), they also serve to entrench labour in the process of generating surplus value. As Stephen Resnick and Richard Wolff (1987, 22) note, the effects of political and legal processes help workers, in part, participate in their own exploitation. The dominant message of corporate crime law reform therefore becomes: "You've got your new law and legal protections, now get back to work so that we, the corporation, can continue to exploit and make money."

All of this starkly illustrates the limits to corporate crime law reform within the capitalist social formation. Although the engagement of law and politics holds much promise for those interested in protecting workers, it also helps (re)enforce and (re)produce dominant class relations. In many respects, the development and implementation of corporate crime laws constitute a form of class struggle over the power of corporate capitalists to control the conditions for appropriating and distributing surplus values (Resnick and Wolff 1987). However, although these struggles are not without merit and their results are far from predetermined, they fail to address the fundamental exploitation that constitutes the primary focus of Marx's surplus labour theory of class (Resnick and Wolff 1987; Wolff 2010a).

From a Marxian perspective, it is therefore imperative to move beyond lobbying for new corporate crime laws to transform the manner in which surplus values are generated, appropriated, and distributed (Eagleton 2010; Harvey 2010; Wolff 2010a). A vital point herein is recognizing that measures to deal with the effects of corporate capitalism (such as the Westray bill) fail to address the legal constitution of the modern corporate form, which separates those who produce (labourers) from the conditions of their production, the bailiwick of those who control the production process. As Resnick and Wolff (1987, 144) note, Marx's notion of class processes clearly illustrates how the separation of some members of society from possessing the means of production is a necessary condition for the reproduction of capitalism. In essence, it allows for workers to produce surplus value for the capitalist owner to appropriate and distribute in ways that help (re)secure capitalism. According to this logic, by removing an important element of this process, namely the separation of workers from "effective possession of the means of production," we can begin to transform capitalism itself (144-45).

Richard Wolff (2010b, 10) argues that pro-regulatory forces, including the Left and unions/labour, need to augment their efforts to better control corporations through law with a strategy that brings an end to the "exclusion of workers from the appropriation and distribution of the surpluses they produced." Wolff argues that this anti-capitalist strategy calls for workers to take responsibility for their workplace in order to constitute the board of directors that decides how to appropriate and distribute surpluses. By ending the exploitation that is inherent to capitalism, workers would take control of the enterprise and organize the workplace in more democratic and safer ways, including a more equitable distribution of surplus values (Wolff 2010b). The point is to strive for an *"alternative* common sense," as Michael Lebowitz (2010, 57-58 [emphasis in original]) argues: *"Be realistic – change the system, not its barriers!"*

Do Not Forget the Role of the State

The various legal, economic, and cultural discourses that permeated the development and introduction of Canada's corporate criminal liability legislation do not suggest that state discursive formations were insignificant to the reform process (an observation first made in Chapter 4). On the contrary, although the advent of neo-liberal political and economic reasoning has recast the state in more market-friendly, pro-capital ways, the state's role is not usurped "entirely by faith in the markets" (Fudge and Cossman 2002; Glasbeek 2002; Haines and Sutton 2003, 12). Indeed, the state played an important role when it came to defining and responding to corporate crime through law, providing the space for various discourses to define and set parameters to the reform process.

The Westray bill's very evolution was rooted in parliamentary politics. It was, after all, the efforts of pro-labour politicians from the New Democratic Party (NDP) and, to a lesser extent, members of parliament (MPs) from the Progressive Conservative (PC) Party that helped keep corporate criminal liability on the political radar. Absent these efforts (along with those of union and labour representatives), it is questionable whether the law would have ever come to fruition. In addition, the Justice Committee played a significant role in shaping the nature and scope of the legislation, providing the conduit for the expression of various perspectives regarding corporate crime and corporate criminal liability. Further, it was the government's legislative drafters (essentially, the Department of Justice) that were left to interpret the Justice Committee's proceedings when creating the new law. As these examples therefore illustrate, it is empirically incorrect and theoretically blind to ignore the fact that the state acts as a site where different discourses and discursive formations coalesce to animate particular legal and policy matters (Comack 1999) – a process that, in the case of the Westray bill, also helps reproduce capitalism's hegemonic status (Jessop 2002).

Resnick and Wolff (1987, 231-32) argue that the state is in a contradictory position in capitalist society, guarding against its excesses while also supporting and maintaining the conditions necessary for "the capitalist fundamental class process." For example, laws that support the creation of corporations or the "freedom" to purchase and sell labour exemplify how the state provides ongoing support to capitalist endeavours. Subsumed class payments from capital to the state have helped to defray the costs of providing these services, a cycle that helps ensure that fundamental class processes continue in a profitable manner (Resnick and Wolff 1987, 235). At the same time, however, the state must occasionally enact laws that do not necessarily favour capitalist class interests, as was the case with the Westray bill. The point is the state "does not merely derive from and reflect some subset of its constituent processes," including the capitalist economy (Resnick and Wolff 1987, 252). As Resnick and Wolff (1987, 253) argue, "rather than an entity determined by the economy or a particular economic class, the state is a specific subset of social processes, each of which is overdetermined by the other processes in that subset and by all the other political, natural, cultural, as well as economic processes in the society."

Corporations beyond the Law?

A key message of *Still Dying for a Living* is that the assumptions that have animated Canada's corporate criminal liability legislation and the meanings inscribed in its provisions throw serious doubt on its ability to hold corporations legally accountable for their harmful, anti-social acts. As Laureen Snider (2004, 180) argues, "if neither the law nor the public can 'see' crime except through the body of the individual bad acts, the possibilities of disciplining the most powerful entities in the modern social order – the organizations dominating our economic and political system – appear slim." What is more, the possibilities of disciplining the corporate form seem all the more daunting in the face of neo-liberalism's globalizing efforts, a hegemonic project that has transformed the corporation (along with its illegalities) into a transnational actor (Tombs and Whyte 2003a). There is thus little reason to believe that the law will produce a crackdown on safety crimes or seriously challenge companies to address workplace injuries and death in industries where fixing these problems is an expensive proposition. Although the Westray bill will hold some corporations and corporate actors accountable – and, thus far, it has been the smallest and weakest that have been subject to the law's gaze – the primary causes of workplace injury and death (for example, the tension between profit maximization and the costs of safety and the relative worth of workers/employees versus owners and investors) will continue.

Despite this gloomy outlook, it would be erroneous to conclude that the production of corporate criminal liability legislation has been pre-determined or its future complete. J.K. Gibson-Graham and David Ruccio (2001, 159) caution against over-analyzing the downsides of capitalist hegemony, particularly the tendency to view it as all-encompassing and dominating, therein diminishing our ability to think of alternatives and causing us to pessimistically believe that "cultural practices of resistances" lack the "potential for development." Non-capitalist positions are thus seen to be the "opposite" of capitalism, too weak or marginal to make a difference, or simply "complementary" in that they support the status quo (168). We therefore need to conceptualize capitalism's effects within the framework of class processes of "producing, appropriating and distributing surplus labour" (169) – a process of becoming, not a necessity within a structure.

We cannot lose site of the fact that the evolution of the Westray bill was, and is, a process of becoming, one in which capitalism is both challenged and reinforced. The law was not a predetermined result but, rather, a process that emerged through various legal, political, and economic discourses. It was, in Althusserian terms, a "result produced by a history" (Althusser and Balibar [1968] 1997, 64). After all, the mere fact that this legislation was introduced speaks to the incompleteness of capitalism's hegemony. What is more, the United Steelworkers of America's ongoing lobbying for the Westray bill's enforcement, most notably their recent attempt to launch a private prosecution, reminds us that the law's fate is far from predetermined. It illustrates that corporate and economic dominance is always uncertain, fluid, and open to contestation; that powerful interests that favour the corporate agenda are not automatic, the state is not always an instrument of capital; and that implementing laws to protect workers is not impossible (Tombs and Whyte 2007). It reminds us that dominant economic logic does not automatically impose its will but instead "depends on the outcome of political and ideological struggles around political process and hegemonic visions as well as the ecological dominance of the circuit of capital" (Jessop 2002, 30).

From this vantage point, we should recall that the Westray bill is a new and symbolically important way to speak of corporate wrongdoing – a language that departs from regulatory approaches to corporate offences that have dominated for more than two decades. In this respect, it is emblematic of growing concerns with the dangers of corporate power in the absence of accountability (Pearce and Snider 1995). At the very least, it creates the possibility for change, an important foundation for future struggles to ensure workers' safety.

Appendix A

Members of the Standing Committee on Justice and Human Rights

The following is a list of members of the Standing Committee on Justice and Human Rights whose names appear in the minutes from the committee's study of corporate criminal liability legislation in May 2002. Members' names are listed in alphabetical order.

Michel Bellehumeur, Bloc Québécois
Bill Blaikie, New Democratic Party
Chuck Cadman, Canadian Alliance Party
Beverly Desjarlais, New Democratic Party
Hedy Fry, Liberal Party
Ivan Grose, Liberal Party
Jay Hill, Canadian Alliance Party
Mario Laframboise, Bloc Québécois
Robert Lanctôt, Bloc Québécois
Derek Lee, Liberal Party
Peter MacKay, Progressive Conservative Party
Paul Harold Macklin, Liberal Party
John Maloney, Liberal Party
John McKay, Liberal Party
Lorne Nystrom, New Democratic Party
Andy Scott, Chair, Standing Committee on Justice and Human Rights, Liberal Party
Kevin Sorenson, Canadian Alliance Party
Vic Toews, Canadian Alliance Party

Appendix B

Details Regarding Data Sources

The following is a detailed summary of the data sources used in this study. The first data source includes approximately thirty-five hours of Hansard documents, verbatim transcripts of various proceedings from Canada's Parliament. The timeline of these documents ranges from discussion and debate regarding the first version of the New Democratic Party's (NDP) private members' legislation tabled in February 1999 to the royal assent of Bill C-45, *An Act to Amend the Criminal Code (Criminal Liability of Organizations)* (Westray bill) in November 2003. They fall into two categories. The first contains statements and debates regarding various iterations of the NDP's private members' bill, the Progressive Conservative (PC) Party's private members' motion, and the government's legislation, including questions posed to the government in the House of Commons (for example, during question period), statements from members of parliament (MPs) on the anniversary of the Westray disaster, and general comments concerning the importance of corporate criminal liability law reform. A total of thirty documents were located and examined, twelve of which included significant statements from, and exchanges between, MPs in the House of Commons and Senate. These exchanges produced approximately fourteen and one-half hours of verbatim transcripts. Although the remaining documents contained information relating to Bill C-45, particularly in determining the timelines of various events, they represented brief interventions only (for example, short statements by a single MP) and therefore did not produce significant data for analysis.

The second category includes verbatim transcripts from the Standing Committee on Justice and Human Rights' (Justice Committee) study of corporate criminal liability. During the spring of 2002, the committee held a total of ten meetings, during which members received briefs, heard testimony, and asked questions of thirty-four witnesses representing a range of opinions and positions. These witnesses included lawyers and legal experts, union representatives, sociologists, criminologists, family members of victims of corporate disasters, and non-governmental organizations. The Justice Committee's hearings produced approximately twenty-one and one-half hours of verbatim transcripts. In addition, some witnesses provided written submissions to the committee in support of their appearance. Hard and electronic copies of these submissions were provided by the clerk of the Justice Committee. A majority of these documents represented the speaking notes that witnesses used in support of their committee appearance.

The second data source includes twenty-three semi-structured interviews, conducted to gain insight into the varied constitution of corporate criminal liability throughout the reform process, the knowledge claims that helped frame the Westray bill. Participants were purposively selected for their knowledge of corporate criminal liability law reform and related issues. At the end of each interview, participants were asked for suggestions for additional interview participants. The goal was to ensure that I interviewed a broad cross-section of individuals with a range of opinions. In addition to individuals who appeared before the Justice Committee – the voices that helped constitute the law – this list includes individuals familiar with the law's development and enforcement. Participants included union and labour representatives, corporate and private sector lawyers, legal academics, government employees, politicians, non-governmental organization workers, and private sector representatives.

The interviews took place from early September to mid-December 2008 (due to scheduling difficulties, one interview with a private sector representative was conducted in March 2009). The average interview length was one hour and the median length was fifty-seven minutes. The longest interview lasted almost ninety minutes, while the shortest was just over thirty minutes. In all but two cases, respondents agreed to have the interviews audio-recorded. For the unrecorded interviews, extensive notes were taken both during and immediately following the interviews to ensure the greatest possible accuracy of the information collected. For recorded interviews, notes were taken during the interviews (for backup purposes), and the majority of each interview was transcribed from the audio recording as soon as possible afterwards. These recordings produced approximately 136 single-spaced pages of transcription.

The third data source includes Internet searches to glean additional details regarding the Westray bill. The Internet was useful for tracking charges and convictions, a strategy made necessary by the fact that no government body is responsible for this task. In addition, the Internet provided an opportunity to explore some of the reaction to the Westray bill, including education and training programs in relation to the new law (as examined in Chapter 6).

Appendix C

Witnesses Appearing before the Standing Committee on Justice and Human Rights

Thursday, 2 May 2002

- Dave Whellams, Criminal Law Policy Section, Department of Justice Canada
- Greg Yost, Criminal Law Policy Section, Department of Justice Canada
- Dominique Vaillancourt, vice-president, director of outreach and communication, Canadian Council for the Rights of Injured Workers
- Maria York, president, Canadian Council for the Rights of Injured Workers
- Doug Perrault, president, Ottawa and District Injured Workers Group
- Vern Theriault, individual presenter, former Westray mine employee

Tuesday, 7 May 2002

- Allen Martin, Westray Families Group
- David Miezenger, Ottawa and District Labour Council
- Duff Conacher, chairperson, Corporate Responsibility Coalition

Wednesday, 8 May 2002

- Lawrence McBrearty, national director, United Steelworkers of America
- Andrew King, department leader, Health, Safety, and Environment, United Steelworkers of America

Thursday, 9 May 2002

- Bev Desjarlais, member of parliament, New Democratic Party, and sponsor of private member's bill on corporate criminal liability
- David Bennett, national director, Health, Safety and Environment, Canadian Labour Congress
- Hassan Yussuff, executive vice-president, Canadian Labour Congress
- Barbara Davidson, OC Transpo Widows
- Terrie Lemay, OC Transpo Widows.

Wednesday, 22 May 2002

- Susan Dodd, sociologist

Thursday, 23 May 2002

- Louis Erlichman, International Association of Machinists and Aerospace Workers in Canada
- Poonam Puri, individual presenter, Osgoode Hall Law School
- Anne-Marie Boisvert, individual presenter, University of Montreal Law School
- Tamara Thomson, director, Legislation and Law Reform, Canadian Bar Association
- Greg DelBiggio, member, National Criminal Justice Section, Canadian Bar Association
- Chris McCormick, individual presenter, St. Thomas University (Criminology)

Thursday, 28 May 2002

- Patrick Healy, individual presenter, McGill University Law School
- Clare Mocherie, director, Aurora Institute
- William Trudell, chair, Canadian Council of Defence Lawyers

Wednesday, 29 May 2002

- Honourable Justice K. Peter Richard, commissioner, Westray Mine Public Inquiry (In Camera Evidence)

Appendix C

Thursday, 30 May 2002

- William Lenton, assistant commissioner, Federal Services, Royal Canadian Mounted Police
- Gil Yaron, director, Law and Policy, Shareholder Association for Research and Education

Wednesday, 22 October 2003

- Richard Mosley, assistant deputy minister, Criminal Law Policy Section, Department of Justice Canada
- Donald Piragoff, Criminal Law Policy Section, Department of Justice Canada
- Greg Yost, Criminal Law Policy Section, Department of Justice Canada
- Joanne Klineberg, Criminal Law Policy Section, Department of Justice Canada
- William Bartlett, Criminal Law Policy Section, Department of Justice Canada
- Lucie Angers, Criminal Law Policy Section, Department of Justice Canada

Appendix D

Interview Participants

A total of twenty-three interviews were conducted as part of this research. The interviews are listed by number, category of interviewee, and date of interview. For reasons of confidentiality, the names of participants are not provided. The breakdown of the interviews, by category, is as follows: government officials (2); non-governmental representatives (3); corporate lawyers (3); criminal lawyers/legal academics (4); union representatives (4); politicians (3); regulators (1); and private sector representatives (3).

Interview 1: Government official, 9 September 2008
Interview 2: Non-governmental representative, 11 September 2008
Interview 3: Government official, 3 October 2008
Interview 4: Corporate lawyer, 7 October 2008
Interview 5: Criminal lawyer, 8 October 2008
Interview 6: Union representative, 8 October 2008
Interview 7: Corporate lawyer, 9 October 2008
Interview 8: Legal academic, 9 October 2008
Interview 9: Union representative, 9 October 2008
Interview 10: Non-governmental representative, 23 October 2008
Interview 11: Politician, 3 November 2008
Interview 12: Union official, 11 November 2008
Interview 13: Non-governmental representative, 11 November 2008
Interview 14: Private sector representative, 18 November 2008
Interview 15: Politician, 19 November 2008

Interview 16: Union representative, 20 November 2008
Interview 17: Legal academic, 20 November 2008
Interview 18: Corporate lawyer, 28 November 2008
Interview 19: Legal academic, 8 December 2008
Interview 20: Politician, 9 December 2008
Interview 21: Regulator, 15 December 2008
Interview 22: Private sector representative, 16 December 2008
Interview 23: Private sector representative, 2 March 2009

Appendix E

Interview Schedule

Part I: Introduction: The Meaning of Corporate Crime and Corporate Criminal Liability

(1) What do you think of when you hear the term corporate crime?

(2) What do you think of when you hear the term occupational health and safety offences?

(3) What do you think of when you hear the term corporate criminal liability?

(4) What do you consider to be the main causes of corporate crime?

(5) What do you consider to be main factors that contribute to occupational health and safety offences?

(6) How do you think the government should respond to corporate crime?

(7) How should the government respond to serious injury in the workplace?

(8) How should the government respond to cases involving death in the workplace?

Part II: The Introduction of Corporate Criminal Liability Legislation

(1) What influence do you think the Westray disaster had for the introduction of corporate criminal liability legislation in Canada?

(2) In your opinion, are there any other factors that provided the impetus for Canada's corporate criminal liability legislation?

(3)   Can you tell me who was involved in lobbying for the introduction of corporate criminal liability legislation?

(4)   Were you involved in the federal government's consultations that preceded this legislation?
(a) If so, can you please tell me what your position was regarding the need for corporate criminal liability legislation?
(b) Has your position changed since then?

(5)   If yes to question 4: Can you please tell me about your experiences testifying before the House of Commons Standing Committee on Justice and Human Rights?
(a) What did you think of the process?
(b) What did you think of the questions that were posed by Justice Committee members?

(6)   Are you familiar with the different individuals and groups who appeared before the House of Commons Standing Committee on Justice and Human Rights?
(a) If so, in your opinion, were there any omissions in terms of the witness list?

(7)   Are you familiar with the different legislative options that were proposed before the final legislation was tabled in Parliament?
(a) If so, what is your opinion of the different options?

(8)   Can you tell me about the main components of Bill C-45/the Westray bill?
(a) How does it assign corporate criminal liability?

(9)   What was your response to the legislation (Bill C-45) following its introduction?
(a) In your opinion, is this legislation necessary?
(b) Are there elements that you believe are missing from the law?

(10) Are you familiar with the sentencing regime contained in the Bill C-45/the Westray bill?
(a) If so, what are your impressions of these punishment options?
(b) In your opinion, are there any punishment options that are missing from the law?

(11) What message do you believe the federal government sent with the introduction of Bill C-45/the Westray bill?

(12) In your opinion, does this legislation represent a fundamental change in corporate criminal liability?

Part III: Expectations for Bill C-45/the Westray Bill

(1)   What are your expectations for this legislation?

(2)   In your opinion, what will the legislation achieve?

(3)   Can you tell me how the Westray bill has been enforced since its enactment?

(4)   Are you familiar with any of the cases for which charges have been laid under this legislation?
(a) If so, how were charges laid?
(b) Did the charges proceed to court?
(c) What was the final outcome of the case(s)?

(5)   In your opinion, how should the government enforce this legislation?

(6)   What legal evidence do you think will be needed to secure a charge under this new law?

(7)   Are you aware of any problems with enforcing this law since its enactment?

(8)   Some observers have noted that the new law blurs the line between regulatory and criminal offences. What is your opinion of this statement?

(9)   Other observers have suggested that the new law will make relations between regulators and corporations increasingly adversarial. In other words, companies will be less inclined to cooperate with regulators if there is a possibility of future criminal charges. What is your opinion of this position?

(10) Some observers suggest that regulatory offences are more effective because they encourage corporations to establish safe working environments. Do you agree?
(a) If yes, why?
(b) If no, why not?

(11) What other strategies, besides the use of criminal law, do you think the government should consider when addressing occupational health and safety offences?

(12) Are you aware of similar legislation in other countries/jurisdictions?
(a) If so, how do they compare to the Westray bill?

Appendix E

Part IV: Conclusion

(1) Is there anything else that you would like to discuss?
(2) Is there anything that you feel that I omitted to ask?
(3) Do you have any final comments?

Notes

Foreword

1 *Public Company Accounting Reform and Investor Protection Act of 2002,* Public Law 107-204, 107th Congress [*Sarbanes-Oxley Act*].
2 The Who, "Won't Get Fooled Again," from the album *Who's Next* (1971), produced by The Who and Glyn Johns.
3 Bill C-45, *An Act to Amend the Criminal Code (Criminal Liability of Organizations),* RC 2003, c 21.
4 *Corporate Manslaughter and Corporate Homicide Act,* 2007 Chapter 19 (United Kingdom).

Preface

1 *Criminal Law,* RSC 1985, c C-46.
2 Bill C-45, *An Act to Amend the Criminal Code (Criminal Liability of Organizations),* RC 2003, c 21.

Chapter 1: Introduction

1 The authors attribute the increase over the two years to fatalities related to occupational diseases, such as "exposure to harmful substances and environments" (for example, asbestos), which take years to develop and detect (Sharpe and Hardt 2006, 43).
2 According to Statistics Canada, police "solved" (meaning someone was charged in) 75 percent of reported homicides in 2004, a conservative estimate given that many cases are not solved until a number of years after the incident is reported in official statistics (Dauvergne 2005, 12).
3 Bill C-45, *An Act to Amend the Criminal Code (Criminal Liability of Organizations),* RC 2003, c 21.
4 *Criminal Law,* RSC 1985, c C-46.
5 The Royal Canadian Mounted Police (the provincial police in Nova Scotia) waited nearly two weeks before launching a criminal investigation and another three months before seizing company records and equipment as evidence (McMullan 2001, 135-36). From the outset, the prosecution was underfunded and inadequately staffed, leading to the eventual resignation of the prosecution team and leaving the responsibility for assembling the case largely in the hands of the police, who

were ill-equipped to deal with such legal complexities (McMullan 2005, 28). Although the case eventually proceeded under the guidance of a new team of prosecutors, it was derailed after the defence successfully argued for a mistrial based on the non-disclosure of evidence. Upon appeal, a new trial was ordered, but the Crown decided against renewing its efforts, citing considerable disagreement among experts as to the cause of the explosion and, therefore, the unlikelihood of securing a conviction (30).

6 Despite this prompt announcement, it was five years later, after much legal wrangling about whether the inquiry could proceed, while a criminal trial was pending, before the inquiry began hearing evidence from more than seventy-one witnesses, including miners, mine and labour experts, government representatives, and elected officials. Conspicuously absent from the witness list was the chief executive officer of Curragh Resources, Clifford Frame, who called the inquiry a "railroad job and a farce," insisting the disaster was an "accident" (McMullan 2005, 31). Despite repeated legal attempts to compel Frame to appear before the inquiry, he never testified.

7 In addition to exposing the ineffectiveness of the Department of Labour's compliance-oriented approach to mine safety, which effectively encouraged a "culture of indifference" between mine management and inspectors, the disregard for workplace safety stood as a perilous reminder of what happens when the pursuit of profit takes priority over human life (McMullan 2005, 26).

8 According to the Parliament of Canada's website, "Private Members' Bills are bills introduced in the House of Commons by individual Members who are not cabinet ministers and in the Senate by individual Senators who are not members of the Ministry" (Parliament of Canada, http://www2. parl.gc.ca). The order paper is the business agenda for the House of Commons.

9 See House of Commons Standing Committee on Justice and Human Rights, Fifteenth Report, 1st Session, 37th Parliament.

10 Bill C-284, *An Act to Amend the Criminal Code (Offences by Corporations, Directors and Officers)*, 1st Session, 37th Parliament, 49-50 Elizabeth II, 2001.

11 For exceptions from the corporate crime literature, see Doran (1996), Pearce and Tombs (1998), and Snider (1990).

Chapter 2: Criminal Liability and the Corporate Form

1 Bill C-45, *An Act to Amend the Criminal Code (Criminal Liability of Organizations)*, RC 2003, c 21.

2 Hansard is the official recording (transcripts) of all proceedings in Parliament (see Hansard Association of Canada, http://www.hansard.ca). All Hansard recordings referenced throughout this book were taken from the Parliament of Canada's website, http://www.parl.gc.ca. References include the date of the parliamentary proceeding and, where appropriate, the individual speaker, his or her political party, and the time at which they spoke. *Criminal Code*, RSC 1985, c C-46.

3 *Salomon v Salomon and Company, Ltd; Salomon and Company, Ltd v Salomon*, [1895-1899] All ER Rep 33; [1895-1899] All ER 33 (HL), established the legal principle that any company adhering to the "statutory requirements for incorporation" is a "legal entity separate and distinct from the individual members of the company" (Yalden et al. 2008, 135). *Companies Act*, 1862, 25 & 26 Vict, c. 89.

4 Yalden et al. (2008, 251-54) catalogue these benefits as: providing shareholders with limited liability; establishing the corporate form in perpetuity; permitting the transfer of shares between interested parties (a process that is limited only by certain securities laws or express limitations imposed by corporate bylaws); preventing individual shareholders from obligating the "body corporate" (corporate authority is commonly delegated to management); enabling the corporation to secure additional capital that is beyond the capacity of any particular shareholder; and ensuring particular tax advantages.

5 The courts have also imposed limits on the limited liability corporation by occasionally "piercing" or "lifting" the "corporate veil" in the interests of justice. For example, the courts have held shareholders responsible when principal investors have used the corporation for purely fraudulent reasons;

when intentional torts have been committed; where the company has avoided taxation; and when the court has determined that "equity or the interests of justice are better served by disregarding the corporate form" (Yalden et al. 2008, 168). Limits also emerge in the context of small businesses. First, banks that finance these ventures will often require that the principals involved personally guarantee the "company's indebtedness." Second, there is often considerable overlap between those who invest in the corporation and those who are involved in the firm's daily operations – a convergence between owners and workers (148-49).

6   *Canada Business Corporations Act,* RSC 1985, c 44.

7   *Peoples Department Store Inc. (Trustee of) v Wise* ([2004] 3 SCR 461, 2004 SCC 68).

8   For some observers, the question that must be asked is whether the modern corporate form has evolved from being a site of production to a vehicle for generating financial capital, making the venture inherently criminogenic (Tomisac 2002; see also Glasbeek 2004).

9   The development of the corporate form in Canada was not seamless in terms of adopting English law. For example, until the 1970s, Canada had both letters patent and memorandum jurisdictions governing the creation of corporations. Letter patents systems were more prescriptive than memorandum jurisdictions in terms of the structure of the corporation, and responsible ministers in letter patent systems had ultimate power to decide whether or not to grant the letter patent. In comparison, memorandum jurisdictions were more akin to the process of modern incorporation, including that the process of granting corporations took a less restrictive approach to paperwork and approval. Today, there is relative harmony across Canada in regard to the legal formation of the corporate form (Yalden et al. 2008, 221).

10   *Lennard's Carrying Co Ltd v Asiatic Petroleum Co Ltd,* [1915] AC 705 (House of Lords). It was in 1842 that a corporation was first dealt with via criminal law for "failure to satisfy absolute statutory duties" (Slapper and Tombs 1999, 27).

11   See *DPP v Kent and Sussex Contractors,* [1944] 1 KB 810; *R v ICR Road Haulage Ltd,* [1944] 1 KB 551; *Moore v Bresler,* [1944] 2 All ER 515 (see, by way of comparison, Slapper and Tombs 1999, 29).

12   Anand and Penley (2005, 950) suggest that the introduction of Bill C-45 stands as the most recent example of the limits that are imposed upon corporations.

13   *Canadian Dredge and Dock Company v The Queen,* [1985] 1 SCR 662.

14   The Standing Committee on Justice and Human Rights' (Justice Committee) proposal was modelled after the recommendations of the Law Reform Commission of Canada (LRCC). In 1987, as part of its proposed recodification of criminal law in Canada, the LRCC argued that "the sort of harm prohibited by criminal law may well result from corporate activity involving negligence in the organizational process rather than in the conduct of any single individual" (Law Reform Commission of Canada 1987, 26). Prior to this, the LRCC recommended changes to criminal law to include corporate responsibility for *"acts and omissions of corporate agents and employees where it appeared that the acts or omissions were tied to policy choices made by someone to whom important decision-making functions had been delegated"* (Law Reform Commission of Canada 1976, 21-22 [emphasis in original]).

15   The report recommended that, for offences requiring proof of intent, a corporation commits an offence when one or more of its representatives commits the offence and one or more of the corporation's representatives knew that the offence would or could take place, directed the offence to take place, either explicitly or implicitly, and had the requisite state of mind for committing the offence. For cases requiring proof of negligence, the minister recommended that a corporation commits an offence when one or more of its representatives has the requisite authority to commit the offence or contribute to its occurrence and the representative(s) fails to exercise reasonable care to prevent the offence from occurring (Minister of Justice Canada 1993, 6-7). A representative is defined broadly as "a director, officer, employee, member or agent" (7).

16   The report also suggests that the Westray disaster was set in motion from the point that Curragh became interested in the Pictou coal project, which was based on significant government support

Notes to pages 19-22

as opposed to the "merits of the project" itself (Richard 1997, 610). In particular, it was only because of the provincial government's support and commitment, which included pre-purchasing a set amount of coal at above-market prices, that the project was even able to take shape (610).

17 *Occupational Health and Safety Act,* 1996, c 7, s 1.

18 The main political parties in Canada's Parliament at the time were the Liberal Party (the government, centrist in orientation), the Canadian Alliance Party (right-wing/conservative), the Progressive Conservative Party (centre-right), the Bloc Québécois Party (independence movement), and the New Democratic Party (left-wing).

19 The NDP tabled private members' bills on five occasions: Alexa McDonough tabled private members' bills on 5 February 1999, 21 October 1999, 7 February 2001, and 20 March 2003. Bev Desjarlais tabled her private members' bill on 26 February 2001.

20 The Parliament of Canada's website notes that private members' motions are "used to introduce a wide range of issues and are framed either as orders or resolutions." Even if adopted by members of the House of Commons, a motion is non-binding given that it is "only stating its opinion or making a declaration of purpose." House of Commons Procedures, Parliament of Canada, http://www.parl.gc.ca.

21 Bill C-284, *An Act to Amend the Criminal Code (Offences by Corporations, Directors and Officers),* 1st Session, 37th Parliament, 49-50 Elizabeth II, 2001. Bills must pass through a number of stages in Canada's Parliament before becoming law. The first stage is when a member of parliament (MP) introduces a bill in the House of Commons, usually offering a brief overview of the proposed legislation. The second stage provides MPs with an opportunity to discuss and debate the bill, the results of which may lead to amendments. The second stage also involves sending the bill to a parliamentary committee for study and to approve it or make modifications. At the third stage, the bill is returned to the House of Commons where MPs decide whether it should be passed. If passed, the bill is then sent to the Senate where it proceeds through a process that is similar to the first and second stages. Once a bill is passed in the Senate, it receives Royal Assent and officially becomes an Act of Parliament. House of Commons Procedure, Parliament of Canada, http://www.parl.gc.ca.

22 House of Commons Standing Committee on Justice and Human Rights, Fifteenth Report, 1st Session, 37th Parliament.

23 All bills die on the order paper when a session of Parliament is prorogued. For a bill to get back on the order paper (to be reconsidered), it must be reintroduced when Parliament resumes sitting. Parliament of Canada, http://www.parl.gc.ca.

24 Although both bills were virtually identical, Desjarlais' version provided for larger fines (Hansard, 20 September 2001, 17:35). The difference was necessary because parliamentary rules and procedures stipulate that a private member's bill can only be tabled by one MP at a time. Providing for different sentences therefore rendered the bills to be separate private members' initiatives.

25 Still unsure whether the government would introduce corporate criminal liability legislation, the NDP tabled one more version of their private members' bill on 20 March 2003 (Hansard, 20 March 2003, 15:10).

26 Within the Australian legislation, there is a "due diligence" defence in which the onus can be refocused on the individual if it can be shown the person lacked "reasonable grounds" to justify that their action or omission was permissible (Department of Justice Canada 2002a).

27 All references to the Justice Committee were taken from the Parliament of Canada's website, http://www.parl.gc.ca.

28 For House of Commons debates concerning MacKay's motion, see the following: 23 April 1999, 18 February 2000, 3 March 2000, 13 March 2000, 21 March 2000, 7 June 2000, 5 October 2000 (all taken from Hansard). The Justice Committee did not hear from any witnesses during its consideration of the motion (the meeting lasted approximately 2.5 hours). However, representatives of the United Steelworkers of America, who were on Parliament Hill at the time lobbying for the introduction of corporate criminal liability legislation, spoke to the committee near the end of the meeting.

The comments they provided underscored the importance of introducing new legislation; however, they did not factor into the committee's discussion or vote concerning the motion (Justice Committee, 6 June 2000).

29 See also House of Commons Standing Committee on Justice and Human Rights, Fifth Report, 2nd Session, 36th Parliament, 7 June 2000.

30 The thirty-seventh general election was held on 27 November 2000. The Liberal Party was returned to power with 41 percent of the vote, equating to 57 percent of the seats in the House of Commons (for election results, see Elections Canada, http://www.elections.ca).

31 All sessions began with presentations from the witness(es), lasting approximately ten minutes each, followed by comments and questions from the Justice Committee members. Witnesses could also provide written briefs for the committee's consideration. Committees are comprised of members of the House of Commons or Senate (or both) who are asked by the House of Commons to study specific matters (for example, proposed legislation). Committees typically have twelve members, the distribution of which is determined by each party's distribution in the House of Commons. There are a variety of committees in Canada's Parliament (legislative, special, standing, joint, subcommittees, Committees of the Whole, and the Liaison Committee). Standing committees are permanent committees that may "study matters referred to it by special order or, within its area of responsibility in the Standing Orders, may undertake studies on its own initiative." Once a committee has completed its work, they may issue a report with findings to the House of Commons (see Parliament of Canada's website, http://www2.parl.gc.ca).

32 Standing Committee on Justice and Human Rights, Fifteenth Report, 1st Session, 37th Parliament.

33 The government also introduced changes to the *Canada Labour Code,* RSC 1985, c L-2, which strengthened the role of workplace health and safety committees and established the right to know about workplace hazards and the right to refuse unsafe working conditions (Hansard, 15 September 2003, 13:35-13:40). The *Canada Labour Code* applies to only federal government employees, who constitute approximately 10 percent of the Canadian workforce.

34 *Criminal Code, supra* note 2 at s 2.

35 Ibid at s 22.1.

36 Ibid at s 22.2.

37 Another approach is specific legislation relating to corporate manslaughter. Recently enacted in the United Kingdom, chapter 19 of the Corporate Manslaughter and Corporate Homicide Act, 2007 Chapter 19 (United Kingdom), introduces the offence of corporate manslaughter (corporate homicide in Scotland) when senior management grossly departs from a duty of care owed to an individual and that departure causes a person's death. In Canada, this approach was criticized for creating a specific offence when laws already exist to deal with this type of behaviour and for narrowly focusing on death only at the expense of workplace accidents (Department of Justice Canada, 2002a).

38 Individuals found guilty will be subject to penalties already prescribed by the *Criminal Code, supra* note 2.

39 Ibid at s 718.21.

40 Ibid at s 735.

41 Ibid at s 732.1.

42 Reference to the Westray bill is also found in *R v Ontario Power Generation,* [2006] OJ No 4659 (see also *R v Tammadge,* [2006] OJ No 5103). Two Ontario Power Generation (OPG) employees were charged with criminal negligence causing death after two people were killed and seven seriously injured when the employees opened the sluice gates for a hydro dam at Barrett Chute (near Calabogie, Ontario), immediately flooding a spillway known to be frequented by swimmers. In a motion from the co-accused for a direct verdict of acquittal (which was dismissed), the judge noted that the law had changed "significantly" with the introduction of Bill C-45. Although the judge could not apply the new law retroactively, he nonetheless stated that its introduction meant that the corporation could now be held responsible for the "aggregated results of the actions of its key officials and their

delegates" (*Ontario Power Generation* at paras. 6 and 7). The judge also noted that, although one of the accused could not be considered a "directing mind of OPG" under the identification doctrine, the situation would be different if Bill C-45 was in effect. As the judge stated, "this case illustrates vividly why the law changed in 2003. Clearly the same result would not obtain today but I am bound to apply the law as it existed" at the time of the incident (para. 36). The two accused were eventually acquitted of all charges when the judge ruled that their actions were not criminal, even if they were negligent in not taking all necessary steps to address the hazards associated with opening the sluice gates (*Tammadge*).

43 *R v Fantini*, [2005] OJ No 2361.

44 *Occupational Health and Safety Act*, RSO 1990, c 0.1.

45 *Fantini, supra* note 42 at para. 20.

46 *R c Transpavé inc*, [2008] JQ no 1857 [*Transpavé*].

47 *R v Scrocca*, [2010] QCCQ 8218 [*Scrocca*].

48 Other Westray bill-related cases were concluding or pending as of the final edits to the book. For example, two employees of a Quebec railway company were charged with criminal negligence causing death and criminal negligence causing bodily harm after an employee was killed and three workers injured when the maintenance vehicle they were driving collided with a train. The court found the accused not guilty as a result of the Crown's failure to prove criminal negligence beyond a reasonable doubt. No charges were brought against the company (Keith and Abbott 2011). The officer of a BC ferry was charged with two counts of criminal negligence causing death after the ferry he was responsible for navigating ran aground and sank off the north coast of Vancouver Island. While fifty-seven passengers and forty-two crew members made it off the ferry before it sank, two passengers were never found and were declared dead. The case continues to make its way through the courts (Baily 2010). Finally, a service manager at a Quebec Volkswagen dealership was charged with criminal negligence causing death after an employee was burned to death while using a broken fuel pump. A preliminary inquiry revealed that the pump had been broken for years (Keith 2011).

49 *Fantini, supra* note 42; *Scrocca, supra* note 46; *Transpavé, supra* note 45.

50 The concepts of discourse and discourse analysis are considered as vague and highly contestable terms (Fairclough et al. 2004, 3; Mills 1997). Helping fuel the debate is the variety of approaches to discourse analysis used by researchers over the years (Fairclough 1992, 3), and that there is no "blue print" for "doing discourse analysis" (225). As Fairclough (1992, 225) notes, "people approach it in different ways according to the specific nature of the project, as well as their own views of discourse." In recent years, researchers have explored more systematic and detailed methods of collecting and analyzing discourse. As part of this transition, they have "turned to more developed frameworks," such as critical discourse analysis, "conversation analysis," and "discursive psychology," to guide their work (Fairclough et al. 2004, 3). In the process, discourse analysis has become an established field within "social theory and research" (3).

51 The authors use semiosis in reference to language and discourse (Fairclough, Jessop, and Sayer 2002).

52 The roots of critical discourse studies trace back to various strands of Marxism and neo-Marxist approaches, a tradition that concerned itself with the intersections between discourse and social structure. Over the past twenty years, this critical theory of discourse was thrown into disrepute by the "Foucauldian revolution" as well as feminist perspectives that questioned the Marxist understanding of power and commitment to structuralism (McKenna 2004, 10-11). Recently, however, there are indications that this hostility has run its course and that it is time to consider the complementary nature of Foucauldian post-structuralism with neo-Marxism (see, for example, Fairclough 1992; Fairclough, Jessop, and Sayer 2002).

53 These documents were obtained from the Parliament of Canada's website using keyword searches of "corporate criminal liability," "Bill C-45," "Westray bill," and "Westray." See Parliament of Canada, http://www.parl.gc.ca.

54 The transcripts from these meetings were available on the Parliament of Canada's website, http://www.parl.gc.ca. Nine of the meetings were held on 2-30 May 2003, while the final meeting was held on 22 October 2003, after the government's legislation was referred to the Justice Committee for its review. One meeting on 29 May 2002, with Justice K. Peter Richard, chair of the Westray inquiry, was held in camera.

55 Of the twenty-seven people that I contacted to participate in this research, three declined. One labour representative had retired and believed that he no longer understood the issues well enough to participate (he referred me to a colleague). Another individual declined as the organization that he worked for was now defunct and he was not comfortable speaking to the issue given his new work responsibilities. An academic agreed to participate, but scheduling conflicts made it difficult to conduct the interview (I eventually interviewed another academic instead). In addition, I also had some difficulties finding individuals from the private sector who were willing to participate in the research. This final issue is discussed further in Chapter 6 of this book.

Chapter 3: Theorizing Corporate Harm and Wrongdoing

1 There is also a range of literature that is beyond this chapter, which theorizes about the causes of corporate malfeasance (for a summary of these theories, see Snider 1993).

2 Examples of this influence include: contemporary control theorists (Tittle 1995, 1997, 2004; Lattimore, Tittle, and Grasmick 2006); general strain theory (Agnew 1992, 2006; Froggio and Agnew 2007); life-course approaches (Sampson and Laub 2005a, 2005b; Sampson, Laub, and Wimer 2006); symbolic interactionism studies (Heimer 1996; De Coster and Heimer 2001); and integrationist research (Miethe and Meier 1990, 1994).

3 This includes, for example, critical feminist (for example, see Balfour and Comack 2006; Carlen 1985; Chunn and Lacombe 2000) and critical race scholars (for example, Backhouse 1999; Razack 2002). Foucault's (1978a, 1978b, 1979, 1980) work also provides innumerable contributions to the study of crime and deviance, particularly his examinations of a "disciplinary society" (power as dispersed throughout the entire social body) and the relationship between knowledge and power.

4 Coleman's (1987) integrated theory of corporate crime combines elements of interactionist theory with broader considerations of the "culture of competition." Braithwaite (1989) argues that combining aspects of opportunity, subcultural, and control theories can explain why some corporate actors and corporations commit crimes, while others do not.

5 Tombs and Whyte (2007, 4) focus on safety rather than health since the two concepts involve "common, but many distinct" issues. While the impact of occupational safety crime is often immediate (for example, death resulting from a catastrophic event), health offences are more difficult to measure in that establishing causation is complex and unfolds over a long period (for example, cancers and other occupational diseases). This distinction is relevant to this research in that Canada's corporate criminal liability legislation emerged in response to safety crimes, and it is therefore unclear whether legislators envisioned health offences as part of the equation.

6 However, Slapper and Tombs (1999, 2-3) point out that the concept of corporate crime dates back to the work of Proudhon ([1840] 1966), Marx and Engels, as well as Bonger's ([1905] 1969) characterization of capitalism as criminogenic and Morris's ([1877] 1947) list of "upperworld" criminals.

7 Bill C-45, *An Act to Amend the Criminal Code (Criminal Liability of Organizations)*, RC 2003, c 21.

8 Mitnick (1980, 20) defines regulatory law as "the intentional restriction of a subject's choice of activity by an entity not directly party or involved in that activity" (as quoted in Snider 1990, 38).

9 Although unionized workers were better able to profit from joint health and safety committees, this benefit was tempered by the fact that unions were simultaneously in rapid decline (Tucker 1995a, 258).

10 *Ontario Factories Act,* 1884, 47 Vic, c 39, s 41.

Notes to pages 37-48

11 Snider (1993, 100-1) also documents the considerable resistance by the corporate elite to Canada's anti-combines legislation, introduced in the late 1800s in response to concerns that corporate mergers would produce monopolies and reduce competition. The business community eventually accepted new legislation, conceding that it contributed to a predictable market environment (103).

12 *Public Company Accounting Reform and Investor Protection Act of 2002*, Public Law 107-204, 107th Congress [*Sarbanes-Oxley Act*].

13 Bill C-13, *An Act to Amend the Criminal Code (Capital Markets Fraud and Evidence Gathering)*, SC 2004, c 3.

14 An exchange between Pearce and Tombs (1990, 1991) and compliance scholar Hawkins (1990, 1991) encapsulates this debate.

15 Compliance scholars argue that there is no way of knowing if accidents were based on an amoral calculation – that it is a post-hoc analysis to attribute the offence as resulting from economic decision making (Hawkins 1990, 454).

16 To borrow a familiar Marxist adage, people choose but not in conditions of their own choosing.

17 For example, Haines and Sutton (2003, 10-11) argue that, regardless of the dominance of "free enterprise ideology," the state will develop mechanisms to safeguard against situations where the "market lets them down." In this respect, "general understandings about the role of the state may have changed, but they have not been replaced entirely by faith in the markets" (12).

18 It is difficult to examine questions of crime, deviance, and punishment without reference to the many contributions of Foucault (Cohen 1985, 10; see also Garland 1990). In addition to revealing the nature of the carceral archipelago, particularly in relation to the "normalization" of discipline, Foucault (1972, 3 and passim) challenged us to reconsider the relationship between power and knowledge, arguing that power is not a series of "linear successions" or "continuities" but, instead, a complex array of "discontinuities" that coalesce in different ways to contribute to the present state of knowledge (see also Foucault 1965, 1966, 1979, 1980).

19 There is an important difference between the current study and Doran's work. Doran (1996, 525) argues against an understanding of state power within a "theoretically prior capitalist system," in favour of viewing power as a "largely discursive phenomenon." In contrast, my theoretical framework suggests that state power and discursive formations are mutually constitutive. In this respect, I disagree with Doran's view of both the state and capitalism in such static terms. Their relationship with various discourses is more complex and fluid than he suggests.

20 In two key texts, *Reading Capital* ([1968] 1997) and *For Marx* (1969), Althusser brings traditional Marxism into a post-Marxist phase (Resch, 1992, 2). In doing so, he attempts to rescue Marxism from its Hegelian tendency of characterizing the economic as determinate of the social realm as well as the teleological belief that class struggle will logically transform capitalism into socialism. Although Althusser was a "child of more than one history," making it difficult to suture together his many diverse philosophical thoughts, and his relatively impenetrable style of theorizing dissuaded more than a few readers from fully exploiting his theoretical and philosophical contributions, his work remains invaluable for those interested in moving beyond "vulgar" Marxism (Jameson, 2001, vii).

21 Carroll's (2004) research illustrates that twenty-two of the top 250 Canadian companies are government owned (many of which are provincial power companies) (see, by way of comparison, Clement 2006, 147). In terms of employment, Fudge (2002, 86) notes that the federal government has a significant workforce and is the "largest single employer of women in Canada."

22 Glasbeek (2002, 31) refers to the fact that, in 1984, less than 1 percent of Canadian retail companies accounted for more than 40 percent of the country's assets and more than 50 percent of its equity. Similarly, using Statistics Canada data, he notes that in 1987 the "top 1 per cent of all enterprises controlled 86 per cent of Canada's assets and made 75 per cent of all profits."

23 Globalization is a contested concept, the parameters for which are far too great to discuss in this book. In official terms, the globalization of economic relations represents an opportunity to provide

enrichment for the entire global population. However, for many observers, it is about creating a borderless economic venture for the benefit of the few, "principally transnational corporations and some of their dependent subcontractors" (Glasbeek 2002, 3; Woodiwiss 1997, 90). Regardless of the differences of opinion about the nature and scope of globalization, there are few doubts about its many impacts.

24 As Pearce and Snider (1995, 21) note, "of the one hundred largest economies in the world in 1989, forty-seven were corporations, not countries."

25 Today, roughly 30 percent of the Canadian workforce is unionized, a figure that is undoubtedly supported by the large number of union jobs in the public sector (Glasbeek 2002, 83).

26 Despite this shift, women continue to bear the majority of responsibility for "unpaid work necessary for social reproduction" (Fudge and Cossman 2002, 27).

27 It is also more fruitful to conceptualize class processes as elements of "producing" the appropriation and distribution of surplus labour (Gibson-Graham, Resnick and Wolff 2001, 18).

Chapter 4: Constituting the Corporate Criminal through Law

1 Bill C-45, *An Act to Amend the Criminal Code (Criminal Liability of Organizations)*, RC 2003, c 21.

2 *Criminal Code*, RSC 1985, c C-46.

3 All references from the interviews conducted for this study are identified by the category of respondent and the interview number. See Appendix D for a complete list of participants.

4 *Public Company Accounting Reform and Investor Protection Act of 2002*, Public Law 107-204, 107th Congress [*Sarbanes-Oxley Act*].

5 This changed in 2011 when the New Democratic Party (NDP) became the official opposition, winning 102 seats (a majority of which were from the province of Quebec). Prior to this victory, the party's connections to eastern Canada were more pronounced. For instance, following Canada's thirty-seventh general election on 27 November 2000, the NDP won thirteen seats in the House of Commons, four of which were from ridings in eastern Canada (three seats in Nova Scotia and one in New Brunswick) (see Elections Canada, *Thirty-Seventh General Election 2000: Official Voting Results: Synopsis,* http://www.elections.ca).

6 Like the NDP, the Progressive Conservative (PC) Party owed much of its political existence to election results in eastern Canada. Prior to merging with the Reform Party to form the Conservative Party in 2003, the PC Party had lost most of its seats in the House of Commons following the defeat of Brian Mulroney's PC government. Following Canada's thirty-seventh general election on 27 November 2000, the PCs won twelve seats in the House of Commons, four of which were from Nova Scotia (see Elections Canada, *Thirty-Seventh General Election 2000: Official Voting Results: Synopsis,* http://www.elections.ca)

7 For a list of previous explosions related to the Foord seem, where Westray is located, see Comish (1993, 1-2).

8 MacKay reiterated his position when the motion was brought forward a second time in February 2000 (Peter MacKay, PC, Hansard, 18 February 2000).

9 Immediately following the disaster, there were some questions as to whether the mine would reopen (Jobb 1994).

10 *Occupational Health and Safety Act*, SNS 1996, c 7, s 1.

11 *Canadian Charter of Rights and Freedoms,* Part 1 of the *Constitution Act, 1982*, being Schedule B to the *Canada Act 1982* (UK), 1982, c 11.

12 One legal academic suggested that the notion of corporate culture was not jettisoned completely from the government's legislation, although there is no specific reference to it in the law (Interview 17). For example, she argued that factors associated with a corporation's culture could be used to determine if the requisite duty of care was taken to ensure the safety of workers. Nevertheless, this position does not undermine the fact that traditional notions of criminal law dominated the reform

process and that alternatives, such as the corporate culture model, were considered too much of a departure from the status quo to be given serious consideration.

Chapter 5: Visions of Economic Grandeur

1 *Criminal Law,* RSC 1985, c C-46.
2 Bill C-45, *An Act to Amend the Criminal Code (Criminal Liability of Organizations),* RC 2003, c 21.
3 Although the award was rescinded, the sponsoring agency's website still lists the Westray mine as receiving a national award for coal-mining safety in 1991 (see archives of past winners at http://www.cim.org/awards/JohnTRyanTrophiesPW2.cfm). What is more, as Jobb (1994, 228) notes, workers noted in the media shortly after the disaster that "mine management had fudged accident figures to capture the award."
4 The perspective was reiterated in the Canadian Bar Association's written submission: "An overly inclusive and over-broad model of corporate criminal liability will have the effects of deterring qualified people from becoming directors or officers of Canadian corporations, particularly if we are to fear the imposition of criminal consequences based on an external assessment of what should have been known. We are concerned that Bill C-284 [the NDP's private member's bill] could have a very chilling effect on corporate relations, causing Canadian corporations to operate with less expertise and less qualified leadership than currently available" (Canadian Bar Association 2002, 3).
5 Ironically, the fact that the Westray workers were not unionized when the disaster occurred was a lost detail by those who raised this issue.
6 The notion of shared responsibility also emerged through reference to unions acting as good corporate citizens, effectively placing them on the same level of authority and control as corporations. In a statement following a presentation by representatives of the United Steelworkers of America, one member stated: "I want to commend the witnesses for their presentation and for their educational efforts in respect of workplace safety and health. It certainly fits with the mandate of occupational health and safety legislation, workplace safety and health legislation, right across Canada. It's important to see the unions actively involved in that. I think it shows good corporate responsibility on their part" (Vic Toews, Conservative Alliance, Justice Committee, 8 May 2002, 15:50).

Chapter 6: Obscuring Corporate Crime and the Corporate Criminal

1 Bill C-45, *An Act to Amend the Criminal Code (Criminal Liability of Organizations),* RC 2003, c 21.
2 The title of this section is based on a quote from a senior executive from Westinghouse in response to questions about why he had been involved in a major price-fixing scandal (as quoted in Glasbeek 2002, 155).
3 *R c Transpavé inc,* [2008] JQ no 1857.
4 There are some exceptions to this rule. For example, if an offender is sentenced to more than two years in prison, they are sent to a federally run institution, while those sentenced to less than two years are sent to a provincial custody institution. Further, the provinces have the power to enact some regulatory laws (for example, with highway traffic offences).
5 The exception is that the federal government is responsible for establishing health and safety laws for workplaces under federal jurisdiction, which accounts for approximately 10 percent of Canada's workforce. These rules are laid out in Part II of the *Canada Labour Code,* RSC 1985, c L-2. As Keith (2004, 97-98) notes, while roughly 10 percent of Canadian employees are regulated federally, "90 per cent are provincially regulated for the purposes of labour relations, employment standards, workers' compensation and OHS."
6 For example, see *The National Public Survey on White Collar Crime* (Rebovich and Layne 2000).
7 *Criminal Code,* RSC 1985, c C-46.

8 In March 2009, a Google Internet search of the terms "Bill C-45" and "Westray bill" yielded 12,500 and 1,100 hits, respectively. The majority of these sites offered general information on the law and its implications for employers and employees and originated from law firms, occupational health and safety consultants, unions and labour groups, industry associations, and online magazines. Although this does not constitute an overwhelming volume of Internet activity, it is nevertheless significant given the Westray bill's virtual disuse.

9 For a discussion of the traditional crime control industry, see Christie (1993, 2004).

10 Abicus Safety Training Software, http://www.abacussafety.com.

11 Gowlings Lafleur Henderson, http://www.ohslaw.ca/ [emphasis in original].

12 Abicus Safety Training Software, http://www.abacussafety.com.

13 OHS Canada, Bill C-45 Overview, http://www.ohscanada.com/ elearning/whatis.asp.

14 Sundown Interactive Communication Corporation, http://www.sundowncorp.com/SundownWSIT_Web/Bill%20C45.htm.

15 Excellence in Manufacturing Consortium, http://www.emccanada.org.

16 Canadian Onsite Medical Incorporated, http://www.canadianonsite.com.

17 Group 4 Securicor, http://www.g4s.com.

18 Canadian Centre for Occupational Health and Safety, http://www.ccohs.ca.

19 For an examination of risk discourse in relation to the traditional crime control realm, see Garland (2001).

20 For a critical discussion of corporate social responsibility, see Bakan (2004), Laufer (2006), and Shamir (2005).

Chapter 7: Disciplining Capital

1 Bill C-45, *An Act to Amend the Criminal Code (Criminal Liability of Organizations)*, RC 2003, c 21.

2 *Criminal Code*, RSC 1985, c C-46.

3 An important aspect of this goal was to avoid conceptualizing discourse as a catalyst of meaning, a form of "discourse imperialism" that equated language with "strong social constructionism" (Fairclough, Jessop, and Sayer 2002, 4).

4 The pitfalls and challenges associated with engaging the law are best illustrated by feminist researchers who critically examine the use of law in response to violence against women (see Bonnycastle 2000; Chunn and Lacombe 2000; Comack 2006; Smart 1989).

References

Agnew, R. (1992) "Foundation for a General Strain Theory of Crime and Delinquency." *Criminology* 30: 47-87.

– (2006) *Pressured into Crime: An Overview of General Strain Theory.* Los Angeles, CA: Roxbury.

Allen, J. (2010-11) "Competition in the Canadian Mortgage Market." *Bank of Canada Review* 11: 1-9.

Althusser, L. (1969) *For Marx.* London: New Left.

– [1971] (2001) *Lenin and Philosophy and Other Essays.* New York: Monthly Review Press.

– (1994) Le courant souterrain du matérialisme de la rencontre, in *Écrits philosophiques et politiques,* volume 1. Paris: Stock/IMEC.

– (1999) *Machiavelli and Us.* London and New York: Verso

Althusser, L., and E. Balibar [1968] (1997) *Reading Capital.* London and New York: Verso.

Anand, A., and J. Penley (2005) "Review of the Corporation: The Pathological Pursuit of Profit and Power." *Queen's Law Journal* 9: 938-52.

Archibald, T., K. Jull, and K. Roach (2004) "The Changed Face of Corporate Criminal Liability." *Criminal Law Quarterly* 48: 367-96.

Arthurs, H., and C. Mumme (2007) "From Governance to Political Economy: Insights from a Study of Relations between Corporations and Workers." *Osgoode Hall Law School Journal* 45: 439-70.

Association of Workers' Compensation Boards of Canada (2006) *National Work Injuries Statistics Program – February 2006,* http://www.awcbc.org/en/nationalworkinjurydiseasesandfatality statistic.asp.

Ayres, I., and J. Braithwaite (1992) *Responsive Regulation: Transcending the Deregulation Debate.* Oxford: Oxford University Press.

Backhouse, C. (1999) *Colour-Coded: A Legal History of Racism in Canada, 1900-1950.* Toronto: University of Toronto Press.

Baily, I. (2010) "Ferry Officer Faces Charges in Queen of the North Sinking." *Globe and Mail,* 16 March, http://www.theglobeandmail.com/news/national/british-columbia/charges-laid -in-sinking-of-queen-of-the-north-ferry/article1502269/.

Balfour, G., and E. Comack (eds.) (2006) *Criminalizing Women.* Halifax, NS: Fernwood Publishing.

Bakan, J. (2004) *The Corporation: The Pathological Pursuit of Profit and Power.* Toronto: Penguin Canada.

Bardach, E., and R. Kagan (1982) *Going by the Book: The Problem of Regulatory Unreasonableness.* Philadelphia, PA: Temple University Press.

Barnetson, B. (2010) *The Political Economy of Workplace Injury in Canada.* Edmonton, AB: Athabasca University Press.

Barry, A., T. Osborne, and N. Rose (1996) *Foucault and Political Reason: Liberalism, Neo-Liberalism and Rationalities of Government.* Chicago: University of Chicago Press.

Beccaria, C. [1764] (1986) *On Crimes and Punishments,* translated by David Young. Indianapolis, IN: Hackett Publishing.

Bentham (1789) *An Introduction to the Principles of Morals and Legislation.* Oxford: Claredon Press.

Berle, A., and G. Means (1967) *The Modern Corporation and Private Property.* New York: Harcourt, Brace and World.

Bernard, T.J. (1984) "The Historical Development of Corporate Criminal Liability." *Criminology* 22(3): 3-17.

Bittle, S., and L. Snider (2006) "From Manslaughter to Preventable Accident: Shaping Corporate Criminal Liability." *Law and Policy* 28(4): 470-96.

– (2011) "Moral Panics" Deflected: The Failed Legislative Response to Canada's Safety Crimes and Markets Fraud Legislation." *Crime, Law and Social Change* 56: 373-87.

Bonger, W. [1905] (1969) *Criminality and Economic Conditions.* Bloomington, IN: Indiana University Press.

Bonnycastle, K. (2000) "Rape Uncodified: Reconsidering Bill C-49 Amendments to Canadian Sexual Assault Laws," in D. Chunn and D. Lacombe (eds.), *Law as a Gendering Practice.* Oxford: Oxford University Press.

Box, S. (1983) *Power, Crime and Mystification.* London: Tavistock.

Boyd, S.C, D.E. Chunn, and R. Menzies (eds.) (2001) *[Ab]Using Power: The Canadian Experience.* Halifax, NS: Fernwood Publishing.

Braithwaite, J. (1982) "Enforced Self Regulation: A New Strategy for Corporate Crime Control." *Michigan Law Review* 80: 1466-1507.

– (1984) *Corporate Crime in the Pharmaceutical Industry.* Cambridge: Cambridge University Press.

– (1989) *Crime, Shame and Reintegration.* Cambridge: Cambridge University Press.

– (2005) *Markets in Vice, Markets in Virtue.* Annandale, Australia: Federation Press.

Braithwaite, J., and B. Fisse (1985) "Varieties of Responsibility and Organisational Crime." *Law and Policy* 7: 315-43.

– (1987) "Self Regulation and the Control of Corporate Crime," in C. Shearing and P. Stenning (eds.), *Private Policing.* Beverly Hills, CA: Sage.

British Columbia Criminal Justice Branch (2011) "Media Statement: Criminal Justice Branch – Private Prosecution of Weyerhaeuser Company Limited," http://www.ag.gov.bc.ca/prosecution -service/media-statements/pdf/11-16_WeyerhaeuserCo-PrivatePros-Stay-24Aug2011.pdf.

Brown, D. (2004) "Criminal Charges Laid under New Corporate Killing Law." *Canadian HRReporter* 17(16): 1.

Burdis, K., and S. Tombs (2012) "After the Crisis: New Directions in Theorizing Corporate and White Collar Crime," in S. Hall and S. Winlow (eds.), *New Directions in Criminological Theory.* London: Routledge.

Cahill, S., and P. Cahill (1999) "Scarlet Letters: Punishing the Corporate Citizen." *International Journal of the Sociology of Law* 27: 153-65.

Callari, A., and D.F. Ruccio (1996) *Postmodern Materialism and the Future of Marxist Theory.* Hanover, NH: Wesleyan University Press.

References

Canadian Bar Association (2002) "Subject Matter of Bill C-284: Criminal Code Amendments (Offences by Corporations, Directors and Officers)," http://www.cba.org/cba/submissions/pdf/02-23-eng.pdf.

Canadian Human Rights Reporter (2008) "Quebec Company Fined $110,000 in Worker's Death." *Canadian Human Rights Reporter*, 18 March.

Canadian Labour Congress (2008) "Justice Denied Courts Maintain Status Quo with Weak Ruling on Corporate Killing," http://canadianlabour.ca.

Canadian Labour Reporter (2011) "B.C. Crown Stays Death-Related Criminal Prosecution of Weyerhaeuser," 26 August, http://www.labour-reporter.com/articleview/11065-bc-crown-stays-death-related-criminal-prosecution-of-weyerhaeuser.

Canadian Press (2008) "Quebec Company Fined $110,000 for Criminal Negligence in Employee Death," http://www.cbc.ca/news/canada/montreal/story/2008/03/18/qc-transpavesentence0318.html.

Carlen, P. (1985) *Criminal Women: Autobiographical Accounts.* Cambridge: Polity Press.

Carroll, W.K. (2004) *Corporate Power in a Globalizing World: A Study in Elite Social Organization.* Don Mills, ON: Oxford University Press.

Carson, W.G. (1970) "White Collar Crime and the Enforcement of Factory Legislation." *British Journal of Criminology* 10: 383-98.

– (1980) "The Institutionalization of Ambiguity: Early British Factory Acts," in G. Geis and E. Stotland (eds.), *White-Collar Crime Theory and Research.* Beverly Hills, CA: Sage.

Chandler, A.D. (1977) *The Managerial Revolution in American Business.* Cambridge, MA: Harvard University Press.

Cherry, P. (2008) "Company Fined $100,000 in Death of Employee." *Montreal Gazette,* 18 March, A8.

Christie, N. (1993) *Crime Control as Industry: Towards Gulags, Western Style,* 3rd edition. London and New York: Routledge.

– (2004) *A Suitable Amount of Crime.* London and New York: Routledge.

Chunn, D., and D. Lacombe (eds.) (2000) *Law as a Gendering Practice.* Oxford: Oxford University Press.

Clarke, T. (ed.) (2004) *Theories of Corporate Governance: The Philosophical Foundations of Corporate Governance.* London and New York: Routledge.

Clement, W. (2001) "Canadian Political Economy's Legacy for Sociology." *Canadian Journal of Sociology* 26(3): 405-20.

– (2006) "Review: *Corporate Power in a Globalizing World: A Study in Elite Social Organization,* by William Carroll." *Canadian Journal of Sociology* 31(1): 146-48.

Cohen, S. (1985) *Visions of Social Control: Crime, Punishment and Classification.* Cambridge: Polity.

– (1996) "Human Rights and Crimes of the State: The Culture of Denial," in J. Muncie, E. McLaughlin, and M. Langan (eds.), *Criminological Perspectives: A Reader.* London: Sage.

Coleman, J. (1987) "Towards an Integrated Theory of White-Collar Crime." *American Journal of Sociology* 93(2): 406-39.

Comack, E. (ed.) (1999) *Locating Law: Race/Class/Gender Connections.* Halifax, NS: Fernwood Publishing.

– (ed.) (2006) *Locating Law: Race/Class/Gender Connections,* 2nd edition. Halifax, NS: Fernwood Publishing.

Comish, S. (1993) *The Westray Tragedy: A Miner's Story.* Halifax, NS: Fernwood Publishing.

Conlin, R.J. (2008) "Transpavé Inc. Bill C-45 Update: Prosecutor and Defence Recommend $100,000 Fine to the Court," in *Occupational Safety and Health Due Diligence Update.* Toronto: Stringer Brisbin Humphrey Management Lawyers.

Cranford, C.J., J. Fudge, E. Tucker, and L. Vosko (2005) *Self-Employed Workers Organize: Law, Policy and Unions*. Montreal and Kingston: McGill-Queen's University Press.

Creswell, J. (1994) *Research Design: Qualitative and Quantitative Approaches*. Thousand Oaks, CA: Sage Publications.

Daily Commercial News (and Construction Record) (2008) "Judge Orders Transpavé to Pay $110,000 Fine in Death of Worker," 20 March, Daily Commercial News (and Construction Record), http://www.dailycommercialnews.com.

Data, R.P. (2007) "From Foucault's Genealogy to Aleatory Materialism: Realism, Nominalism, and Politics," in J. Frauley and F. Pearce (eds.), *Critical Realism and the Social Sciences: Heterodox Elaborations*. Toronto: University of Toronto Press.

Dauvergne, M. (2005) "Homicide in Canada, 2005," Catalogue no. 85-002-XIE. *Juristat* 26(6): 1-26.

Davis, C. (2000) Corporate Violence, Regulatory Agencies and the Management and Deflection of Censure. Ph.D. dissertation, University of Southampton, Southampton, UK.

De Coster, S., and K. Heimer (2001) "The Relationship between Law Violation and Depression: An Interactionist Analysis." *Criminology* 39(4): 799-836.

Deflem, M. (2008) *Sociology of Law: Visions of a Scholarly Tradition*. Cambridge: Cambridge University Press.

Denzin, N.K., and Y.S. Lincoln (1994) "Introduction: Entering the Field of Qualitative Research," in N.K. Denzin and Y.S. Lincoln (eds.), *Handbook of Qualitative Research*. Thousand Oaks, CA: Sage Publications.

Department of Justice Canada (2002a) *Corporate Criminal Liability: Discussion Paper*. Ottawa: Department of Justice Canada.

– (2002b) *Government Response to the Fifteenth Report of the Standing Committee on Justice and Human Rights: Corporate Liability*. Ottawa: Department of Justice Canada.

– (2003) *Criminal Liability of Organizations: A Plain Language Guide to Bill C-45*. Ottawa: Department of Justice Canada.

Dienst, R. (2011) *The Bonds of Debt: Borrowing against the Common Good*. London: Verso.

Doran, N. (1996) "From Embodied 'Health' to Official 'Accidents': Class Codification and British Factory Legislation 1831-1844." *Social and Legal Studies* 5(4): 423-65.

Dupont, D., and F. Pearce (2001) "Foucault contra Foucault: Rereading the 'Governmentality' Papers." *Theoretical Criminology* 5(2): 123-58.

Durkheim, E. (1966) *Suicide: A Study in Sociology,* translated by J.A. Spaulding and G. Simpson. New York: Free Press.

Eagleton, T. (2010) *Why Marx Was Right*. New Haven, CT: Yale University Press.

Easterbrook, F., and D. Fischel (1985) "Limited Liability and the Corporation." *University of Chicago Law Review* 52: 93-101.

Edelhertz, H. (1970) *The Nature, Impact and Prosecution of White-Collar Crime*. Washington, DC: National Institute of Law Enforcement and Criminal Justice, Department of Justice.

Edwards, C., and J. Thibault (2009) "Corporate Criminal Liability: Coming to a Construction Project Near You?" Heenan Blaikie, http://www.heenanblaikie.com.

Edwards, C.A., and R.J. Conlin (2006) "First Corporate Charged with Workplace Safety Crime Post Bill C-45," in *Occupational Health and Safety Due Diligence Update*. Toronto, ON: Stringer Brisbin Humphrey Management Lawyers.

Edwards, C.A, S.D. Todd, and J. Warning (2010) "Bill C-45 Lives: Worker Death Sparks Criminal Negligence Charges," Canadian Occupational Health and Safety, http://www.cos-mag.com.

Elston, S. (2005) "Bill C-45 and You: What Principals Need to Know (A Guide for Dealing with Life-Threatening Allergies and Other Medical Conditions)," http://www.legalexpenseinsurance. ca/BillC45.doc.

References

Emond and Harnden (law firm) (2008) "$100,000 Fine Imposed on First Corporation Convicted of Criminal Negligence in a Workplace Fatality," Labour and Employment Law for Employers, April, http://www.ehlaw.ca/whatsnew/0804/Focus0804.shtml.

Erickson and Partners (law firm) (2009) "Bill C-45: Criminal Liability of Organizations," http://www.erickson-law.com.

Ericson, R., P.M. Baranek, and J.B.L. Chan (1991) *Representing Order: Crime, Law and Justice in the News Media*. Toronto: University of Toronto Press.

Ericson, R., and K.D. Haggerty (1997) *Policing the Risk Society*. Oxford: Clarendon Press.

Fairclough, N. (1992) *Discourse and Social Change*. Cambridge: Polity Press.

Fairclough, N., P. Graham, J. Lemke, and R. Wodak (2004) "Introduction." *Critical Discourse Studies* 1(1): 1-7.

Fairclough, N., B. Jessop, and A. Sayer (2002) "Critical Realism and Semiosis." *Journal of Critical Realism* 5(1): 2-10.

Ferguson, G. (1998) "Corruption and Corporate Criminal Liability," International Centre for Criminal Law Reform and Criminal Justice Policy, http://www.icclr.law.ubc.ca/Site%20Map/Publications%20Page/Gerry_Ferguson.htm.

Ferretter, L. (2006) *Louis Althusser*. Oxford: Routledge.

Foucault, M. [1965] (1988) *Madness and Civilization: A History of Insanity in the Age of Reason*. New York: Vintage Books.

– [1966] (2002) *The Order of Things*. London and New York: Routledge.

– [1972] (2001) *The Archaeology of Knowledge*. London and New York: Routledge.

– (1979) *Discipline and Punish: The Birth of the Prison*. New York: Vintage Books.

– (1980) *Power/Knowledge: Selected Interviews and Other Writings*, edited by Colin Gordon. New York: Pantheon Books.

Frauley, J., and F. Pearce (2007) "Critical Realism and the Social Sciences: Methodological and Epistemological Preliminaries," in J. Frauley and F. Pearce (eds.), *Critical Realism and the Social Sciences: Heterodox Elaborations*. Toronto: University of Toronto Press.

Friedrichs, D.O. (1992) "White-Collar Crime and the Definitional Quagmire: A Provisional Solution." *Journal of Human Justice* 3(2): 5-21.

– (2010) *Trusted Criminals: White Collar Crime in Contemporary Society*, 4th edition. Belmont, CA: Wadsworth Cengage Learning.

– (2011) "Occupy Wall Street Does Have a Clear Message. Commentary: A Call to Recognize the Crimes of High Finance, Marketwatch, 24 October, http://www.marketwatch.com/story/occupy-wall-street-does-have-a-clear-message-2011-10-24.

Froggio, G., and R. Agnew (2007) "The Relationship between Crime and 'Objective' versus 'Subjective' Strains." *Journal of Criminal Justice* 35: 81-87.

Fudge, J. (2002) "From Segregation to Privatization: Equality, the Law, and Women Public Servants, 1908-2001," in J. Fudge and B. Cossman (eds.), *Privatization, Law and the Challenge to Feminism*. Toronto: University of Toronto Press.

Fudge, J., and B. Cossman (2002) "Introduction," in J. Fudge and B. Cossman (eds.), *Privatization, Law and the Challenge to Feminism*. Toronto: University of Toronto Press.

Gamble, A. (2009) *The Spectre at the Feast: Capitalist Crisis and the Politics of Recession*. London: Palgrave Macmillan.

Garland, D. (1990) *Punishment and Modern Society: A Study in Social Theory*. Chicago: University of Chicago Press.

– (1999) "'Governmentality' and the Problem of Crime," in Russell Smandych (ed.), *Governable Places: Readings on Governmentality and Crime Control*. Aldershot, UK: Ashgate Dartmouth.

– (2001) *The Culture of Control: Crime and Social Order in Contemporary Society*. Chicago: University of Chicago Press.

Geis, G., and J.F.C. DiMento (1995) "Should We Prosecute Corporations and/or Individuals?" in F. Pearce and L. Snider (eds.), *Corporate Crime: Contemporary Debates*. Toronto: University of Toronto Press.

Gibson-Graham, J.K., S. Resnick, and R. Wolff (2001) "Toward a Poststructuralist Political Economy," in J.K. Gibson-Graham, Stephen Resnick, and Richard Wolff (eds.), *Re/Presenting Class: Essays in Postmodern Marxism*. Durham, NC: Duke University Press.

Gibson-Graham, J.K., and D. Ruccio (2001) "'After' Development: Re-Imagining Economy and Class," in J.K. Gibson-Graham, Stephen Resnick, and Richard Wolff (eds.), *Re/Presenting Class: Essays in Postmodern Marxism*. Durham, NC: Duke University Press.

Glasbeek, H. (2002) *Wealth by Stealth: Corporate Crime, Corporate Law, and the Perversion of Democracy*. Toronto: Between the Lines.

– (2004) "Enron and Its Aftermath: Can Reforms Restore Confidence?" in A.I. Anand, J.A. Connidis, and W.F. Flannagan (eds.), *Crime in the Corporation*. Queen's Annual Business Law Symposium, Queen's University, Kingston, ON.

– (2005) "More Criminalization in Canada: More of the Same?" *Flinders Journal of Law Reform* 8(1): 39-56.

Glasbeek, H., and E. Tucker (1993) "Death by Consensus: The Westray Mine Story." *New Solutions*, 14-39.

Goetz, D. (2003) *Bill C-45: An Act to Amend the Criminal Code (Criminal Liability of Organizations)*, Legislative Summary LS-457E. Ottawa: Library of Parliament.

Goff, C.H., and C.E. Reasons (1978) *Contemporary Crime in Canada: A Critical Analysis of Anti-Combines Legislation*. Scarborough, ON: Prentice-Hall.

Gonzalez, G. (2005) "Safety Law Scares Canadian Firms Straight." *Business Insurance* 39(38): 4.

Gowlings (law firm) (2004) "First Bill C-45 Charge Pending." *Occupational Health and Safety Law Report*, September, http://www.gowlings.com.

Grabosky, P., and N. Shover (2010) "Editorial Conclusion: Forestalling the Next Epidemic of White-Collar Crime – Linking Policy to Theory," Special Issue: The Global Economy, Economic Crisis, and White-Collar Crime. *Criminology and Public Policy* 9(3): 641-54.

Gramsci, A. (1971) *Selections from the Prison Notebooks of Antonio Gramsci*, translated by Q. Hoare and G. Novell Smith. New York: International Publishers.

– (1975) *Quaderno del Carcere*, edited by V. Gerratan, 4 volumes. Turrin, Italy: Einaudi Editore.

Gray, G.C. (2006) "The Regulation of Corporate Violations: Punishment, Compliance, and the Blurring of Responsibility." *British Journal of Criminology* 46(5): 875-92.

– (2009) "The Responsibilization Strategy of Health and Safety: Neo-Liberalism and the Reconfiguration of Individual Responsibility for Risk." *British Journal of Criminology* 49: 326-42.

Green, G.S. (1990) *Occupational Crime*. Chicago: Nelson Hall.

Greenfield, K. (2005) "New Principles for Corporate Law." *Hastings Business Law Journal* 1. 87 118, http://lawdigitalcommons.bc.edu/lsfp/56.

Gunningham, N., and P.N. Grabosky (1998) *Smart Regulation: Designing Environmental Policy*. Oxford: Clarendon Press.

Gunningham, N., and R.A. Kagan (2005) "Regulation and Business Behaviour." *Law and Policy* 27(2): 213-18.

Gunningham, N., R.A. Kagan, and D. Thornton (2003) *Shade of Green: Business, Regulation and Environment*. Stanford: CA: Stanford University Press.

Gunningham, N., D. Thornton, and R.A. Kagan (2005) "Motivating Management: Corporate Compliance in Environmental Protection." *Law and Policy* 27(2): 289-316.

Guthrie, B. (2003) "Regulatory Reform in Light of Regulatory Character: Assessing Industrial Safety Change in the Aftermath of the Kader Toy Factory Fire in Bangkok, Thailand." *Social and Legal Studies* 12(4): 461-87.

– (2004) "Westray's Legacy." *Canadian Business* 77(21): 167-70.

Haines, F., and A. Hall (2004) "The Law and Order Debate in OHS." *Journal of Occupational Health and Safety* 20(3): 263-73.

Haines, F., and A. Sutton (2003) "The Engineer's Dilemma: A Sociological Perspective on Juridification and Regulation." *Crime, Law and Social Change* 39: 1-22.

Hamilton, G. (2008) "Sentencing for Workplace Death a First." *National Post,* 26 February, A8.

Hannah-Moffat, K. (2001) *Punishment in Disguise: Penal Governance and Federal Imprisonment of Women in Canada.* Toronto: University of Toronto Press.

Harvey, D. (2009) "Is This Really the End of Neoliberalism?" *Counterpunch,* 14-15 March, http://www.counterpunch.org/2009/03/13/is-this-really-the-end-of-neoliberalism/.

– (2010) *The Enigma of Capital and the Crises of Capitalism.* Oxford: Oxford University Press.

Hawkins, K. (1984) Environment and Enforcement: Regulation and the Social Definition of Pollution. Oxford: Clarendon Press.

– (1990) "Compliance Strategy, Prosecution Policy and Aunt Sally: A Comment on Pearce and Tombs." *British Journal of Criminology* 30: 444-66.

– (1991) "Enforcing Regulation: More of the Same from Pearce and Tombs." *British Journal of Criminology* 31(4): 427-30.

– (ed.) (1997) *The Human Face of Law.* Oxford: Clarendon Press.

– (2002) Law as a Last Resort: Prosecution Decision Making in a Regulatory Authority. Oxford: Oxford University Press.

Heimer, K. (1996) "Gender, Interaction, and Delinquency: Testing a Theory of Differential Social Control." *Social Psychology Quarterly* 59(1): 39-61.

Henry, S., and M.M. Lanier (2004) *Essential Criminology,* 2nd edition. Boulder, CO: Westview.

Hills, S. (1987) "Epilogue: Corporate Violence and the Banality of Evil," in S. Hills (ed.), *Corporate Violence: Injury and Death for Profit.* Totowa, NJ: Rowman and Littlefield.

Hillyard, P., C. Pantazis, S. Tombs, and D. Gordon (eds.) (2004) *Beyond Criminology: Taking Harm Seriously.* London: Pluto Press.

Hillyard, P., and S. Tombs (2004) "Beyond Criminology," in P. Hillyard, C. Pantazis, S. Tombs, and D. Gordon (eds.), *Beyond Criminology: Taking Harm Seriously.* London: Pluto Press.

Hindess, B., and P.Q. Hirst (1975) *Pre-Capitalist Modes of Production.* London: Routledge and Kegan Paul.

Hirschi, T. (1969) *Causes of Delinquency.* Berkeley, CA: University of California Press.

Hirst, P.Q., and G. Thompson (1996) *Globalization in Question: The International Economy and the Possibilities of Governance.* Cambridge, MA: Blackwell

Hunt, A. (2004) "Getting Marx and Foucault into Bed Together!" *Journal of Law and Society* 31(4): 592-609.

Hunt, A., and G. Wickham (1994) *Foucault and Law: Towards a Sociology of Law as Governance.* Boulder, CO: Pluto Press.

Hutter, B. (1988) *The Reasonable Arm of the Law? The Law Enforcement Procedures of Environmental Health Officers.* Oxford: Clarendon Press.

International Labour Organization (2005) *World Day for Safety and Health at Work 2005: A Background Paper.* Geneva: International Labour Office.

Jameson, F. (2001) "Introduction," in L. Althusser (ed.), *Lenin Philosophy and Other Essays.* New York: Monthly Review Press.

Jessop, B. (2002) *The Future of the Capitalist State.* Cambridge: Polity Press.

– (2004) "Critical Semiotic Analysis and Cultural Political Economy." *Critical Discourse Studies* 1(2): 159 74.

– (2007) "From Micro-Powers to Governmentality: Foucault's Work on Statehood, State Formation, Statecraft and State Power." *Political Geography* 26: 34-40.

– (2008) *State Power*. Cambridge, MA: Polity Press.

Jobb, D. (1994) *Calculated Risk: Greed, Politics and the Westray Tragedy*. Halifax, NS: Nimbus Publishing.

Kagan, R., and J. Scholz (1984) "The Criminology of the Corporation and Regulatory Enforcement Strategies," in K. Hawkins and J. Thomas (eds.), *Enforcing Regulation*. Boston: Kluwer-Hijhoff.

Keith, N. (2004) *Workplace Health and Safety Crimes*. Markham, ON: Butterworths.

– (2009) *Workplace Health and Safety Crimes*, 2nd edition. Markham, ON: Butterworths.

– (2011a) "Regulators Gone Wild! Occupational Health and Safety and Criminal Charges Laid in Christmas Eve Scaffolding Deaths." *Canadian Occupational Safety* 8(6): 1-2.

– (2011b) *Corporate Crime and Accountability in Canada: From Prosecutions to Corporate Social Responsibility*. Markham, ON: LexisNexis.

Keith, N. and A. Abbott (2011) "Acquittal in Quebec Bill C-45 Charges," Occupational Health and Safety Newsflash, http://www.gowlings.com/KnowledgeCentre/enewsletters/ohslaw/HtmFiles/ohslaw20110427.en.html.

Keith, N., and C. Walsh (2008) "Bill C-45 Alert: Sentence Handed Down in First OHS Criminal Negligence Conviction." Occupational Health and Safety Newsflash, http://www.gowlings.com/resources/PublicationPDFs/Keith_Walsh_March2008.pdf.

Kirby, D., and B. Perrin (2004) "Do Your Commercial Agreements Reflect the Bill C-45 Amendments to Canada's Criminal Code?" Osler Update, http://www.osler.com/resources.aspx?id=8572.

Lacey, N. (1995) "Contingency and Criminalisation," in I. Loveland (ed.), *Frontiers of Criminality*. London, UK: Sweet and Maxwell.

Lattimore, L.T., C.R. Tittle, and H.G. Grasmick (2006) "Childrearing, Self-Control, and Crime: Additional Evidence." *Sociological Inquiry* 76(3): 343-71.

Lau, A. (2011) "Charges Stayed in Mill Death: Sawmill Worker Was Killed in Workplace Accident in 2004." *The Record*, 26 August, http://www.canada.com/health/Charges+stayed+mill+death/5310464/story.html.

Laufer, W. (2006) *Corporate Bodies and Guilty Minds*. Chicago: University of Chicago Press.

Law Reform Commission of Canada (1976) *Criminal Responsibility for Group Action*, Working Paper no. 16. Ottawa: Information Canada.

– (1987) *Recodifying Criminal Law*, revised and enlarged edition. Ottawa: Law Reform Commission of Canada.

Liazos, A. (1972) "The Sociology of Nuts, Sluts and Perverts. *Social Problems* 20: 103-20.

Lebowitz, M. (2010) "Change the System, Not Its Barriers." *Socialism and Democracy* 24(3): 46-59.

Lombroso, C. [1876] (1911) *The Criminal Man*. Montclair, NJ: Patterson Smith.

Lowman, J., and B. MacLean (eds.) (1992) *Realist Criminology: Crime Control and Policing in the 1990s*. Toronto: University of Toronto Press.

MacPherson, D.L. (2005) "Review: *The Company: A Short History of a Revolutionary Idea*, by H. Micklethwait and A. Wooldridge." *Manitoba Law Journal* 31: 377-99.

MacPherson, Leslie, and Tyerman (law firm) (2005) "Bill C-45: The Changing Law Corporate Criminal Liability," in *Labour and Employment* Regina, Calgary, and Saskatoon: MacPherson Leslie and Tyerman.

Mahon, R. (2005) *The OECD and the Reconciliation Agenda: Competing Blueprints*. Toronto: Childcare Resources and Research Unit, University of Toronto.

Mann, M. (2004) "Corporate Criminals." *Canada Business* 77(2): 29.

Marx, K. (1976) *Capital*, volume 1. New York: Penguin Books.

McGurrin, D., and D.O. Friedrichs (2010) "Victims of Economic Crime on a Grand Scale." *Journal International de Victimologie* 23: 1848-2030, http://www.jidv.com/njidv/index.php/archives/par-numero/jidv-23/150-jidv-23/428-victims-of-economic-crime-on-a-grand-scale.

McKenna, B. (2004) "Critical Discourse Studies: Where To from Here?" *Critical Discourse Studies* 1(1): 9-39.

McMillan Binch (law firm) (2004) "Westray Bill Impacts Canadian Workers." *Employee and Labour Relations Bulletin,* McMillan Binch [on file with the author].

McMullan, J. (1992) *Beyond the Limits of the Law: Corporate Crime and Law and Order.* Halifax, NS: Fernwood Publishing.

– (2001) "Westray and After: Power, Truth and News Reporting of the Westray Mine Disaster," in S. Boyd, D.E. Chunn, and R. Menzies (eds.), *[Ab]Using Power: The Canadian Experience.* Halifax, NS: Fernwood Publishing.

– (2005) *News, Truth and Crime: The Westray Disaster and Its Aftermath.* Halifax, NS: Fernwood Publishing.

Menzies, R., D.E. Chunn, and S. Boyd (2001) "Introduction," in S. Boyd, D.E. Chunn, and R. Menzies (eds.), *[Ab]Using Power: The Canadian Experience.* Halifax, NS: Fernwood Publishing.

Merton, R. (1938) "Social Structure and Anomie." *American Sociological Review* 3: 672-82.

Micklethwait, J., and A. Wooldridge (2003) *The Company: A Short History of a Revolutionary Idea.* New York: Random House.

Miethe. T.D., and R.F. Meier (1990) "Opportunity, Choice and Criminal Victimization: A Test of a Theoretical Model." *Journal of Research in Crime and Delinquency* 27(3): 243-66.

– (1994) *Crime and Its Social Context: Toward an Integrated Theory of Offenders, Victims, and Situations.* New York: State University of New York Press.

Millan, L. (2008) "Company Fined $110,000 for Death of Employee." *Lawyers Weekly,* http://www.lawyersweekly.ca/index.php?section=article&articleid=645.

Mills, S. (1997) *Discourse.* London and New York: Routledge.

Minister of Justice Canada (1993) *Proposals to Amend the Criminal Code (General Principles),* 28 June. Ottawa: Government of Canada.

Mitnick, B.M. (1980) *The Political Economy of Regulation.* New York: Columbia University Press.

Morris, W. [1877] (1947) *On Art and Socialism: Essays and Lectures.* London: John Lehmann.

Morrison, W. (1995) *Theoretical Criminology: From Modernity to Post-Modernity.* London and Sydney: Cavendish Publishing.

Mosco, V. (1989) *The Pay-Per Society: Computers and Communication in the Information Age.* Toronto: Garamond Press.

Naffine, N. (1990) *The Law and the Sexes: Exploration in Feminist Jurisprudence.* Sydney, Australia: Allen and Unwin.

Nelken, D. (1994) "White Collar Crime," in M. Maguire, R. Morgan, and R. Reiner (eds.), *Oxford Handbook of Criminology.* Oxford: Oxford University Press.

Nicholls, C. (2005) *Corporate Law.* Toronto: Emond Montgomery.

Noble, C. (1995) "Regulating Work in a Capitalist Society," in F. Pearce and L. Snider (eds.), *Corporate Crime: Contemporary Debates.* Toronto: University of Toronto Press.

Norton, B. (2001) "Reading Marx for Class," in J.K. Gibson-Graham, Stephen Resnick, and Richard Wolff (eds.), *Re/Presenting Class: Essays in Postmodern Marxism.* Durham, NC: Duke University Press.

O'Ferrall, K. (2011) "Crown Drops Criminal Negligence Charges under Bill C-45," Canadian Employment and Pension Law, http://www.canadianemploymentpensionlaw.com/employment -standards/crown-drops-criminal-negligence-charges-under-bill-c-45/.

Palys, T. (1997) *Research Decisions: Quantitative and Qualitative Perspectives.* Toronto: Harcourt Brace.

Panitch, L. (1999) "The Impoverishment of State Theory." *Socialism and Democracy* 13(2): 19-35.

Paton, P.D. (2006-07) "Review: Allan C. Hutchinson's *The Companies We Keep: Corporate Governance for a Democratic Society." Ottawa Law Review* 38(2): 229-39.

Pearce, F. (1976) *Crimes of the Powerful: Marxism, Crime and Deviance.* London: Pluto Press.

– (1990) "Responsible Corporations and Regulatory Agencies." *Political Quarterly* 61(4): 415-30.

– (1992) "The Contribution of 'Left Realism' to the Study of Commercial Crime," in J. Lowman and B. MacLean (eds.), *Realist Criminology: Crime Control and Policing in the 1990s.* Toronto: University of Toronto Press.

Pearce, F., and S. Snider (eds.) (1995) *Corporate Crime: Contemporary Debates.* Toronto: University of Toronto Press.

Pearce, F., and S. Tombs (1989) "Bhopal: Union Carbide and the Hubris of the Capitalist Technocracy." *Social Justice* 16(2): 116-44.

– (1990) "Ideology Hegemony and Empiricism: Compliance Theories of Regulation." *British Journal of Criminology* 30: 423-43.

– (1991) "Policing Corporate 'Skid Rows.'" *British Journal of Criminology* 31: 415-26.

– (1997) "Hazards, Law and Class: Contextualizing the Regulation of Corporate Crime." *Social and Legal Studies* 6(1): 79-107.

– (1998) *Toxic Capitalism: Corporate Crime and the Chemical Industry.* Toronto: Canadian Scholars' Press.

Pfohl, S.J. (1985) *Images of Deviance and Social Control: A Sociological History.* New York: McGraw-Hill.

Proudhon, P.J. [1840] (1966) *Qu'est-ce que la propriété/ou recherches sur le principe du droit et du gouvernement, premier mémoire.* Paris: Garnier-Flammarion.

Razack, S.H. (ed.) (2002) *Race, Space and the Law: Unmapping a White Settler Society.* Toronto: Between the Lines Press.

Read, J. (2002) "Primitive Accumulation: The Aleatory Foundation of Capitalism." *Rethinking Marxism: A Journal of Economics, Culture and Society* 14(2): 24-49.

– (2003) *The Micro-Politics of Capital: Marx and the Prehistory of the Present.* New York: State University of New York Press.

Rebovich, D.J., and J. Layne (2000) *The National Public Survey on White Collar Crime.* Morgantown, PA: National White Collar Crime Centre.

Reiman, J. (1979) *The Rich Get Richer and the Poor Get Prison: Ideology, Class and Criminal Justice.* New York: Wiley.

– (2004) *The Rich Get Richer and the Poor Get Prison: Ideology, Class and Criminal Justice,* 7th edition. London: Pearson Publishing.

Resch, R.P. (1992) *Althusser and the Renewal of Marxist Social Theory.* Berkeley, CA: University of California Press.

Resnick, S.A., and R.D. Wolff (1985) "Introduction: Solution and Problems," in S.A. Resnick and R.D. Wolff (eds.), *Rethinking Marxism: Struggles in Marxist Theory.* New York: Autonomedia Incorporated.

– (1987) *Knowledge and Class: A Marxian Critique of Political Economy.* Chicago: University of Chicago Press.

– (eds.) (2006) *New Departures in Marxian Theory.* London and New York: Routledge.

– (2010) "The Economic Crisis: A Marxian Interpretation." *Rethinking Marxism: A Journal of Economics, Culture and Society* 22: 170-86.

Richard, Justice K.P. (1997) *The Westray Story: A Predictable Path to Disaster,* Report of the Westray Mine Public Inquiry, Justice K. Peter Richard, Commissioner. Halifax, NS: Government of Nova Scotia.

Rose, N. (2000) "Government and Control." *British Journal of Criminology* 40(2): 231-339.

Rose, N., and P. Miller (1992) "Political Power beyond the State: Problematics of Government." *British Journal of Sociology* 43(2): 172-205.

Rosoff, S.N., H.N. Pontell, and R. Tillman (2005) *Profit without Honor: White-Collar Crime and the Looting of America.* Upper Saddle River, NJ: Pearson/Prentice Hall.

Saint-Cyr, Y. (2005) "Criminal Code Charges under Bill C-45 Withdrawn." *International Human Resources Guide,* April, http://www.hrmguide.net.

Sampson, R., and J.H. Laub (2005a) "A Life-Course View of the Development of Crime." *Annals of the American Academy* 602: 12-45.

– (2005b) "When Prediction Fails: From Crime-Prone Boys to Heterogeneity in Adulthood." *Annals of the American Academy* 602: 73-79.

Sampson, R., J.H. Laub, and C. Wimer (2006) "Does Marriage Reduce Crime? A Counterfactual Approach to Within-Individual Causal Effects." *Criminology* 44(3): 465-508.

Shareholder Association for Research and Education (2002) "Submission to the House of Commons Standing Committee on Justice and Human Rights by the Shareholder Association for Research and Education" [copy of submission on file with author].

Shamir, R. (2005) "Mind the Gap: The Commodification of Corporate Social Responsibility." *Symbolic Interaction* 28(2): 229-53.

Sharpe, A., and J. Hardt (2006) *Five Deaths a Day: Workplace Fatalities in Canada: 1993-2005,* Research Paper no. 2006-04. Ottawa, ON: Centre for the Study of Living Standards.

Shearing, C. (2001) "Punishment and the Changing Face of Governance." *Punishment and Society* 3(2): 203-20.

Silverman, RA., J.J. Teevan, and V.F. Sacco (2000) *Crime in Canadian Society,* 6th edition. Toronto: Harcourt Brace.

Simon, D.R., and D.S. Eitzen (1986) *Elite Deviance.* Toronto: Allyn and Bacon.

Simpson, S. (2002) *Corporate Crime, Law and Social Control.* Cambridge: Cambridge University Press.

Sinclair, J. (2011) "Employers Must Be Held Accountable for Deaths." *Vancouver Sun,* 22 September, A15.

Slapper, G., and S. Tombs (1999) *Corporate Crime.* Essex, UK: Pearson Education.

Smandych, R. (1991) "The Origins of Canadian Anti-Combines Legislation, 1890-1920," in E. Comack and S. Brickey (eds.), *The Social Basis of Law,* 2nd edition. Halifax, NS: Garamond Press.

Smart, C. (1989) *Feminism and the Power of Law.* London and New York: Routledge.

Smith, A. (1937) *The Wealth of Nations.* New York: Modern Library.

Snider, L. (1978) "Corporate Crime in Canada: A Preliminary Report." *Canadian Journal of Criminology* 20: 142-68.

– (1987) "Towards a Political Economy of Reform, Regulation and Corporate Crime." *Law and Policy* 9(1): 37-68.

– (1990) "Cooperative Models and Corporate Crime: Panacea or Cop-Out?" *Crime and Delinquency* 36(2): 373-90.

– (1993) *Bad Business: Corporate Crime in Canada.* Toronto: Nelson Canada.

– (2000) "The Sociology of Corporate Crime: An Obituary (or: Whose Knowledge Claims Have Legs?)" *Theoretical Criminology* 4(2): 196-206.

– (2001) "Abusing Corporate Power: The Death of a Concept," in S. Boyd, D. Chunn, and R. Menzies (eds.), *(Ab)Using Power: The Canadian Experience.* Halifax, NS: Fernwood Publishing.

– (2002) "Theft of Time: Disciplining through Science and Law." *Osgoode Hall Law Journal* 40(1): 90-112.

– (2004) "Poisoned Water, Environmental Regulation, and Crime: Constituting the Nonculpable Subject in Walkerton, Ontario," in Law Commission of Canada (ed.), *What Is a Crime? Defining Criminal Conduct in Contemporary Society.* Vancouver and Toronto: UBC Press.

– (2008) "'But They're Not Real Criminals': Downsizing Corporate Crime," in B. Schissel and C. Brooks (eds.), *Marginality and Condemnation.* Halifax, NS: Fernwood Publishing.

– (2009) "Accommodating Power: The Common Sense of Regulators." *Social and Legal Studies* 18(2): 179-97.

Soederberg, S. (2008) "Deconstructing the Official Treatment for 'Enronitis': The Sarbanes-Oxley Act and the Neoliberal Governance of Corporate America." *Critical Sociology* 34(5): 657-80.

– (2010) *Corporate Power and Ownership in Contemporary Capitalism: The Politics of Resistance and Domination*. London and New York: Routledge.

South, N. (1998) "Corporate and State Crimes against the Environment: Foundations for a Green Perspective in European Criminology," in V. Ruggiero, N. South, and I. Taylor (eds.), *The New European Criminology: Crime and Social Order in Europe*. London and New York: Routledge.

Standryk, L.E. (2009) "Bill C-45, An Act to Amend the Criminal Code: Criminal Liability and Accountability for Workplace Safety," Lancaster, Brooks, and Welch, http://www.lbwlawyers.com/publications/bc45.php.

Statistics Canada (2006) *The Daily: Homicides,* Statistics Canada, http://www.statcan.gc.ca/daily-quotidien/061108/dq061108b-eng.htm.

Stewart McKelvey Stirling Scales (law firm) (2005) "Bill C-45: Expansion of Criminal Liability for Corporations and Officers," http://www.stewartmckelvey.com/en/home/default.aspx#.

Stone, A. (1982) *Regulation and Its Alternatives*. Washington, DC: Congressional Quarterly Press.

Storey, R., and E. Tucker (2005) "All That Is Solid Melts into Air: Worker Participation and Occupational Health and Safety Regulation in Ontario, 1970-2000," in V. Mogensen (ed.), *Worker Safety under Siege: Labor, Capital and Politics of Workplace Safety in a Deregulated Work*. Armonk, NY: Sharpe.

Sumner, C. (1994) *The Sociology of Deviance: An Obituary*. Buckingham, UK: Open University Press.

Sutherland, E. (1939) *Principles of Criminology,* 3rd edition. Philadelphia, PA: Lippincott.

– [1940] (1995) "White Collar Criminality," reprinted in G. Geis, R.F. Meier, and L.M. Salinger (eds.), *White-Collar Crime, Classic and Contemporary Views*. New York: Free Press.

– (1949) *White Collar Crime. The Uncut Version,* New Haven, CT: Yale University Press.

– (1983) *White Collar Crime: The Uncut Version,* revised edition. New Haven, CT: Yale University Press.

Tappan, P. (1947) "Who Is the Criminal?" *American Sociological Review* 12: 96-102.

Taylor, I. (1999) *Crime in Context: A Critical Criminology of Market Societies*. Cambridge: Westview Press.

Taylor, I., P. Walton, and J. Young (1973) *The New Criminology: For a Social Theory of Deviance*. London: Routledge and Kegan Paul.

Thornton, D., N.A. Gunningham, and R.A. Kagan (2005) "General Deterrence and Corporate Environmental Behaviour." *Law and Policy* 27(2): 262-88.

Tillman, R.H., and M.L. Indergaard (2005) *Pump and Dump: The Rancid Rules of the New Economy*. Piscataway, NJ: Rutgers University Press.

Tittle, C.R. (1995) *Control Balance: Toward a General Theory of Deviance*. Boulder, CO: Westview.

– (1997) "Thoughts Stimulated by Braithwaite's Analysis Control Balance Theory." *Theoretical Criminology* 1(1): 99-110.

– (2004) "Refining Control Balance Theory." *Theoretical Criminology* 8(4): 395-428.

Tombs, S. (1995) "Corporate Crime and New Organizational Forms," in F. Pearce and L. Snider (eds.), *Corporate Crime: Contemporary Debates*. Toronto: University of Toronto Press.

– (2004) "Workplace Injury and Death: Social Harm and the Illusion of Law," in P. Hillyard et al. (eds.), *Beyond Criminology? Taking Harm Seriously*. London: Pluto Press.

– (2006) "'Violence,' Safety Crimes and Criminology." *British Journal of Criminology* 47(4): 531-50.

Tombs, S., and D. Whyte (2003a) "Introduction: Corporations beyond the Law? Regulation, Risk and Corporate Crime in a Globalised Era." *Risk Management: An International Journal* 5(2): 9-16.

– (2003b) "Two Steps Forward, One Step Back: Towards Accountability for Workplace Deaths?" *Policy and Practice in Health and Safety* 1(1): 9-30.

– (eds.) (2003c) *Unmasking the Crime of the Powerful: Scrutinizing States and Corporations*. New York: Peter Lang Publishing.

– (2007) *Safety Crimes*. Cullompton, UK: Willan Publishing.

Tomisac, R. (2002) "Corporate Collapse, Crime and Governance: Enron, Anderson and Beyond. *Australia Journal of Corporate Law* 14(1): 183-201.

Tucker, E. (1990) *Administering Danger in the Workplace: The Law and Politics of Occupational Health and Safety Regulations in Ontario, 1850-1914*. Toronto: University of Toronto Press.

– (1995a) "And Defeat Goes On: An Assessment of Third-Wave Health and Safety Regulation," in F. Pearce and S. Snider (eds.), *Corporate Crime: Contemporary Debates*. Toronto: University of Toronto Press.

– (1995b) "The Westray Mine Disaster and Its Aftermath: The Politics of Causation." *Canadian Journal of Law and Society* 10(1): 91-123.

– (ed.) (2006) *Working Disasters: The Politics of Recognition and Response*. Amityville, NY: Baywood Publishing Company.

United Steelworkers of America (2006) *Whatever Happened to the Westray Bill? Why Are We Still Dying for a Living?* March, http://www.usw.ca/workplace/health/issues?id=0007.

– (2011) "News Release: USW Condemns Refusal to Prosecute Weyerhaeuser," http://www.usw.ca/media/news/releases?id=0680.

Walters, V., W. Lewchuk, R.J. Richardson, L.A. Moran, T. Haines, and D. Verma (1995) "Judgements of Legitimacy Regarding Occupational Health and Safety," in F. Pearce and L. Snider (eds.), *Corporate Crime: Contemporary Debates*. Toronto: University of Toronto Press.

Wells, C. (1993) *Corporations and Criminal Responsibility*. Oxford: Clarendon.

Williams, J. (2008) "The Lessons of 'Enron': Media Accounts, Corporate Crimes and Financial Markets." *Theoretical Criminology* 12(4): 471-99.

Wolff, R. (2010a) *Capitalism Hits the Fan: The Global Economic Meltdown and What to Do About It*. Northampton, MA: Olive Branch Press.

– (2010b) "Taking over the Enterprise: A New Strategy for Labor and the Left." *New Labor Forum* 19(1): 8-12.

Woodiwiss, A. (1990) *Social Theory after Postmodernism: Rethinking Production, Law and Class*. London, UK: Pluto Press.

– (1997) "Behind Governmentality: Sociological Theory, Pacific Capitalism and Industrial Citizenship." *Citizenship Studies* 1(1): 87-114.

– (2006) "International Law." *Theory, Culture and Society* 23(2-3): 524-25.

Workers' Health and Safety Centre (2011) "Worker Death Leads to the Second C-45 Conviction," http://www.whsc.on.ca/whatnews2.cfm?autoid=663.

Yalden, R., P.D. Paton, J. Sarra, M. Gillen, and M. Condon (2008) *Business Organizations: Principles, Policies and Practice*. Toronto, ON: Emond Montgomery.

Yalnizyan, A. (2009) *Exposed: Revealing Truths about Canada's Recession*. Ottawa: Canadian Centre for Policy Alternatives.

York Regional Police (2004) "Charges in King Trench Collapse," Media Release. *York Regional Police Communications*, 25 August.

Žižek, S. (2009) *First as Tragedy, Then as Farce*. London: Verso.

Index

Abbott, Jim: statement in House of Commons, 123

An Act to Amend the Criminal Code (Capital Markets Fraud and Evidence Gathering) (2004), xi, 49

An Act to Amend the Criminal Code (Criminal Liability of Corporations, Directors and Officers) (2001), 5, 24-25, 210n19

An Act to Amend the Criminal Code (Criminal Liability of Organizations) (2003). *See* Bill C-45

An Act to Amend the Criminal Code (Offences by Corporations, Directors and Officers), 5

aleatory materialism, 56

Althusser, Louis, 56, 59-60, 64, 214n20

Angers, Lucie, 200

anti-combines legislation, 214n11

Aurora Institute, 99-100, 104-5, 199

Australia: corporate culture in legislation, 25, 105, 107, 109, 112, 210n26

Balibar, Étienne, 8, 59-60

Bardach, Eugene, 51, 52

Bartlett, William, 200

Beccaria, Cesare, 41

Bellehumeur, Michel, 194

Bennett, David, 199

Bentham, Jeremy, 41

Bhopal, India, 38, 58

Bill C-45, xv-xvi, 4, 14-15, 27; corporate responses to, 2; debate in House of Commons, 27-28; emergence of consulting services concerning, 150, 170-77, 187; impact on safety policies and practices, 11, 150, 164-70, 176-82; individual liability vs corporate culture, 30, 89-98, 106-14, 186; initial characterization, 2; prosecutions following enactment, xi, xvi, 2, 4, 31-33, 149, 156-63, 184, 211n42; public interest in, 2; resistance to, 2, 77; revisions of proposed legislation, 29-30; Senate approval, 29; sentencing regime, 31; symbolic impact, 150, 164-67, 177-82. *See also Criminal Code* amendment

bills, 210n21, 210n23; Bill C-13, xi, 49; Bill C-284, 5; Bill C-418, 5, 24-25, 210n19; private members' bills, 208n8, 210n20. *See also* Bill C-45; *Criminal Code* amendment

Blaikie, Bill, 194; statements in Justice Committee, 103-4, 132, 142

Boccanfuso, Aniello, 33, 34

Boisvert, Anne-Marie, 199; statements before Justice Committee, 105

Box, Steven, 39, 44

Braithwaite, John, 43, 47, 50, 161, 213n4

British Columbia: workplace accidents, 33-34, 212n48

Bryden, John: statements in House of Commons, 77, 90-91

Cadman, Chuck, 194; statements in Justice Committee, 4-5, 94-95, 154, 155

Canada, Dept. of Justice, 23, 28, 29, 198, 200; concern for *Charter* challenge, 106-7; drafting of legislation, 6, 27-28, 29, 123, 156, 191

Canada, Parliament, 191; composition, 210n18, 211n30, 215n5; dominant corporate perspectives, 11, 119-25, 145-46; Hansard, 208n2. *See also* bills

Canada Business Corporations Act, 1985, 18-19

Canada Labour Code (1985), 211n33, 216n5

Canadian Bar Association, 126, 199; submission to Justice Committee, 97, 108, 216n4

Canadian Centre for Occupational Health and Safety, 175

Canadian Council for the Rights of Injured Workers, 198

Canadian Council of Defence Lawyers, 199

Canadian Dredge and Dock Company v The Queen, 21

Canadian Labour Congress, 32-33, 199

Canadian Onsite Medical, 174

Canadian social formation, 61-64

capitalist mode of production: corporate crime and, xvi, 7, 8-9, 168, 188-89, 192, 208n7

capitalist social formation, 12, 192-93; mutually-reinforcing discourses and, 185, 188-91

Carroll, Aileen: statement in House of Commons, 136-37

Casey, Bill: statement in House of Commons, 79

class politics, 9, 64-70, 138, 141, 185, 190, 214n20

Coleman, James, 43, 213n4

companies, 214n22; Canadian government ownership, 214n21

Companies Act, 1862 (England), 17

compliance scholarship, 50-53, 215n15

Conacher, Duff, 139, 198

Conservative Party, 215n6

constitutional issues, 158-60

consulting services, 2, 11, 150, 170-77, 187

corporate crime, 38-39, 151-54, 213n6; academic study of, 39-40, 43-68; accountability under Bill C-45, 30-31; *actus rea,* 45, 106; as accident, 48, 105, 149; as committed by rogue corporations, 153, 156, 181; as regulatory offences, 153-54, 157-62; as wrongdoing, 152-53; capitalist mode of production and, xvi, 7, 8-9, 168, 188-89, 192, 208n7; conceptualized as individualistic, 16, 30, 54, 72, 186; definitions, 43-46; evolution of concept, 3, 6, 16-23, 74-75; identification doctrine and, 21, 24, 156-57, 211n42; "invisibility" of, 39, 41, 149, 151-52; *mens rea* (guilty mind) issue, 21, 29, 31, 45, 72, 85, 89, 90, 91-98, 106-7, 111, 113, 187; organizational production of, 44-45, 153; shaping discourses, 6-7, 8-9, 12, 54, 151-55, 157, 182; social-political-economic contexts, 53-57. *See also* workplace accidents

corporate criminal liability legislation, 7, 31, 46, 49; regulatory measures, 46-53; social structures and, 53-56, 192. *See also* Bill C-45; corporate crime; *Criminal Code* amendment

corporate culture: in Australian legislation, 25, 112, 210n26; concept excluded from Bill C-45, 103-14, 186, 215n12; criminogenic aspects, 25, 54, 104, 209n8

Corporate Manslaughter and Corporate Homicide Act (2007) (United Kingdom), xiv, 211n37

Corporate Responsibility Coalition, 198

corporations, 208n3, 209n8; as an inherent good, 50; conceived as private property, 20; concern about legislative reform, 11, 119-25, 145-46; directing minds, 21, 30-31, 211n42; distributed responsibility issues, 21; evolution of the form, 16-17, 19-20, 209n9; fiduciary responsibility and public interests, 18-19, 20; lack of obvious representation in reform process, 11, 117, 119-25, 145-46; limited liability, 17-18, 20, 208n4-5; management of, 18-19, 20, 21; perceived as critical to the economy, 149; possible departure from Canada, 129-31; possible impact of "director chill," 125-29; profit maximization, xvi, 69, 119, 134, 138, 192; representatives of, 30; resistance to

232   Index

regulations and laws, 48-49, 119; senior officers, 30-31; shareholder interests, 18-19, 20, 208n4-5; stakeholder interests, 19. *See also* organizations

Crête, Paul: statement in House of Commons, 125

crime: conceptualized as individualistic, 16, 30; cultural constructions of, 187; negligence, 30; social construction of, 42, 149, 150-52; subjective intent, 30-31. *See also* corporate crime

crime and deviance scholarship, 40-43; critical corporate crime scholarship, 51-56, 212n52; definitions of corporate crime, 43-46; extra-discursive considerations, 59-70; marginalization of corporate crime, 39, 41, 42, 43; self-regulation/compliance scholarship, 50-53, 215n15

crime control discourse. *See* law-and-order discourse

crime (un)control industry, 2, 11, 150, 170-77, 187

crimes of the powerful. *See* corporate crime

Criminal Code amendment, 84-85; counter-hegemonic perspectives, 131-34; feared economic impacts, 125-31; Justice Committee hearings (2002), 6, 198-200, 211n31; Justice Committee recommendations (1993), 5, 23, 209n14; Justice Committee recommendations (2000), 5, 26-27; Law Reform Commission of Canada recommendations, 209n14; legal context, 85-89; Ministry of Justice white paper recommendations (1993), 5, 23, 209n15; political context, 76, 77, 83, 84, 170; private members' bills (NDP) (1999), 5, 23-24, 82; private members' bill (NDP; Bill C-418) (2001), 5, 24-25, 210n19; private members' bill (NDP; Bill C-284) (2001), 5, 24, 25, 210n19; private members' bill (NDP) (2003), 24, 82; private members' motion (PC) (1999), 24, 26, 76, 77-80, 210n28; role of compromise, 112-13, 144, 145, 180-81; role of pro-labour politicians, 189; role of the state, 191-92; role of United Steelworkers of America, 81-84, 189; "selling" of Bill-45, 155-56; Westray disaster inquiry recommendations, 5, 22-23, 73, 74, 80, 81-82, 89, 142, 209n16. *See also* Bill C-45

criminal intent. *See mens rea*

criminal prosecutions, xi, xvi, 2, 4, 31-33, 149, 156-63, 184, 211n42

cultural discourses: crime control, 149-57, 164; nature of crime, 186, 187

Curragh Resources, 4, 77, 208n6, 209n16; coal mining safety award, 121, 216n3. *See also* Westray mine

Davidson, Barbara, 199

DelBiggio, Greg, 199; statements before Justice Committee, 88-89, 95, 108, 126-27

deregulation, ix-xii, 117-18, 152. *See also* regulatory issues

Desjarlais, Bev, 194, 199; private members' bill, 25, 210n19, 210n24; statements before Justice Committee, 132, 153; statements in House of Commons, 28, 76, 153

discourse analysis. *See* methodology

discourses. *See* cultural discourses; discursive formations; economic discourse; legal discourse

discursive formations, xvi, 56-58, 212n50; contradictory messages, 71-72, 186; law-and-order discourse, 1-2, 3, 11, 39, 152, 154-55, 172; mutually reinforcing, 184-85, 186, 191; power relations and, 9, 12, 85, 87; privileging of, 9, 11, 36; related to social structures, 8-9, 185; state, 72, 73, 185, 191-92. *See also* cultural discourses; economic discourse; legal discourse

Dockrill, Michelle: statement in House of Commons, 79

Dodd, Susan, 199; statements before Justice Committee, 93, 94-95, 104, 132-33

Doran, Nob, 58, 214n19

due diligence discourse, 173-77

Durkheim, Émile, 41-42

East India Company, 17

economic crimes. *See* corporate crime

economic discourse, 116-47, 186-87; director chill, 125-29; lack of corporate representatives in reform process, 117, 119-25, 145-46, 186; possible corporate lobbying of MPs, 121-25. *See also* class politics

economic structures, xi; Canada, 61-64; financial crisis, ix-xii

elite deviance. *See* corporate crime
enforcement issues, 168-69, 184; crown prosecutors unfamiliar with legislation, 157,
160-62; marginalized position of corporate crime, 150-55, 157, 163-64; police
unfamiliar with legislation, 157, 160-62;
relationship with provincial regulations,
157-60, 169
Erlichman, Louis, 199
Excellence in Manufacturing Consortium, 174

Fairclough, Norman, 9, 35-36, 58, 212n52
Fantini, Domenico, 31-32, 34
fear of crime, 1, 11
financial crime, x, 38, 43, 49, 75
for-fee services. *See* consulting services
Foucault, Michel, 8, 35, 56-58, 185, 212n52,
213n3, 214n18
Fry, Hedy, 194; statement in Justice Committee, 99

Garrido, Ameth, 31-32, 34
Gibson-Graham, J.K., 59, 65-68, 193
globalization, 62, 214n23
Gramsci, Antonio, 58, 146
Grose, Ivan, 194; statements in Justice
Committee, 140, 159
Group 4 Securicor, 174-75

Hansard, 208n2
Hawkins, Keith, 51
health and safety committees, 213n9
health and safety regulation, ix-xii; health
and safety differentiated, 213n5; history
of, 47-49; self-regulation/compliance
approach, 49-52
health offences, 213n5
Healy, Patrick, 106, 108, 199; statements
before Justice Committee, 96-97, 108-9,
154
Hewer, Lyle, 33-34, 161
Hill, Jay, 194
Hindess, Barry, 64-65
Hirschi, Travis, 42
Hirst, Paul, 64-65

identification doctrine, 21, 24, 156-57, 211n42
Industry Committee, 115-16
Integrated Market Enforcement Teams
(IMETs), 49

International Association of Machinists and
Aerospace Workers in Canada, 199

Jennings, Marlene: statement in House of
Commons, 158
Jessop, Bob, 9, 35-36, 55, 58, 64, 68, 212n52
John T. Ryan award, 121, 216n3
joint stock companies, 17
Justice Committee, 191; consideration of private members' bill (2002), 27-28, 115-
16; consideration of private members'
motion (2000), 26; discourse surround-
ing interpersonal violence, 154-55; lack
of witnesses from corporate world, 117,
119-20; members, 194; recommendations (June 2000), 5, 26-27; witnesses,
198-200

Kagan, Robert, 51, 52
King, Andrew, 198; statements before Justice
Committee, 97-98, 112
Klineberg, Joanne, 200

Laframboise, Mario, 194
Lanctôt, Robert, 194; statements in Justice
Committee, 139, 141, 159
law, 85-87, 186; as specialized knowledge, 72,
98-100, 108; constitution of laws, 12-13;
ideology and, 12, 86-87; perceived infallibility, 100-3; role in reproducing
social order, 156. *See also* legal discourse
law-and-order discourse, 1-2, 3, 11, 39, 152,
154-55, 172
law reform. *See Criminal Code* amendment
L'Ecuyer, Steve, 32-33, 34, 156-57, 164
Lee, Derek, 194; statement in Justice
Committee, 93
legal discourse, 72-73, 85-87, 116; marginalization of non-legal experts, 98-100, 108;
role in *Criminal Code* reform, 87-114,
186. *See also* law
Lemay, Terrie, 199
Lenton, William, 200
Lill, Wendy: statement in House of
Commons, 141-42
Lombroso, Cesare, 41
Lunn, Gary: statement in House of
Commons, 90, 130

MacKay, Elmer, 77

MacKay, Peter, 77, 194; private members' motion, 24, 26, 77-80, 136; statements in House of Commons, 26, 78, 79, 136; statements in Justice Committee, 90, 93, 101-2, 104, 133, 154, 155

Macklin, Paul Harold, 194; statements in House of Commons, 14, 28; statements in Justice Committee, 102, 131

mala prohibita v. malum in se, 3

Maloney, John, 194; statements in Justice Committee, 90, 94, 127-28, 131

Mancini, Peter: statements in House of Commons, 27

Mark, Inky: statement in House of Commons, 136

market economy: neo-liberalism and, 117-19

Martin, Allen, 14, 198

Martin, Debbie, 14

Martin, Pat: statements in House of Commons, 77, 79, 132, 164-65

Marxist theory, 65-67. *See also* neo-Marxist analytical perspectives

McBrearty, Lawrence, 198; statement before Justice Committee, 82

McCormick, Chris, 199

McDonough, Alexa: private members' bill, 24-25, 210n19; statements in House of Commons, 15, 29, 123

McKay, John, 194; statement in Justice Committee, 107, 126

McLellan, Anne: statements in House of Commons, 125

McMullan, John, 51, 53

mens rea, 21, 29, 31, 45, 72, 85, 89, 90, 91-98, 106-7, 111, 113, 187

Merton, Robert, 42

methodology, 7-10, 15-16, 35-36; data sources, 9-10, 36-37, 195-97; discourse analysis, 9, 35-36, 56-58, 212n50, 212n52; extra-discursive analysis, 57-70; interviews, 201-6, 213n55; reticence of corporate representatives to participate, 178. *See also* crime and deviance scholarship

Metron Construction Corporation, 33

Miezenger, David, 198

Millennium Crane Rentals, 33

Mocherie, Clare, 199; statement before Justice Committee, 104-5

Morrison, Lee: statement in House of Commons, 101

Mosley, Richard, 200

NDP. *See* New Democratic Party (NDP)

negligence, 30

neo-liberalism, 61-64, 117-19, 131, 186-87; individual free choice and, 134-36, 147, 187

Neo-Marxist analytical perspectives, 8-9, 35, 55-56, 59-60, 212n52; class politics, 64-70, 185

New Democratic Party (NDP), 73, 76-77, 103-5, 189, 215n5; private members' bill (2003), 24, 82; private members' bills, 5, 23-25, 76, 82, 210n19; private members' bills (1999), 5, 23-24, 82; private members' bill (Bill C-284) (2001), 5, 24, 25, 210n19; private members' bill (Bill C-418) (2001), 5, 24-25, 210n19

Nova Scotia, 4-5. *See also* Westray mine

Nystrom, Lorne, 194; statement in House of Commons, 134

OC Transpo Widows, 199

occupational crimes. *See* corporate crime

Occupational Health and Safey (OHS) Canada, 173

Ontario: Ontario Power Generation, 211n42; Walkerton water poisoning disaster, 75; workplace accidents, 31-32, 33, 34

Ontario Factories Act (1884), 48

organizations, 143-45; individual criminal liability within, 30. *See also* corporations

Ottawa and District Injured Workers Group, 198

Ottawa and District Labour Council, 198

Paulson Plan, ix

Pearce, Frank, xvii-xviii, 40, 44-45, 51, 52-53, 54, 58

Peoples Department Store Inc. (Trustee of) v Wise, 19

Perrault, Doug, 198; statement before Justice Committee, 104

power relations: law and, 9, 12, 85-87

powerlessness: law enforcement and, 12

private members' bills, 208n8, 210n20. *See also* New Democratic Party (NDP)

Progressive Conservative Party (PC), 76, 77-78, 215n6; private members' motion (1999), 24, 26, 76, 77-80, 210n28 provincial health and safety regulations, 157-60

Public Company Accounting Reform and Investor Protection Act of 2002, 49, 75

public opinion: corporate accountability, 26

Puri, Poonam, 199; statement before Justice Committee, 111

QFL. *See* Quebec Federation of Labour (QFL)

Quebec: workplace accidents, 32-33, 34, 156-57, 212n48

Quebec Federation of Labour (QFL), 32, 157

R c Transpavé inc, 32-33, 34, 156-57, 164

R v Fantini, 31-32, 34

R v Ontario Power Generation, 211n42

R v Scrocca, 33, 34

RCMP. *See* Royal Canadian Mounted Police

Reform Party, 215n6

regulated companies, 17

regulatory issues, ix-xii; academic scholarship and, xiii; history, 46-53; "infallibility" of the law and, 101-3; self-regulation/ compliance approach, xiii-xiv, 47, 49-52, 141. *See also* health and safety regulation

Reid, Scott: statements in House of Commons, 92

research methods. *See* methodology

Resnick, Stephen, 59, 65-68

Richard, Justice K. Peter, 5, 22-23, 73, 74, 80, 81-82, 89, 142, 191-92, 199, 209n16

Royal Canadian Mounted Police, 200, 207n5

Ruccio, David, 193

safety crimes. *See* corporate crime

safety offences, 213n5

safety regulation. *See* health and safety regulation

Salomon v Salomon and Company (1892), 17, 208n3

Sarbanes-Oxley Act (United States), xi, 49, 75

Sayer, Andrew, 9, 35-36, 58, 212n52

Scholz, John, 51

Scott, Andy, 194; statement in Justice Committee, 95

Scrocca, Pasquale, 33, 34

self-regulation/compliance approach, xiii-xiv, 47, 49-52, 141

semiosis, 35-36

Senate Standing Committee on Legal and Constitutional Affairs, 29

senior officers, 31

Shareholder Association for Research and Education, 200; submission to Justice Committee, 105

shareholders, 18-19, 20, 208n4-5

Slapper, Gary, 39, 44, 51, 54

Snider, Laureen, xviii, 48, 51, 53

social formations. *See* Canadian social formation; capitalist social formation

Sorenson, Kevin, 194; statement in Justice Committee, 93-94, 130, 137-38

St. Denis, Brent: statement in House of Commons, 158-59

Standing Committee on Industry, Science and Technology, 115-16

Standing Committee on Justice and Human Rights. *See* Justice Committee

the state: role in society, 73, 185, 191-92. *See also* Canada, Parliament; *Criminal Code* amendment

Steelworkers. *See* United Steelworkers of America

street-level crime: conceptualization contrasted to corporate crime, 11, 12, 150-52, 181-82; contrasted to corporate crime, 50, 100, 183-84

Sundown Interactive Communication Corporation, 173-74

Sutherland, Edwin, 42, 43-44, 45

Tappan, Paul, 44

Theriault, Vern, 14, 137-38, 198

Thomson, Tamara, 199

Toews, Vic, 194; statements in House of Commons, 126, 130; statements in Justice Committee, 88, 92, 94, 98-99, 138-40, 142-43, 154-55, 216n6

Tombs, Steve, 39, 44-45, 51-54, 58

Transpavé, 32-33, 34, 156-57, 164

Trudell, William, 108, 199; statements before Justice Committee, 88, 92-93, 100, 102, 108-9, 126, 127

Tucker, Eric, 47-48, 54, 55

Union Carbide, 38, 58

unions, 189, 215n25; shared responsibility for workplace safety, 97-98, 136-43, 144, 145, 216n6

United Kingdom, ix, x, xiii, 211n37; historical conditions, 17, 20-21; identification doctrine, 21

United States, ix, xi; *Public Company Accounting Reform and Investor Protection Act of 2002,* xi, 49, 75; vicarious liability, 31

United Steelworkers of America, 29, 198, 216n6; poll concerning corporate wrongdoing, 26; private prosecution concerning death of Lyle Hewer, 33-34, 161; role in *Criminal Code* reform, 73, 80, 81-84, 89, 112, 139, 179, 189, 193, 210n28; role in Westray mine disaster inquiry, 23, 81-82; unionization of Westray mine, 80-81

Vaillancourt, Dominique, 198
vicarious liability, 30-31

Walkerton water poisoning disaster, 75
welfare state, 63-64
Westray bill. *See* Bill C-45
Westray Families Group, 14, 198
Westray mine: disaster, 4-5, 14, 38-39, 54, 69, 74, 77, 102, 207n5, 208n6-7; inquiry recommendations, 5, 22-23, 73, 74, 80, 81-82, 89, 142, 209n16; unionization, 80-81
The Westray Story: A Predictable Path to Disaster, 4-5, 22-23, 73, 74, 80, 81-82, 89, 142, 209n16

Weyerhaeuser, 33-34, 161
Whellams, Dave, 198; statements before Justice Committee, 106-7
white-collar crime. *See* corporate crime
Whyte, D., 45, 51-53
Wolff, Richard, 59, 65-68, 191-92
workers' interests, 19
working conditions: historical conditions, 20
workplace accidents, xii, 3, 105, 212n48; criminal culpability, xii, xv, 3; death of Ameth Garrido, 31-32, 34; death of Aniello Boccanfuso, 33, 34; death of Lyle Hewer, 33-34, 161; death of Steve L'Ecuyer, 32-33, 34, 156-57, 164; deaths following collapse of scaffolding, 33; deaths following hydro dam flooding, 211n42; defined as "accident," 48, 105, 149; historical conditions, 20-21; statistics, xii, 3; Walkerton water poisoning disaster, 75. *See also* corporate crime; Westray mine, disaster
workplace culture. *See* corporate culture
workplace safety, 3-4; as worker responsibility, 136-43, 146-47

Yaron, Gil, 200
York, Maria, 198
Yost, Greg, 198, 200
Yussuff, Hassan, 199

David R. Boyd
The Right to a Healthy Environment: Revitalizing Canada's Constitution (2012)

David Milward
Aboriginal Justice and the Charter: Realizing a Culturally Sensitive Interpretation of Legal Rights (2012)

Shelley A.M. Gavigan
Hunger, Horses, and Government Men: Criminal Law on the Aboriginal Plains, 1870-1905 (2012)

Jacqueline D. Krikorian
International Trade Law and Domestic Policy: Canada, the United States, and the WTO (2012)

Michael Boudreau
City of Order: Crime and Society in Halifax, 1918-35 (2012)

Lesley Erickson
Westward Bound: Sex, Violence, the Law, and the Making of a Settler Society (2011)

David R. Boyd
The Environmental Rights Revolution: A Global Study of Constitutions, Human Rights, and the Environment (2011)

Elaine Craig
Troubling Sex: Towards a Legal Theory of Sexual Integrity (2011)

Laura DeVries
Conflict in Caledonia: Aboriginal Land Rights and the Rule of Law (2011)

Jocelyn Downie and Jennifer J. Llewellyn (eds.)
Being Relational: Reflections on Relational Theory and Health Law (2011)

Grace Li Xiu Woo
Ghost Dancing with Colonialism: Decolonization and Indigenous Rights at the Supreme Court of Canada (2011)

Fiona Kelly
Transforming Law's Family: The Legal Recognition of Planned Lesbian Motherhood (2011)

Colleen Bell
The Freedom of Security: Governing Canada in the Age of Counter-Terrorism (2011)

Andrew S. Thompson
In Defence of Principles: NGOs and Human Rights in Canada (2010)

Aaron Doyle and Dawn Moore (eds.)
Critical Criminology in Canada: New Voices, New Directions (2010)

Joanna R. Quinn
The Politics of Acknowledgement: Truth Commissions in Uganda and Haiti (2010)

Patrick James
Constitutional Politics in Canada after the Charter: Liberalism, Communitarianism, and Systemism (2010)

Louis A. Knafla and Haijo Westra (eds.)
Aboriginal Title and Indigenous Peoples: Canada, Australia, and New Zealand (2010)

Janet Mosher and Joan Brockman (eds.)
Constructing Crime: Contemporary Processes of Criminalization (2010)

Stephen Clarkson and Stepan Wood
A Perilous Imbalance: The Globalization of Canadian Law and Governance (2009)

Amanda Glasbeek
Feminized Justice: The Toronto Women's Court, 1913-34 (2009)

Kim Brooks (ed.)
Justice Bertha Wilson: One Woman's Difference (2009)

Wayne V. McIntosh and Cynthia L. Cates
Multi-Party Litigation: The Strategic Context (2009)

Renisa Mawani
Colonial Proximities: Crossracial Encounters and Juridical Truths in British Columbia, 1871-1921 (2009)

James B. Kelly and Christopher P. Manfredi (eds.)
Contested Constitutionalism: Reflections on the Canadian Charter of Rights and Freedoms (2009)

Catherine Bell and Robert K. Paterson (eds.)
Protection of First Nations Cultural Heritage: Laws, Policy, and Reform (2008)

Hamar Foster, Benjamin L. Berger, and A.R. Buck (eds.)
The Grand Experiment: Law and Legal Culture in British Settler Societies (2008)

Richard J. Moon (ed.)
Law and Religious Pluralism in Canada (2008)

Catherine Bell and Val Napoleon (eds.)
First Nations Cultural Heritage and Law: Case Studies, Voices, and Perspectives (2008)

Douglas C. Harris
Landing Native Fisheries: Indian Reserves and Fishing Rights in British Columbia, 1849-1925 (2008)

Peggy J. Blair
Lament for a First Nation: The Williams Treaties of Southern Ontario (2008)

Lori G. Beaman
Defining Harm: Religious Freedom and the Limits of the Law (2007)

Stephen Tierney (ed.)
Multiculturalism and the Canadian Constitution (2007)

Julie Macfarlane
The New Lawyer: How Settlement Is Transforming the Practice of Law (2007)

Kimberley White
Negotiating Responsibility: Law, Murder, and States of Mind (2007)

Dawn Moore
Criminal Artefacts: Governing Drugs and Users (2007)

Hamar Foster, Heather Raven, and Jeremy Webber (eds.)
Let Right Be Done: Aboriginal Title, the Calder *Case, and the Future of Indigenous Rights* (2007)

Dorothy E. Chunn, Susan B. Boyd, and Hester Lessard (eds.)
Reaction and Resistance: Feminism, Law, and Social Change (2007)

Margot Young, Susan B. Boyd, Gwen Brodsky, and Shelagh Day (eds.)
Poverty: Rights, Social Citizenship, and Legal Activism (2007)

Rosanna L. Langer
Defining Rights and Wrongs: Bureaucracy, Human Rights, and Public Accountability (2007)

C.L. Ostberg and Matthew E. Wetstein
Attitudinal Decision Making in the Supreme Court of Canada (2007)

Chris Clarkson
Domestic Reforms: Political Visions and Family Regulation in British Columbia, 1862-1940 (2007)

Jean McKenzie Leiper
Bar Codes: Women in the Legal Profession (2006)

Gerald Baier
Courts and Federalism: Judicial Doctrine in the United States, Australia, and Canada (2006)

Avigail Eisenberg (ed.)
Diversity and Equality: The Changing Framework of Freedom in Canada (2006)

Randy K. Lippert
Sanctuary, Sovereignty, Sacrifice: Canadian Sanctuary Incidents, Power, and Law (2005)

James B. Kelly
Governing with the Charter: Legislative and Judicial Activism and Framers' Intent (2005)

Dianne Pothier and Richard Devlin (eds.)
Critical Disability Theory: Essays in Philosophy, Politics, Policy, and Law (2005)

Susan G. Drummond
Mapping Marriage Law in Spanish Gitano Communities (2005)

Louis A. Knafla and Jonathan Swainger (eds.)
Laws and Societies in the Canadian Prairie West, 1670-1940 (2005)

Ikechi Mgbeoji
Global Biopiracy: Patents, Plants, and Indigenous Knowledge (2005)

Florian Sauvageau, David Schneiderman, and David Taras,
with Ruth Klinkhammer and Pierre Trudel
The Last Word: Media Coverage of the Supreme Court of Canada (2005)

Gerald Kernerman
Multicultural Nationalism: Civilizing Difference, Constituting Community (2005)

Pamela A. Jordan
Defending Rights in Russia: Lawyers, the State, and Legal Reform in the Post-Soviet Era (2005)

Anna Pratt
Securing Borders: Detention and Deportation in Canada (2005)

Kirsten Johnson Kramar
Unwilling Mothers, Unwanted Babies: Infanticide in Canada (2005)

W.A. Bogart
*Good Government? Good Citizens? Courts, Politics, and Markets
in a Changing Canada* (2005)

Catherine Dauvergne
*Humanitarianism, Identity, and Nation: Migration Laws in Canada
and Australia* (2005)

Michael Lee Ross
First Nations Sacred Sites in Canada's Courts (2005)

Andrew Woolford
Between Justice and Certainty: Treaty Making in British Columbia (2005)

John McLaren, Andrew Buck, and Nancy Wright (eds.)
Despotic Dominion: Property Rights in British Settler Societies (2004)

Georges Campeau
From UI to EI: Waging War on the Welfare State (2004)

Alvin J. Esau
*The Courts and the Colonies: The Litigation of Hutterite Church
Disputes* (2004)

Christopher N. Kendall
Gay Male Pornography: An Issue of Sex Discrimination (2004)

Roy B. Flemming
Tournament of Appeals: Granting Judicial Review in Canada (2004)

Constance Backhouse and Nancy L. Backhouse
*The Heiress vs the Establishment: Mrs. Campbell's Campaign for Legal
Justice* (2004)

Christopher P. Manfredi
Feminist Activism in the Supreme Court: Legal Mobilization and the Women's Legal Education and Action Fund (2004)

Annalise Acorn
Compulsory Compassion: A Critique of Restorative Justice (2004)

Jonathan Swainger and Constance Backhouse (eds.)
People and Place: Historical Influences on Legal Culture (2003)

Jim Phillips and Rosemary Gartner
Murdering Holiness: The Trials of Franz Creffield and George Mitchell (2003)

David R. Boyd
Unnatural Law: Rethinking Canadian Environmental Law and Policy (2003)

Ikechi Mgbeoji
Collective Insecurity: The Liberian Crisis, Unilateralism, and Global Order (2003)

Rebecca Johnson
Taxing Choices: The Intersection of Class, Gender, Parenthood, and the Law (2002)

John McLaren, Robert Menzies, and Dorothy E. Chunn (eds.)
Regulating Lives: Historical Essays on the State, Society, the Individual, and the Law (2002)

Joan Brockman
Gender in the Legal Profession: Fitting or Breaking the Mould (2001)

Printed and bound in Canada by Friesens

Set in Kozuka Gothic and Minion by Artegraphica Design Co. Ltd.

Copy editor: Stacy Belden

Proofreader: Steph VanderMeulen

Indexer: Christine Jacobs